The Criminal Justice Process
A Reader

The Criminal Justice Process
A Reader

edited by

William B. Sanders
University of Florida

and

Howard C. Daudistel
University of Texas, El Paso

Praeger Publishers
New York

Published in the United States of America in 1976
by Praeger Publishers, Inc.
111 Fourth Avenue, New York, N.Y. 10003

Library of Congress Cataloging in Publication Data
Main entry under title:

The Criminal justice process.

    1. Criminal justice, Administration of--Address-
es, essays, lectures. I. Sanders, William B.
II. Daudistel, Howard C.
HV8665.C76   364   75-3749

ISBN 0-275-89320-0

Printed in the United States of America

For Eli, Sandy, Billy, and David

Preface

The study of criminal justice has suffered from a lack of cohesion. It has been the stepchild of the sociology of law and of deviance, especially criminology, but has only rarely been approached as an area of investigation in its own right. Encumbered by narrow legal interpretations, police science orientations (often nothing more than "war stories" and technological suggestions), and reforming zeal, sociologists have found it difficult to treat criminal justice in the same way they approach the study of the traditional areas of inquiry. This book is a step toward treating criminal justice like any other phenomenon of sociological interest, and we claim no special privileges or exemptions because the subject matter we deal with is criminal justice.

To this end we have organized the subject matter into various components, compared empirical studies and methodologies, and presented various theoretical frameworks. After having read the book, the student, we hope, will be familiar with some of the basic issues in criminal justice, will understand the day-to-day processes that constitute criminal justice in operation, and will be able to interpret several different criminal justice situations. In short, we hope that the student will be able to understand criminal justice in the same way sociologists understand any other social process.

We have chosen studies of the criminal justice process based on their relevance to key issues. Some of these issues are substantive, such as the studies of police discretion; others are theoretical, dealing with frameworks for understanding various procedures and activities. Each, we believe, is interesting, and many could be called controversial. Our task, however, is not to condemn or justify the criminal justice process but to encourage students of introductory criminal justice and sociology to think about this massive and complex process and perhaps pursue their inquiry further. Nothing would please us more than to find students endeavoring to determine on their own whether what we say is true.

We are grateful to many who have assisted us in putting this book together. Our own orientation to criminal justice was guided by Don Zimmerman, D. Lawrence Wieder, and Donald R. Cressey; without their inspiration, it is unlikely that this book would have ever been prepared. We are most grateful to the authors and publishers who allowed us to reprint their materials. In our own research we are indebted to those who have allowed us into their world to study what they do in criminal justice, especially the detectives of the Santa Barbara County Sheriff's Office, whose guests we were for a year. Jackie Moore and Peggy Dever gave us invaluable assistance in preparing the editorial material. Gladys Topkis, our outstanding editor, was our most valuable asset in this work's preparation. Finally, we owe our wives, Eli Sanders and Sandy Daudistel, our unedited affection for their understanding during the period we were working on the book.

W.B.S.
H.C.D.

Contents

The Criminal Justice Process
A Reader

I
Situational Structures and the Criminal Justice Process

The study of criminal justice for the most part has been conducted in a theoretical vacuum or as an offshoot of other focal concerns. The most common approach has been a "systems" perspective, which examines the workings of criminal justice from a practical, non-theoretical point of view (Coffey, 1974). The sociological approach, on the other hand, has made some theoretical contributions, but criminal justice generally has been of secondary interest. Thus criminologists of the labeling school have been interested in the impact of the criminal justice system on deviance and crime (Lemert, 1951). They see the criminal justice system as contributing to deviance and criminality by stigmatizing and criminalizing people who enter the criminal justice process (Goffman, 1963; Hartjen, 1974). Students of the sociology of law have developed theories attempting to explain how laws have come to be developed (Pound, 1922; Quinney, 1974). This approach, known as "sociological jurisprudence," seeks to develop theories of the "law in action," but the "action" these theories have been able to explain has been limited for the most part to lawmaking.

Figure 1 shows the formal structure of the criminal justice process, and it is a good example of how the "systems perspective" deals with criminal justice. In the remainder of this introduction we will provide an overview of our perspective and introduce some of the basic concepts in the study of criminal justice.

A Situational Perspective on the Criminal Justice System

We call our approach the "situational perspective" in that we examine critical situations in the criminal justice process, focusing on the face-to-face encounters between people who are a part of the criminal justice system and those who come into contact with it. In these critical situations, decisions are made that have a significant effect on the lives of those who come to the attention of the system, such as whether or not a suspect should be arrested, whether or not a defendant should be charged with a crime, and other matters.

The subject matter of criminal justice has traditionally been divided into four subareas: law enforcement, prosecution/defense, the

1

courts, and corrections. The process of criminal justice begins when the police decide to make an arrest and ends when a person leaves the control of the criminal justice system. Most people brought in by the police are released without entering the correctional system. Moreover, the correctional process is to a large extent independent of the criminal justice process and might best be seen as a place where the process "puts" certain convicted offenders. And finally, corrections and penology constitute so massive an area of study in criminology and sociology that we could not deal with it adequately here. Consequently, in this book we will consider only the processes and organizations that serve to separate the criminal and the non-criminal, that is, law enforcement, prosecution/defense, and the courts.

Our use of "criminal justice" does not refer to a philosophical definition of right and wrong. "Criminal" refers to the violation of some criminal law, and "justice," to the operations of due process as set down in the Constitution of the United States, the Bill of Rights, and other documents that specify how criminal cases are to be handled. These are operational definitions, to be sure, but they provide both a theoretical and a practical sense of what we shall be dealing with. In this book, criminal justice means the way in which due process functions in cases involving violation of a criminal statute. The criminal justice process refers to the procedures and agencies used for handling people who have been accused of violating the criminal law.

Legally defined, a "crime" is an offense against the state punishable by fine, imprisonment, or some other penalty (Kerper, 1972:30). The important element of this definition is that the act is considered to be *against the state* and *punishable by the state.* If an offense is considered against an individual but not against the state, it is called a "tort," and tort offenses are handled by civil, not criminal, procedures. Many offenses, of course, are against both individuals and the state. For example, burglary is a crime since it is legally defined as against the state and punishable by the state, but at the same time it is typically against a specific individual. There are two courses of action that can be taken against a burglar who is caught. On the one hand, since burglary is a crime, the state can prosecute the burglar and impose a punishment against him if he is convicted. On the other hand, since the offense is against an individual, the victim can take the burglar to civil court and sue him for the loss of property. Typically, however, those who break the criminal law go only to the criminal court, and no civil litigation is brought against them. We might be able to show that any offense against another person is both a crime and a tort and that all public offenses are also offenses against individuals; however, the only way to differentiate between crimes and torts is to see whether or not the law specifies that the offense is against the state and that the punishment is to be carried out by the state. A crime is a crime by definition, and only by definition.

The legal or "official" understanding of crime is thus fairly clear, but the "social" understanding is not. Most people have only a general idea of what is or is not a crime. They may know that if someone breaks into their house and takes something, the act is a crime, but they probably don't know whether the crime is technically a theft, a burglary, or a robbery. This distinction may not seem important, but to the police, the courts, and the prosecuting and defense attorneys it is of great significance. For petty theft, a misdemeanor, the punishment is relatively light compared to robbery, a felony.* Similarly, the general social understanding of the law often includes many acts that the public believes are crimes but that are not so considered by the police and others in the criminal justice system. For example, one study found that although 58 percent of the complaints by citizens to the police involved criminal matters as defined by the people who called, fewer than half of these complaints were regarded as criminal matters by the police (Reiss, 1971:73).

The terms "official" and "social" understandings are somewhat misleading, for any interpretation is a social one (Blumer, 1969) in that it takes place in some kind of social context, whether a barroom or a courtroom, and involves social actors in social roles attempting to make sense of some event. Those involved in the criminal justice process, however, are more likely to be familiar with certain technical language than are laymen. Therefore, when we refer to "legal" or "official" understandings, we mean interpretations of the law by those in various criminal justice roles on occasions when these interpretations are officially consequential. Interpretations by laymen will be called "social."

By now it should be clear that the law of the land is not an unequivocal set of rules like "natural" law but is subject to social mediation before legal sanctions are brought to bear. Consider the differences between a natural law—say, the law of gravity—and a criminal law. Suppose a person is walking across a field and comes upon a wide, deep ditch. If he continues to walk, the law of gravity will cause him to fall into the ditch. There are no ifs, ands, or buts about this law, and in all cases the consequences of "breaking" it will happen immediately.

If someone breaks a criminal law, on the other hand, several things have to happen before the consequences are invoked. Suppose a woman punches a man in the nose. If the act was intentional, it

*The difference between "felony" and "misdemeanor" varies from state to state. For our purposes, it is sufficient to regard felonies as serious offenses and misdemeanors as minor ones.

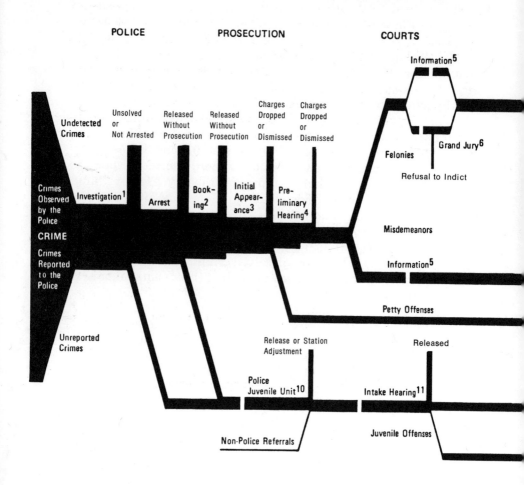

POLICE   PROSECUTION   COURTS

Information[5]

Undetected Crimes

Unsolved or Not Arrested

Released Without Prosecution

Released Without Prosecution

Charges Dropped or Dismissed

Charges Dropped or Dismissed

Grand Jury[6]

Felonies

Refusal to Indict

Crimes Observed by the Police

Investigation[1]

Arrest

Book-ing[2]

Initial Appear-ance[3]

Pre-liminary Hearing[4]

CRIME

Misdemeanors

Crimes Reported to the Police

Information[5]

Petty Offenses

Unreported Crimes

Release or Station Adjustment

Released

Police Juvenile Unit[10]

Intake Hearing[11]

Non-Police Referrals

Juvenile Offenses

[1] May continue until trial.

[2] Administrative record of arrest. First step at which temporary release on bail may be available.

[3] Before magistrate, commissioner, or justice of peace. Formal notice of charge, advice of rights. Bail set. Summary trials for petty offenses usually conducted here without further processing.

[4] Preliminary testing of evidence against defendant. Charge may be reduced. No separate preliminary hearing for misdemeanors in some systems.

[5] Charge filed by prosecutor on basis of information submitted by police or citizens. Alternative to grand jury indictment; often used in felonies, almost always in misdemeanors.

Note: Procedures in individual jurisdictions may vary from the pattern shown here. The differing weights of line indicate the relative volume of cases typically disposed of at various points in the system.

THE CRIMINAL JUSTICE SYSTEM*

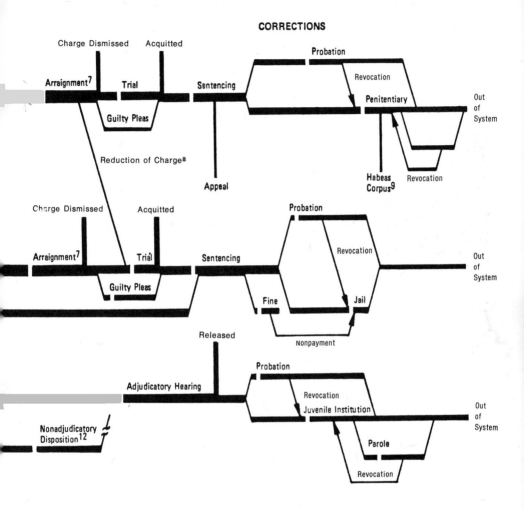

CORRECTIONS

Source: The President's Commission on Law Enforcement and Administration of Justice, *The Challenge of Crime in a Free Society* (Washington, D.C.: U.S. Government Printing Office, 1967), pp. 8–9.

5

constitutes a violation of the criminal law of battery. However, before the penalties for breaking the law are applied, the act must be defined by someone as a violation of the law. Next, the authorities, usually the police, must be summoned. Having arrived, they then must interpret the situation as one in which a criminal act has occurred and make an arrest. Detectives may have to investigate to determine further whether the law has been broken in the context of the situation. Then the prosecutor's office must file an "information" (bring the offense to the attention of the court) based on the evidence gathered by the police or on material they themselves have gathered. Next, the judge must accept the case as one with "reasonable" cause to be tried, after which judge or a jury must determine guilt. If the defendant is found guilty, the judge has to hand down the sentence the law prescribes. Only if all these events occur will the penalties for breaking the law be put into effect. It is unlikely, in the case of a woman who socks a man in the nose, that anyone would define the situation as criminal, and the chance that this reported violation would go all the way to trial is slim indeed. Thus, unlike violation of the law of gravity, for which the penalties are immediate and inexorable, violation of a criminal law is subject to social mediation.

Understanding the law in action, then, is not a simple matter of reading the statutes; we need some framework that will explain the everyday application and execution of the law. Only by examining situations in which the law is interpreted and implemented on a routine, day-to-day basis can we begin to understand what the criminal justice process really is as opposed to how it is supposed to function. We propose, therefore, to examine studies of situations in which the law has been brought to bear to see what typically takes place, to look at typical encounters between the police and the citizenry, at the structure of decision-making in discretionary situations in the adjudication phase, and at patterns of interaction in the courtroom. In other words, we shall look at the actual social structure, roles, attitudes, and practices in the criminal justice process— the situations in which what is called "criminal justice" gets done.

An Overview

Several of the articles included in this book—those by Bittner, Daudistel and Sanders, Sudnow, and Cicourel—have been chosen because they elaborate our point of view. Most of the other articles are included because they focus on the types of occasions we take as central to an understanding of the reality of the criminal justice process, offering critical examinations of day-to-day activities as they occur rather than an idealized version of how they are supposed to occur. Thus they provide support for our theoretical position and pinpoint those everyday situations in which criminal justice in some sense is accomplished.

The Police

The police, those who are charged with enforcing the law and keeping the peace (Manning, 1971), constitute the first subsystem in the criminal justice process. This official task is to detect crime, apprehend lawbreakers, and provide information to the prosecutors and the courts so that the lawbreakers will be penalized. They have the power to make arrests, or official accusations of law violation, thereby separating out those they believe have violated the law. We can see how the police actually function in the criminal justice process by examining occasions on which they decide whether or not to invoke the law and make an arrest.

The occasions for police interest vary, and we find different forms of police-citizen interaction depending on the context of these encounters. Egon Bittner shows that the police on Skid-Row are interested primarily in keeping some semblance of order and that the law is only incidental to their activities. With the assumed power of the law behind them, the police are able to "handle situations" that do not necessarily entail invocation of the law. The everyday scenes they encounter on Skid-Row occasion their activities, and the occasions are elaborated in the overall context of life on Skid-Row.

A second area of interest in the study of police encounters with the citizenry is that of police discretion. "Discretion" here refers to the decision whether or not to make an arrest. Basically, police organizations are divided by function into patrol and investigation, along with supporting and administrative staffs. Officers on patrol cover a given area in cars or on foot, look for criminal violations and respond to calls for police assistance in both criminal and noncriminal matters. Once a crime has been reported by patrol, the detectives of the investigative branch decide whether in fact a crime has occurred that must be investigated and if so what law has been violated. Unless the detectives decide to treat the incident as a crime, no further action will occur. Their decision to investigate or not is the next step in the process, and it too is consequential, for it may activate the mechanisms of the entire criminal justice process.

Piliavin and Briar examine police discretionary situations in terms of the demeanor of juvenile suspects, pointing out that those who defer to police authority are less likely to be arrested than those who do not. On the other hand, Black, who examines not only the suspect's demeanor but also the victim's desire that something be done by the police, found some differences in the outcome of discretionary situations depending on the demeanor of the suspect but concludes that, regardless of the behavior of the accused, the police are most likely to invoke the law if the crime victim or some other involved party insists that they do so. Both studies show that elements of the situation in which whether or not to make an arrest is decided are significant determinants.

The next two articles examine how the police decide whether to apply the law and, if so, what law. Most people assume that a homicide is an "objective fact" out in the world. Terry and Luckenbill, however, show that a vast amount of interpretive work must take place before an event is defined as a homicide. Not only can a number of different legal applications be employed when talking about a person made dead by another but also the characterization of a death as a homicide is dependent on constructing the death occasion in a very specific manner. This point is further elaborated by Daudistel and Sanders as they outline how the police decide on the specific sense of a crime. Rather than provide guidelines for action, the rules are accomplished in an *ad hoc* manner on the occasion of their use.

Prosecution and Defense

Once detectives have decided to make an arrest, they take their information to the prosecutor's office, the next critical situation in the chain. After examining the evidence, the prosecutor's office decides whether it is sufficient to take the case to court. This decision is made in interaction with the defense attorney, who is a privately hired lawyer, a court-appointed attorney, or a public defender. Together the defense and prosecution determine the "worth" of a case and what crime the defendant should be charged with. Sometimes the defense and prosecution play out the roles of adversaries, with the prosecution fighting for maximum punishment and the defense for acquittal; more typically, the decision of what should be done with the defendant is arrived at mutually, through consultation and understandings the two sides develop. Because our aim in this part of the book is to show the day-to-day operation of the prosecution and defense, we have deliberately left out jury-trial preparation. Only about 10 percent of all convictions are the result of a jury trial. Usually defendants plead guilty and make some sort of "deal" with the prosecutor. David Sudnow's study examines how the public defender routinely works with the prosecutor in determining the "worth" of a crime.

Abraham Blumberg's study of private defense attorneys provides another sense of criminal law in action. Blumberg sees the everyday practice of law as a confidence game with the hapless defendant as the "mark." The routine activities of the private criminal attorney are not aspects of an adversary position but measures taken to maximize his profit and minimize his effort, all the time giving the appearance of an active defense.

The remaining studies in this section document the operation of "bargain justice." Martin Mayer examines a highly successful district attorney's office and shows how the goal of a high conviction rate is realized by "dealing" cases (that is, making a deal with a defendant involving a lesser charge in exchange for a guilty plea) in the courts. Jonathan Casper's study of convicted defendants shows how the defendants, those who receive "bargain justice," feel about the practice and at the same time provides insight into the process. Finally, Mendes and Wold examine how bargain justice has permeated the courts, to the extent that cases are "dealt out" at the arraignment phase of an adjudication.

The Courts

As bargain justice takes over the judicial process, courts and judges become less significant; however, the courts still play an important role.

When the case is brought to the attention of the court, the first critical step is bail setting. Interaction in the courtroom during bail setting is consequential, for it determines whether the defendant will remain in custody or will be set free while awaiting trial. The fortunate defendant will be released on his "own recognizance" without bail. A less fortunate defendant may spend up to a year in jail awaiting trial. The situation in which bail is determined is therefore of central importance. Frederic Suffet's study highlights the key role of the courtroom encounter in the determination of bail.

Next we look at the judge, supposedly the impartial referee in the battle between prosecution and defense. However, as we have seen, the prosecution and defense are hardly adversaries, and in the article by Carol Bohmer we learn that the judge is not always impartial. Researching judicial attitudes toward rape victims, Bohmer found that the attitude of the judge may have significant consequences for courtroom outcomes.

Jacqueline Wiseman then offers a glimpse of a court with a phenomenally high production rate. The drunk court processes "criminals" of the most common type, those arrested for drunk and disorderly conduct. The critical situation for the defendant takes about thirty seconds—his "day in court." In this brief time all the necessary "legal" trappings are presented, and "justice" is done.

If a case goes to trial, the occasion of the trial is a series of critical situations as the prosecution and defense bring in key witnesses and evidence. Decisions by the judge—whether to allow certain testimony, accept key evidence, and the like—are consequential in that their effect on the jury (and on the judge himself) determines the outcome of the trial. If the defendant is found guilty, the outcome of most trials, the judge must decide what sentence he is to receive, a decision made on the basis of a presentence report made by the probation officer. Usually the judge goes along with the report's recommendation. Therefore, the critical situation is not when the judge decides on the sentence but when the probation officer compiles the presentence report, thus in effect making the sentencing decision.

Robert Carter and Leslie Wilkins provide insight into the influential role of the probation officer in decision making, thus documenting the extralegal character of the courtroom process.

Finally, we examine the juvenile court process. It again becomes clear that the social-interaction process is the crucial variable in court dispositions. In addition to the nature of the crime, the assessments of the parents and the juvenile are the principal determinants of the courtroom outcome. In the example of "Robert," Aaron Cicourel demonstrates that the mobilization of family resources is an effective way of keeping Robert free of detention.

This series of encounters and discretionary situations points to the importance of the structure of the criminal justice process, for this structure determines the critical situations. However, it is no less important to understand the manner in which these situations are patterned and how they are typically resolved, for it is in these situations that the actual decisions are made. This book, then, presents empirical studies dealing with face-to-face interactions on these occasions and the mechanisms that determine their outcome. We are not denying the importance of the law and the legal requirements of due process. However, it is important to understand that the law is often transcended by nonlegal, not necessarily illegal, social processes. An understanding of these social processes is essential for a realistic understanding of how the criminal justice process operates.

References

Blumer, Herbert. 1969. *Symbolic Interactionism.* Englewood Cliffs, N.J.: Prentice-Hall.

Coffey, Alan R. 1974. *Juvenile Justice as a System: Law Enforcement to Rehabilitation.* Englewood Cliffs, N.J.: Prentice-Hall.

Goffman, Erving. 1963. *Stigma.* Englewood Cliffs, N.J.: Prentice-Hall.

Hartjen, Clayton A. 1974. *Crime and Criminalization.* New York: Praeger.

Kerper, Hazel. 1972. *Introduction to the Criminal Justice System.* St. Paul, Minn.: West Publishing.

Lemert, Edwin. 1951. *Social Pathology.* New York: McGraw-Hill.

Pound, Roscoe. 1922. *An Introduction to the Philosophy of Law.* New Haven: Yale Univ. Press.

Quinney, Richard. 1974. *Criminal Justice in America: A Critical Understanding.* Boston: Little, Brown.

Reiss, Albert J., Jr. 1971. *The Police and the Public.* New Haven, Conn.: Yale Univ. Press.

2
Encounters with the Police

The public's fascination with the police is attested by the plethora of television programs and motion pictures dealing with police activities. These presentations are sometimes entertaining, but they tend to be inaccurate depictions of police work. If there are any slick investigators who solve every single burglary, robbery, rape, and assault that comes to their attention and spend their spare time doing social work, they are few and far between. Even though most people don't take such characterizations seriously, the fact remains that the mass media's customary portrait of law enforcement distorts reality.

There are more than 40,000 municipal, county, state, and federal police agencies in the United States, employing well over 400,000 police officers. Most of the work of these officers is unspectacular, even boring. How exciting can it be to drive a patrol car through the deserted streets of a city at 4:00 A.M.? How thrilling is it to spend two hours writing a report about the theft of a stereo? Police chases, shootouts, and apprehensions of notorious criminals do indeed take place, but they are relatively rare and offer marked contrast to the mundane duties of all police personnel.

The officer's role in society is not always exciting, but it is significant. Policemen can detain and question those they feel need to be questioned, and they have the power to dramatically alter the lives of citizens. The police have been given the "legitimate" right to take the life of another if they deem it necessary to protect the members of the community or their own lives. Clearly, few others in our society are permitted to make such serious decisions individually.

An accurate model of the police role would probably center on the officer's position as a decision-maker. It is his duty to decide how to handle a wide variety of problems he encounters. Generally the law enforcement officer has the responsibility of determining what to do with the dozens of requests made by citizens who want his aid.

The readings in this part focus on the ways in which police officers decide what to do in their encounters with the public. Each author exposes a major aspect of police work in our society that has received little coverage in the popular media.

Egon Bittner documents the diverse nature of the policeman's role in our society, showing that law enforcement is only one part of the policeman's mandate. More salient is the officer's role as peace-keeper, a role whose adequate performance depends not on a technical understanding of the law but on skills developed on the job. One such skill is the ability to use the law as a resource for maintaining order. For example, the problems caused by an intoxicated person who is uncooperative with the police and has no family or friends to care for him may be resolved by arrest and incarceration. In this case, the arrest is not based on some abstract ideal embodied in the law. Rather, the law itself is a device for dealing with the requirements of the situation: clearing the streets of someone who is a threat to public order.

Irving Piliavin and Scott Briar make a unique contribution to our knowledge of police decision-making by focusing on police encounters with juveniles. The criminological literature includes several social-scientific articles and reports of police discretion in the application of the law to adults but contains few good studies that concentrate on the conditions influencing police treatment of minors. The study by Piliavin and Briar was one of the first research efforts to remedy this serious void in criminal justice literature.

Like Bittner, Piliavin and Briar demonstrate that the decisions made by police officers are typically based on more legal evidence that a juvenile has committed a wrongful act. With the exception of those offenders who are wanted by authorities and those who have committed "serious" acts, the disposition of juvenile cases depends on how the youth's character is evaluated by police officers. Such evaluations may be based on information from a wide variety of sources. Nevertheless, Piliavin and Briar have discovered that, in fact, most police decisions about juveniles are based on the limited information police can gather during their encounters with juveniles.

Piliavin and Briar's findings have many implications. For example, they document the weakness of a system of juvenile justice based on informal evaluations of a youth's "life situation." If police officers believe that a youth's demeanor, style of dress, and race are good indicators of his possible future criminality or probity, their arrests will be discriminatory, punishing those who do not fit their idea of normalcy. Piliavin and Briar clearly show that the disadvantages of giving police officers wide freedom to judge juveniles informally far outweigh the benefits of the greater flexibility of individualized justice. The social-scientific implications of their findings relate to the distorted crime rates that may be produced by police reliance on juvenile demeanor as grounds for arrest. For instance, according to Piliavin and Briar, because blacks are more frequently identified as "potential troublemakers" than are whites, there is greater probability that they will be arrested. Social scientists must use police arrest statistics with some caution. All one can say about these data is that they indicate that members of some groups are arrested more often than others.

The third study in this section illustrates that police–citizen encounters can be studied systematically by social scientists. The use of well-formulated observational techniques gave Donald Black the opportunity to discover the most influential situational conditions in police–citizen encounters.

On the basis of an observational study of patrolman–citizen transactions in Boston, Chicago, and Washington, D.C., Black was able to identify a number of variables that influence the likelihood of arrest. Like the other authors in this part, he found that the probability that a criminal act will be detected and sanctioned is significantly dependent on factors that are not legally relevant to the act itself. For example, the role of the citizen complainant is particularly important. Because the police have limited access to social settings, the detection of deviance depends heavily upon citizens' action. If the complainant is present during a police–suspect encounter and prefers that the case be handled by an arrest, the probability of an arrest is greatly increased.

A person who is disrespectful to the police is more likely to be arrested if he is suspected of a crime, and his wishes are less likely to be recognized officially if he is a complainant. Generally, like Piliavin and Briar, Black discovered that one's demeanor significantly affects the outcome of police–citizen contacts. Like Bittner, Black shows that arrest is only one alternative available to the police and its use depends on matters that may not be relevant to the accused's guilt or innocence.

The final two papers in this section examine decision-making by police detectives, taking us one step farther through the criminal justice system. The Terry and Luckenbill and Daudistel and Sanders articles add other dimensions to the discussion of police decision-making by using a theoretical perspective suggested by Bittner's work.

Clinton Terry and David Luckenbill reveal the contextual quality of homicide, showing how the categorization of a death as criminal is dependent on interpretive work done by homicide detectives. No matter how obvious it may seem, the establishment of any death as a criminal homicide requires that members of the police department present it as such. This presentation means that someone must select out the relevant evidence in support of the criminal nature of the event and convince others that this characterization is the correct one. According to Terry and Luckenbill, the "convincing" must be done in every case if it is to be considered a matter worthy of further investigation and processing in the criminal justice system. Even when the corpse is found at the feet of someone who is holding a smoking gun, it is the task of the homicide detective to "create" facts out of all the evidence and put them together so that the case can be presented as a crime.

The socially constructed character of crime is also investigated by Howard Daudistel and William Sanders, who found, as did Terry and Luckenbill, that all the scenes encountered by detectives must be subjected to a "practical analysis" before they are sensible to members of the criminal justice system. Their article focuses on the law itself and how its objective character is created by police detectives.

Daudistel and Sanders argue that the ethnomethodological perspective is useful because it concentrates on the most fundamental aspects of police decision-making. Following an ethnomethodological analysis of how police officers use the law, they argue that an adequate understanding of police discretion requires focus on how the meaning of the law itself is constructed by officers on specific occasions. This approach is distinctive because it concentrates on the legal categories themselves rather than on the persons who are using them or who are being placed in them.

Daudistel and Sanders further illustrate that the meaning of a law is not one specific thing. Nor is the meaning of the law to be found in a literal interpretation of what has been written. They conclude that the law is quite vague. The "elements" of the law, which are assumed to serve as instructions for those who wish to apply it, *do not* function as necessary and sufficient criteria that indicate when an act has been properly categorized as a criminal violation. This finding is important because it suggests that social scientists studying police discretion must recognize that meaning is always being given to the law. Because meanings change, acts are labeled criminal through defining the law rather than being made to fit the law. This means that a thorough study of police decision-making must include an investigation into the interpretive methods used to make the law fit various situations.

The Police on Skid-Row
A Study of Peace Keeping

Egon Bittner

The prototype of modern police organization, the Metropolitan Police of London, was created to replace an antiquated and corrupt system of law enforcement. The early planners were motivated by the mixture of hardheaded business rationality and humane sentiment that characterized liberal British thought of the first half of the nineteenth century. Partly to meet the objections of a parliamentary committee, which was opposed to the establishment of the police in England, and partly because it was in line with their own thinking, the planners sought to produce an instrument that could not readily be used in the play of internal power politics but would, instead, advance and protect conditions favorable to industry and commerce and to urban civil life in general. These intentions were not very specific and had to be reconciled with the existing structures of governing, administering justice, and keeping the peace. Consequently, the locus and mandate of the police in the modern polity were ill-defined at the outset. On the one hand, the new institution was to be a part of the executive branch of government, organized, funded, and staffed in accordance with standards that were typical for the entire system of the executive. On the other hand, the duties that were given to the police organization brought it under direct control of the judiciary in its day-to-day operation.

The dual patronage of the police by the executive and the judiciary is characteristic for all democratically governed countries. Moreover, it is generally the case, or at least it is deemed desirable, that judges *rather than* executive officials have control over police use and procedure.[1] This preference is based on two considerations. First, in the tenets of the democratic creed, the possibility of direct

Source: *American Sociological Review,* 32 (October 1967): 699–715. Reprinted by permission of the author and the American Sociological Association.

Note: This research was supported in part by Grant 64-1-35 from the California Department of Mental Hygiene. I gratefully acknowledge the help I received from Fred Davis, Sheldon Messinger, Leonard Schatzman, and Anselm Strauss in the preparation of this paper.

[1]Jerome Hall, "Police and Law in a Democratic Society," *Indiana Law Journal,* 28 (1953), 133–77. Though other authors are less emphatic on this point, judicial control is generally taken for granted. The point has been made, however, that in modern times judicial control over the police has been asserted mainly because of the default of any other general controlling authority, cf. E. L. Barrett, Jr., "Police Practice and the Law," *California Law Review,* 50 (1962), 11–55.

control of the police by a government in power is repugnant.[2] Even when the specter of the police state in its more ominous forms is not a concern, close ties between those who govern and those who police are viewed as a sign of political corruption. Hence, mayors, governors, and cabinet officers—although the nominal superiors of the police—tend to maintain, or to pretend, a hands-off policy. Second, it is commonly understood that the main function of the police is the control of crime. Since the concept of crime belongs wholly to the law, and its treatment is exhaustively based on considerations of legality, police procedure automatically stands under the same system of review that controls the administration of justice in general.

By nature, judicial control encompasses only those aspects of police activity that are directly related to full-dress legal prosecution of offenders. The judiciary has neither the authority nor the means to direct, supervise, and review those activities of the police that do not result in prosecution. Yet such other activities are unavoidable, frequent, and largely within the realm of public expectations. It might be assumed that in this domain of practice the police are under executive control. This is not the case, however, except in a marginal sense.[3] Not only are police departments generally free to determine what need be done and how, but aside from informal pressures they are given scant direction in these matters. Thus, there appear to exist two relatively independent domains of police activity. In one, their methods are constrained by the prospect of the future disposition of a case in the courts; in the other, they operate under some other consideration and largely with no structured and continuous outside constraint. Following the terminology suggested by Michael Banton, they may be said to function in the first instance as "law officers" and in the second instance as "peace officers."[4] It must be emphasized that the designation "peace officer" is a residual term, with only some vaguely presumptive content. The role, as Banton speaks of it, is supposed to encompass all occupational routines not directly related to making arrests, without, however, specifying what determines the limits of competence and availability of the police in such actions.

[2]A. C. German, F. D. Day and R. R. J. Gallati, *Introduction to Law Enforcement,* Springfield, Ill.: C. C. Thomas, 1966; "One concept, in particular, should be kept in mind. A dictatorship can never exist unless the police system of the country is under the absolute control of the dictator. There is no other way to uphold a dictatorship except by terror, and the instrument of this total terror is the secret police, whatever its name. In every country where freedom has been lost, law enforcement has been a dominant instrument in destroying it" (p. 80).

[3]The executive margin of control is set mainly in terms of budgetary determinations and the mapping of some formal aspects of the organization of departments.

[4]Michael Banton, *The Policeman in the Community,* New York: Basic Books, 1964, pp. 6–7 and 127 ff.

Efforts to characterize a large domain of activities of an important public agency have so far yielded only negative definitions. We know that they do not involve arrests; we also know that they do not stand under judicial control and that they are not, in any important sense, determined by specific executive or legislative mandates. In police textbooks and manuals, these activities receive only casual attention, and the role of the "peace officer" is typically stated in terms suggesting that his work is governed mainly by the individual officer's personal wisdom, integrity, and altruism. Police departments generally keep no records of procedures that do not involve making arrests. Policemen, when asked, insist that they merely use common sense when acting as "peace officers," though they tend to emphasize the elements of experience and practice in discharging the role adequately. All this ambiguity is the more remarkable for the fact that peace-keeping tasks—i.e., procedures not involving the formal legal remedy of arrest—were explicitly built into the program of the modern police from the outset. The early executives of the London police saw with great clarity that their organization had a dual function. While it was to be an arm of the administration of justice, in respect of which it developed certain techniques for bringing offenders to trial, it was also expected to function apart from, and at times in lieu of, the employment of full-dress legal procedure. Despite its early origin, despite a great deal of public knowledge about it, despite the fact that it is routinely done by policemen, no one can say with any clarity what it means to do a good job of keeping the peace. To be sure, there is vague consensus that when policemen direct, aid, inform, pacify, warn, discipline, roust, and do whatever else they do without making arrests, they do this with some reference to the circumstances of the occasion and, thus, somehow contribute to the maintenance of the peace and order. Peace keeping appears to be a solution to an unknown problem arrived at by unknown means.

The following is an attempt to clarify conceptually the mandate and the practice of keeping the peace. The effort will be directed not to the formulation of a comprehensive solution of the problem but to a detailed consideration of some aspects of it. Only in order to place the particular into the overall domain to which it belongs will the structural determinants of keeping the peace in general be discussed. By structural determinants are meant the typical situations that policemen perceive as *demand conditions* for action without arrest. This will be followed by a description of peace keeping in Skid-Row districts, with the object of identifying those aspects of it that constitute a *practical skill.*

Since the major object of this paper is to elucidate peace keeping practice as a skilled performance, it is necessary to make clear how the use of the term is intended.

Practical skill will be used to refer to those methods of doing certain things, and to the information that underlies the use of the methods, that *practitioners themselves* view as proper and efficient. Skill is, therefore, a stable orientation to work tasks that is relatively independent of the personal feelings and judgments of those who employ it. Whether the exercise of this skilled performance is desirable or not, and whether it is based on correct information or not, are specifically outside the scope of interest of this presentation. The following is deliberately confined to a description of what police patrolmen consider to be the reality of their work circumstances, what they do, and what they feel they must do to do a good job. That the practice is thought to be determined by normative standards of skill minimizes but does not eliminate the factors of personal interest or inclination. Moreover, the distribution of skill varies among practitioners in the very standards they set for themselves. For example, we will show that patrolmen view a measure of rough informality as good practice vis-à-vis Skid-Row inhabitants. By this standard, patrolmen who are "not rough enough" or who are "too rough," or whose roughness is determined by personal feelings rather than by situational exigencies are judged to be poor craftsmen.

The description and analysis are based on twelve months of field work with the police departments of two large cities west of the Mississippi. Eleven weeks of this time were spent in Skid-Row and Skid-Row-like districts. The observations were augmented by approximately one hundred interviews with police officers of all ranks. The formulations that will be proposed were discussed in these interviews. They were recognized by the respondents as elements of standard practice. The respondents' recognition was often accompanied by remarks indicating that they had never thought about things in this way and that they were not aware how standarized police work was.

Structural Demand Conditions of Peace Keeping

There exist at least five types of relatively distinct circumstances that produce police activities that do not involve invoking the law and that are only in a trivial sense determined by those considerations of legality that determine law enforcement. This does not mean that these activities are illegal but merely that there is no legal directive that informs the acting policeman whether what he does must be done or how it is to be done. In these circumstances, policemen act as all-purpose and terminal remedial agents, and the confronted problem is solved in the field. If these practices stand under any kind of review at all, and typically they do not, it is only through internal police department control.

1. Although the executive branch of government generally refrains from exercising a controlling influence over the direction of police interest, it manages to extract certain performances from it. Two important examples of this are the supervision of certain licensed services and premises and the regulation of traffic. With respect to the first, the police tend to concentrate on what might be called the moral aspects of establishments rather than on questions relating to the technical adequacy of the service. This orientation is based on the assumption that certain types of businesses lend themselves to exploitation for undesirable and illegal purposes. Since this tendency cannot be fully controlled, it is only natural that the police will be inclined to favor licensees who are at least cooperative. This, however, transforms the task from the mere scrutiny of credentials and the passing of judgments, to the creation and maintenance of a network of connections that conveys influence, pressure, and information. The duty to inspect is the background of this network, but the resulting contacts acquire additional value for solving crimes and maintaining public order. Bartenders, shopkeepers, and hotel clerks become, for patrolmen, a resource that must be continuously serviced by visits and exchanges of favors. While it is apparent that this condition lends itself to corrupt exploitation by individual officers, even the most flawlessly honest policeman must participate in this network of exchanges if he is to function adequately. Thus, engaging in such exchanges becomes an occupational task that demands attention and time.

Regulation of traffic is considerably less complex. More than anything else, traffic control symbolizes the autonomous authority of policemen. Their commands generally are met with unquestioned compliance. Even when they issue citations, which seemingly refer the case to the courts, it is common practice for the accused to view the allegation as a finding against him and to pay the fine. Police officials emphasize that it is more important to be circumspect than legalistic in traffic control. Officers are often reminded that a large segment of the public has no other contacts with the police, and that the field lends itself to public relations work by the line personnel.

2. Policemen often do not arrest persons who have committed minor offenses in circumstances in which the arrest is technically possible. This practice has recently received considerable attention in legal and sociological literature. The studies were motivated by the realization that "police decisions not to invoke the criminal process determine the outer limits of law enforcement." From these researches, it was learned that the police tend to impose more stringent criteria of law enforcement on certain segments of the community than on others.[5] It was also learned that, from the perspective

[5]Jerome Skolnick, *Justice without Trial*, New York: Wiley, 1966.

of the administration of justice, the decisions not to make arrests often are based on compelling reasons. It is less well appreciated that policemen often not only refrain from invoking the law formally but also employ alternative sanctions. For example, it is standard practice that violators are warned not to repeat the offense. This often leads to patrolmen's "keeping an eye" on certain persons. Less frequent, though not unusual, is the practice of direct disciplining of offenders, especially when they are juveniles, which occasionally involves inducing them to repair the damage occasioned by their misconduct.

The power to arrest and the freedom not to arrest can be used in cases that do not involve patent offenses. An officer can say to a person whose behavior he wishes to control, "I'll let you go this time!" without indicating to him that he could not have been arrested in any case. Nor is this always deliberate misrepresentation, for in many cases the law is sufficiently ambiguous to allow alternative interpretations. In short, not to make an arrest is rarely, if ever, merely a decision not to act; it is most often a decision to act alternatively. In the case of minor offenses, to make an arrest often is merely one of several possible proper actions.

3. There exists a public demand for police intervention in matters that contain no criminal and often no legal aspects. For example, it is commonly assumed that officers will be available to arbitrate quarrels, to pacify the unruly, and to help in keeping order. They are supposed also to aid people in trouble, and there is scarcely a human predicament imaginable for which police aid has not been solicited and obtained at one time or another. Most authors writing about the police consider such activities only marginally related to the police mandate. This view fails to reckon with the fact that the availability of these performances is taken for granted and the police assign a substantial amount of their resources to such work. Although this work cannot be subsumed under the concept of legal action, it does involve the exercise of a form of authority that most people associate with the police. In fact, no matter how trivial the occasion, the device of "calling the cops" transforms any problem. It implies that a situation is, or is getting, out of hand. Police responses to public demands are always oriented to this implication, and the risk of proliferation of troubles makes every call a potentially serious matter.[6]

4. Certain mass phenomena of either a regular or a spontaneous nature require direct monitoring. Most important is the controlling

---

[6]There is little doubt that many requests for service are turned down by the police, especially when they are made over the telephone or by mail. ... The uniformed patrolman, however, finds it virtually impossible to leave the scene without becoming involved in some way or another.

of crowds in incipient stages of disorder. The specter of mob violence frequently calls for measures that involve coercion, including the use of physical force. Legal theory allows, of course, that public officials are empowered to use coercion in situations of imminent danger. Unfortunately, the doctrine is not sufficiently specific to be of much help as a rule of practice. It is based on the assumption of the adventitiousness of danger, and thus does not lend itself readily to elaborations that could direct the routines of early detection and prevention of untoward developments. It is interesting that the objective of preventing riots by informal means posed one of the central organizational problems for the police in England during the era of the Chartists.

5. The police have certain special duties with respect to persons who are viewed as less than fully accountable for their actions. Examples of those eligible for special consideration are those who are under age and those who are mentally ill. Although it is virtually never acknowledged explicitly, those receiving special treatment include people who do not lead "normal" lives and who occupy a pariah status in society. This group includes residents of ethnic ghettos, certain types of bohemians and vagabonds, and persons of known criminal background. The special treatment of children and of sick persons is permissively sanctioned by the law, but the special treatment of others is, in principle, opposed by the leading theme of legality and the tenets of the democratic faith.[7] The important point is not that such persons are arrested more often than others, which is quite true, but that they are perceived by the police as producing a special problem that necessitates continuous attention and the use of special procedures.

The five types of demand conditions do not exclude the possibility of invoking the criminal process. Indeed, arrests do occur quite frequently in all these circumstances. But the concerns generated in these areas cause activities that usually do not terminate in an arrest. When arrests are made, there exist, at least in the ideal, certain criteria by reference to which the arrest can be judged as having been made more or less properly, and there are some persons who, in the natural course of events, actually judge the performance.[8] But for actions not resulting in arrest there are no such criteria and no

[7]It bears mentioning, however, that differential treatment is not unique with the police, but is also in many ways representative for the administration of justice in general; cf. J. E. Carlin, Jan Howard and S. L. Messinger, "Civil Justice and the Poor," *Law and Society*, 1 (1966), 9–89; Jacobus tenBroek (ed.) *The Law of the Poor*, San Francisco: Chandler Publishing Co., 1966.

[8]This is, however, true only in the ideal. It is well known that a substantial number of persons who are arrested are subsequently released without ever being charged and tried, cf. Barrett, *op. cit.*

such judges. How, then, can one speak of such actions as necessary and proper? Since there does not exist any official answer to this query, and since policemen act in the role of "peace officers" pretty much without external direction or constraint, the question comes down to asking how the policeman himself knows whether he has any business with a person he does not arrest and, if so, what that business might be. Furthermore, if there exists a domain of concerns and activities that is largely independent of the law enforcement mandate, it is reasonable to assume that it will exercise some degree of influence on how and to what ends the law is invoked in cases of arrests.

Skid-Row presents one excellent opportunity to study these problems. The area contains a heavy concentration of persons who do not live "normal" lives in terms of prevailing standards of middle-class morality. Since the police respond to this situation by intensive patrolling, the structure of peace keeping should be readily observable. Needless to say, the findings and conclusions will not be necessarily generalizable to other types of demand conditions.

The Problem of Keeping the Peace in Skid-Row

Skid-Row has always occupied a special place among the various forms of urban life. While other areas are perceived as being different in many ways, Skid-Row is seen as completely different. Though it is located in the heart of civilization, it is viewed as containing aspects of the primordial jungle, calling for missionary activities and offering opportunities for exotic adventure. While each inhabitant individually can be seen as tragically linked to the vicissitudes of "normal" life, allowing others to say "here but for the Grace of God go I," those who live there are believed to have repudiated the entire role-casting scheme of the majority and to live apart from normalcy. Accordingly, the traditional attitude of civic-mindedness toward Skid-Row has been dominated by the desire to contain it and to salvage souls from its clutches.[9] The specific task of containment has been left to the police. That this task pressed upon the police some rather special duties has never come under explicit consideration, either from the government that expects control or from the police departments that implement it. Instead, the prevailing method of carrying out the task is to assign partrolmen to the area on a fairly permanent basis and to allow them to work out their own ways of

[9]The literature on Skid-Row is voluminous. The classic in the field is Nels Anderson, *The Hobo,* Chicago: University of Chicago Press, 1923. Samuel E. Wallace, *Skid-Row as a Way of Life,* Totowa, New Jersey: The Bedminister Press, 1965, is a more recent descriptive account and contains a useful bibliography. Donald A. Bogue, *Skid-Row in American Cities,* Chicago: Community and Family Center, University of Chicago, 1963, contains an exhaustive quantitative survey of Chicago Skid-Row.

running things. External influence is confined largely to the supply of support and facilities, on the one hand, and to occasional expressions of criticism about the overall conditions, on the other. Within the limits of available resources and general expectations, patrolmen are supposed to know what to do and are free to do it.[10]

Patrolmen who are more or less permanently assigned to Skid-Row districts tend to develop a conception of the nature of their "domain" that is surprisingly uniform. Individual officers differ in many aspects of practice, emphasize different concerns, and maintain different contacts, but they are in fundamental agreement about the structure of Skid-Row life. This relatively uniform conception includes an implicit formulation of the problem of keeping the peace in Skid-Row.

In the view of experienced patrolmen, life on Skid-Row is fundamentally different from life in other parts of society. To be sure, they say, around its geographic limits the area tends to blend into the surrounding environment, and its population always encompasses some persons who are only transitionally associated with it. Basically, however, Skid-Row is perceived as the natural habitat of people who lack the capacities and commitments to live "normal" lives on a sustained basis. The presence of these people defines the nature of social reality in the area. In general, and especially in casual encounters, the presumption of incompetence and of the disinclination to be "normal" is the leading theme for the interpretation of all actions and relations. Not only do people approach one another in this manner, but presumably they also expect to be approached in this way, and they conduct themselves accordingly.

In practice, the restriction of interactional possibilities that is based on the patrolman's stereotyped conception of Skid-Row residents is always subject to revision and modification toward particular individuals. Thus, it is entirely possible, and not unusual, for patrolmen to view certain Skid-Row inhabitants in terms that involve non–Skid-Row aspects of normality. Instances of such approaches and relationships invariably involve personal acquaintance and the knowledge of a good deal of individually qualifying information. Such instances are seen, despite their relative frequency, as exceptions to the rule. The awareness of the possibility

[10]One of the two cities described in this paper also employed the procedure of the "round-up" of drunks. In this, the police van toured the Skid-Row area twice daily, during the midafternoon and early evening hours, and the officers who manned it picked up drunks they sighted. A similar procedure is used in New York's Bowery, and the officers who do it are called "condition men." Cf. *Bowery Project,* Bureau of Applied Social Research, Columbia University, Summary Report of a Study Undertaken under Contract Approved by the Board of Estimate, 1963, mimeo., p. 11.

of breakdown, frustration, and betrayal is ever present, basic wariness is never wholly dissipated, and undaunted trust can never be fully reconciled with presence on Skid-Row.

What patrolmen view as normal on Skid-Row—and what they also think is taken for granted as "life as usual" by the inhabitants —is not easily summarized. It seems to focus on the idea that the dominant consideration governing all enterprise and association is directed to the occasion of the moment. Nothing is thought of as having a background that might have led up to the present in terms of some compelling moral or practical necessity. There are some exceptions to this rule, of course: the police themselves, and those who run certain establishments, are perceived as engaged in important and necessary activities. But in order to carry them out they, too, must be geared to the overall atmosphere of fortuitousness. In this atmosphere, the range of control that persons have over one another is exceedingly narrow. Good faith, even where it is valued, is seen merely as a personal matter. Its violations are the victim's own hard luck, rather than demonstrable violations of property. There is only a private sense of irony at having been victimized. The overall air is not so much one of active distrust as it is one of irrelevance of trust; as patrolmen often emphasize, the situation does not necessarily cause all relations to be predatory, but the possibility of exploitation is not checked by the expectation that it will not happen.

Just as the past is seen by the policeman as having only the most attenuated relevance to the present, so the future implications of present situations are said to be generally devoid of prospective coherence. No venture, especially no joint venture, can be said to have a strongly predictable future in line with its initial objectives. It is a matter of adventitious circumstance whether or not matters go as anticipated. That which is not within the grasp of momentary control is outside of practical social reality.

Though patrolmen see the temporal framework of the occasion of the moment mainly as a lack of trustworthiness, they also recognize that it involves more than merely the personal motives of individuals. In addition to the fact that everybody *feels* that things matter only at the moment, irresponsibility takes an *objectified* form on Skid-Row. The places the residents occupy, the social relations they entertain, and the activities that engage them are not meaningfully connected over time. Thus, for example, address, occupation, marital status, etc., matter much less on Skid-Row than in any other part of society. The fact that present whereabouts, activities, and affiliations imply neither continuity nor direction means that life on Skid-Row lacks a socially structured background of accountability. Of course, everybody's life contains some sequential incongruities, but in the life of a Skid-Row inhabitant every moment is an accident. That a

man has no "address" in the future that could be in some way inferred from where he is and what he does makes him a person of
radically reduced visibility. If he disappears from sight and one
wishes to locate him, it is virtually impossible to systematize the
search. All one can know with relative certainty is that he will be
somehwere on some Skid-Row, and the only thing one can do is to
trace the factual contiguities of his whereabouts.

It is commonly known that the police are expert in finding people
and that they have developed an exquisite technology involving
special facilities and procedures of sleuthing. It is less well appreciated that all this technology builds upon those socially structured
features of everyday life that render persons findable in the first
place.

Under ordinary conditions, the query as to where a person is can
be addressed, from the outset, to a restricted realm of possibilities
that can be further narrowed by looking into certain places and
asking certain persons. The map of whereabouts that normally competent persons use whenever they wish to locate someone is constituted by the basic facts of membership in society. Insofar as
membership consists of status incumbencies, each of which has an
adumbrated future that substantially reduces unpredictability, it is
itself a guarantee of the order within which it is quite difficult to get
lost. Membership is thus visible not only now but also as its own
projection into the future. It is in terms of this prospective availability that the Skid-Row inhabitant is a person of reduced visibility.
His membership is viewed as extraordinary because its extension
into the future is *not* reduced to a restricted realm of possibilities.
Neither his subjective dispositions, nor his circumstances, indicate
that he is oriented to any particular long-range interests. But, as he
may claim every contingent opportunity, his claims are always seen
as based on slight merit or right, at least to the extent that interfering
with them does not constitute a substantial denial of his freedom.

This, then, constitutes the problem of keeping the peace on Skid-
Row. Considerations of momentary expediency are seen as having
unqualified priority as maxims of conduct; consequently, the controlling influences of the pursuit of sustained interests are presumed
to be absent.

The Practices of Keeping the Peace in Skid-Row

From the perspective of society as a whole, Skid-Row inhabitants
appear troublesome in a variety of ways. The uncommitted life
attributed to them is perceived as inherently offensive; its very
existence arouses indignation and contempt. More important, however, is the feeling that persons who have repudiated the entire

role-status casting system of society, persons whose lives forever collapse into a succession of random moments, are seen as constituting a practical risk. As they have nothing to foresake, nothing is thought safe from them.[11]

The Skid-Row patrolman's concept of his mandate includes an awareness of this presumed risk. He is constantly attuned to the possibility of violence, and he is convinced that things to which the inhabitants have free access are as good as lost. But his concern is directed toward the continuous condition of peril *in the area* rather than *for society in general.* While he is obviously conscious of the presence of many persons who have committed crimes outside of Skid-Row and will arrest them when they come to his attention, this is a peripheral part of his routine activities. In general, the Skid-Row patrolman and his superiors take for granted that his main business is to keep the peace and enforce the laws *on Skid-Row,* and that he is involved only incidentally in protecting society at large. Thus, his task is formulated basically as the protection of putative predators from one another. The maintenance of peace and safety is difficult because everyday life on Skid-Row is viewed as an open field for reciprocal exploitation. As the lives of the inhabitants lack the prospective coherence associated with status incumbency, the realization of self-interest does not produce order. Hence, mechanisms that control risk must work primarily from without.

External containment, to be effective, must be oriented to the realities of existence. Thus, the Skid-Row patrolman employs an approach that he views as appropriate to the *ad hoc* nature of Skid-Row life. The following are the three most prominent elements of this approach. First, the seasoned patrolman seeks to acquire a richly particularized knowledge of people and places in the area. Second, he gives the consideration of strict culpability a subordinate status among grounds for remedial sanction. Third, his use and choice of coercive interventions is determined mainly by exigencies of situations and with little regard for possible long-range effects on individual persons.

The Particularization of Knowledge

The patrolman's orientation to people on Skid-Row is structured basically by the presupposition that if he does not know a man personally there is very little that he can assume about him. This

---

[11]An illuminating parallel to the perception of Skid-Row can be found in the more traditional concept of vagabondage. Cf. Alexandre Vexliard, *Introduction à la Sociologie du Vagabondage,* Paris: Libraire Marcel Rivière, 1956, and "La Disparition du Vagabondage comme Fleau Social Universel," *Revue de L'Institut de Sociologie* (1963), 53–79. The classic account of English conditions up to the nineteenth century is C. J. Ribton-Turner, *A History of Vagrants and Vagrancy and Beggars and Begging,* London: Chapman and Hall, 1887.

rule determines his interaction with people who live on Skid-Row. Since the area also contains other types of persons, however, its applicability is not universal. To some such persons it does not apply at all, and it has a somewhat mitigated significance with certain others. For example, some persons encountered on Skid-Row can be recognized immediately as outsiders. Among them are workers who are employed in commercial and industrial enterprises that abut the area, persons who come for the purpose of adventurous "slumming," and some patrons of secondhand stores and pawn shops. Even with very little experience, it is relatively easy to identify these people by appearance, demeanor, and the time and place of their presence. The patrolman maintains an impersonal attitude toward them, and they are, under ordinary circumstances, not the objects of his attention.[12]

Clearly set off from these outsiders are the residents and the entire corps of personnel that services Skid-Row. It would be fair to say that one of the main routine activities of patrolmen is the establishment and maintenance of familiar relationships with individual members of these groups. Officers emphasize their interest in this, and they maintain that their grasp of and control over Skid-Row is precisely commensurate with the extent to which they "know the people." By this they do not mean having a quasi-theoretical understanding of human nature but rather the common practice of individualized and reciprocal recognition. As this group encompasses both those who render services on Skid-Row and those who are serviced, individualized interest is not always based on the desire to overcome uncertainty. Instead, relations with service personnel become absorbed into the network of particularized attention. Ties between patrolmen, on the one hand, and businessmen, managers, and workers, on the other hand, are often defined in terms of shared or similar interests. It bears mentioning that many persons live *and* work on Skid-Row. Thus, the distinction between those who service and those who are serviced is not a clear-cut dichotomy but a spectrum of affiliations.

As a general rule, the Skid-Row patrolman possesses an immensely detailed factual knowledge of his beat. He knows, and knows a great deal about, a large number of residents. He is likely to know every person who manages or works in the local bars, hotels, shops, stores, and missions. Moreover, he probably knows every public and private place inside and out. Finally, he ordinarily remembers countless events of the past which he can recount by citing names, dates and places with remarkable precision. Though

---

[12]Several patrolmen complained about the influx of "tourists" into Skid-Row. Since such "tourists" are perceived as seeking illicit adventure, they receive little sympathy from patrolmen when they complain about being victimized.

there are always some threads missing in the fabric of information, it is continuously woven and mended even as it is being used. New facts, however, are added to the texture, not in terms of structured categories but in terms of adjoining known realities. In other words, the content and organization of the patrolman's knowledge is primarily ideographic and only vestigially, if at all, nomothetic.

Individual patrolmen vary in the extent to which they make themselves available or actively pursue personal acquaintants. But even the most aloof are continuously greeted and engaged in conversations that indicate a background of individualistic associations. While this scarcely has the appearance of work, because of its casual character, patrolmen do not view it as an optional activity. In the course of making their rounds, patrolmen seem to have access to every place, and their entry causes no surprise or consternation. Instead, the entry tends to lead to informal exchanges of small talk. At times the rounds include entering hotels and gaining access to rooms or dormitories, often for no other purpose than asking the occupants how things are going. In all this, patrolmen address innumerable persons by name and are in turn addressed by name. The conversational style that characterizes these exchanges is casual to an extent that by non-Skid-Row standards might suggest intimacy. Not only does the officer himself avoid all terms of deference and respect but he does not seem to expect or demand them. For example, a patrolman said to a man radiating an alcoholic glow on the streets, "You've got enough of a heat on now; I'll give you ten minutes to get your ass off the street!" Without stopping, the man answered, "Oh, why don't you go and piss in your own pot!" The officer's only response was, "All right, in ten minutes you're either in bed or on your way to the can."

This kind of expressive freedom is an intricately limited privilege. Persons of acquaintance are entitled to it and appear to exercise it mainly in routinized encounters. But strangers, too, can use it with impunity. The safe way of gaining the privilege is to respond to the patrolman in ways that do not challenge his right to ask questions and issue commands. Once the concession is made that the officer is entitled to inquire into a man's background, business, and intentions, and that he is entitled to obedience, there opens a field of colloquial license. A patrolman seems to grant expressive freedom in recognition of a person's acceptance of his access to areas of life ordinarily defined as private and subject to coercive control only under special circumstances. While patrolmen accept and seemingly even cultivate the rough *quid pro quo* of informality, and while they do not expect sincerity, candor, or obedience in their dealings with the inhabitants, they do not allow the rejection of their approach.

The explicit refusal to answer questions of a personal nature and the demand to know why the questions are asked significantly enhances a person's chances of being arrested on some minor charge. While most patrolmen tend to be personally indignant about this kind of response and use the arrest to compose their own hurt feelings, this is merely a case of affect being in line with the method. There are other officers who proceed in the same manner without taking offense, or even with feelings of regret. Such patrolmen often maintain that their colleagues' affective involvement is a corruption of an essentially valid technique. The technique is oriented to the goal of maintaining operational control. The patrolman's conception of this goal places him hierarchically above whomever he approaches, and makes him the sole judge of the propriety of the occasion. As he alone is oriented to this goal, and as he seeks to attain it by means of individualized access to persons, those who frustrate him are seen as motivated at best by the desire to "give him a hard time" and at worst by some darkly devious purpose.

Officers are quite aware that the directness of their approach and the demands they make are difficult to reconcile with the doctrines of civil liberties, but they maintain that they are in accord with the general freedom of access that persons living on Skid-Row normally grant one another. That is, they believe that the imposition of personalized and far-reaching control is in tune with standard expectancies. In terms of these expectancies, people are not so much denied the right to privacy as they are seen as not having any privacy. Thus, officers seek to install themselves in the center of people's lives and let the consciousness of their presence play the part of conscience.

When talking about the practical necessity of an aggressively personal approach, officers do not refer merely to the need for maintaining control over lives that are open in the direction of the untoward. They also see it as the basis for the supply of certain valued services to inhabitants of Skid-Row. The coerced or conceded access to persons often imposes on the patrolman tasks that are, in the main, in line with these persons' expressed or implied interest. In asserting this connection, patrolmen note that they frequently help people to obtain meals, lodging, employment, that they direct them to welfare and health services, and that they aid them in various other ways. Though patrolmen tend to describe such services mainly as the product of their own altruism, they also say that their colleagues who avoid them are simply doing a poor job of patrolling. The acceptance of the need to help people is based on the realization that the hungry, the sick, and the troubled are a potential source of problems. Moreover, that patrolmen will help people is part of the background expectancies of life on Skid-Row. Hotel clerks normally call policemen when someone gets so sick as to need attention; merchants expect to be taxed, in a manner of speaking, to meet the pressing needs of certain persons; and the inhabitants do not hesitate to accept, solicit, and demand every kind of aid. The domain of the patrolman's service activity is virtually limitless, and it is no exaggeration to say that the solution of every conceivable problem has at one time or another been attempted by a police officer. In one observed instance, a patrolman unceremoniously entered the room of a man he had never seen before. The man, who gave no indication that he regarded the officer's entry and questions as anything but part of life as usual, related a story of having had his dentures stolen by his wife. In the course of the subsequent rounds, the patrolman sought to locate the woman and the dentures. This did not become the evening's project but was attended to while doing other things. In the densely matted activities of the patrolman, the questioning became one more strand, not so much to be pursued to its solution as a theme that organized the memory of one more man known individually. In all this, the officer followed the precept formulated by a somewhat more articulate patrolman: "If I want to be in control of my work and keep the street relatively peaceful, I have to know the people. To know them I must gain their trust, which means that I have to be involved in their lives. But I can't be soft like a social worker because unlike him I cannot call the cops when things go wrong. I am the cops!"[13]

The Restricted Relevance of Culpability

It is well known that policemen exercise discretionary freedom in invoking the law. It is also conceded that, in some measure, the practice is unavoidable. This being so, the outstanding problem is whether or not the decisions are in line with the intent of the law. On Skid-Row, patrolmen often make decisions based on reasons that the law probably does not recognize as valid. The problem can best be introduced by citing an example.

A man in a relatively mild state of intoxication (by skid-row standards) approached a patrolman to tell him that he had a room in a hotel, to which the officer responded by urging him to go to bed instead of getting drunk. As the man walked off, the officer related the following thoughts: Here is a completely lost soul. Though he probably is no more than thirty-five years old, he looks to be in his fifties. He never works and he hardly ever has a place to stay. He has been on the street for several years and is known as "Dakota." During the past few days, "Dakota" has been seen in the company of "Big

[13] The same officer commented further, "If a man looks for something, I might help him. But I don't stay with him till he finds what he is looking for. If I did, I would never get to do anything else. In the last analysis, I really never solve any problems. The best I can hope for is to keep things from getting worse."

Jim." The latter is an invalid living on some sort of pension with which he pays for a room in the hotel to which "Dakota" referred and for four weekly meal tickets in one of the restaurants on the street. Whatever is left he spends on wine and beer. Occasionally, "Big Jim" goes on drinking sprees in the company of someone like "Dakota." Leaving aside the consideration that there is probably a homosexual background to the association, and that it is not right that "Big Jim" should have to support the drinking habit of someone else, there is the more important risk that if "Dakota" moves in with "Big Jim" he will very likely walk off with whatever the latter keeps in his room. "Big Jim" would never dream of reporting the theft; he would just beat the hell out of "Dakota" after he sobered up. When asked what could be done to prevent the theft and the subsequent recriminations, the patrolman proposed that in this particular case he would throw "Big Jim" into jail if he found him tonight and then tell the hotel clerk to throw "Dakota" out of the room. When asked why he did not arrest "Dakota," who was, after all, drunk enough to warrant an arrest, the officer explained that this would not solve anything. While "Dakota" was in jail "Big Jim" would continue drinking and would either strike up another liaison or embrace his old buddy after he had been released. The only thing to do was to get "Big Jim" to sober up, and the only sure way of doing this was to arrest him.

As it turned out, "Big Jim" was not located that evening. But had he been located and arrested on a drunk charge, the fact that he was intoxicated would not have been the real reason for proceeding against him, but merely the pretext. The point of the example is not that it illustrates the tendency of Skid-Row patrolmen to arrest persons who would not be arrested under conditions of full respect for their legal rights. To be sure, this too happens. In the majority of minor arrest cases, however, the criteria the law specifies are met. But it is the rare exception that the law is invoked merely because the specifications of the law are met. That is, compliance with the law is merely the outward appearance of an intervention that is actually based on altogether different considerations. Thus, it could be said that patrolmen do not really enforce the law, even when they do invoke it, but merely use it as a resource to solve certain pressing practical problems in keeping the peace. This observation goes beyond the conclusion that many of the lesser norms of the criminal law are treated as defeasible in police work. It is patently not the case that Skid-Row patrolmen apply the legal norms while recognizing many exceptions to their applicability. Instead, the observation leads to the conclusion that, in keeping the peace of Skid-Row, patrolmen encounter certain matters they attend to by means of coercive action, e.g., arrests. In doing this, they invoke legal norms that are available, and with some regard for substantive appropriateness.

Hence, the problem patrolmen confront is not which drunks, beggars, or disturbers of the peace should be arrested and which can be let go as exceptions to the rule. Rather, the problem is whether, when someone "needs" to be arrested, he should be charged with drunkenness, begging, or disturbing the peace. Speculating further, one is almost compelled to infer that virtually any set of norms could be used in this manner, provided that they sanction relatively common forms of behavior.

The reduced relevance of culpability in peacekeeping practice on Skid-Row is not readily visible. As mentioned, most arrested persons were actually found in the act, or in the state, alleged in the arrest record. It becomes partly visible when one views the treatment of persons who are not arrested even though all the legal grounds for an arrest are present. Whenever such persons are encountered and can be induced to leave, or taken to some shelter, or remanded to someone's care, then patrolmen feel, or at least maintain, that an arrest would serve no useful purpose. That is, whenever there exist means for controlling the troublesome aspects of some person's presence in some way alternative to an arrest, such means are preferentially employed, provided, of course, that the case at hand involves only a minor offense.[14]

The attenuation of the relevance of culpability is most visible when the presence of legal grounds for an arrest could be questioned, i.e., in cases that sometimes are euphemistically called "preventive arrests." In one observed instance, a man who attempted to trade a pocket knife came to the attention of a patrolman. The initial encounter was attended by a good deal of levity, and the man willingly responded to the officer's inquiries about his identity and business. The man laughingly acknowledged that he needed some money to get drunk. In the course of the exchange it came to light that he had just arrived in town, traveling in his automobile. When confronted with the demand to lead the officer to the car, the man's expression became serious and he pointedly stated that he would not comply because this was none of the officer's business. After a bit more prodding, which the patrolman initially kept in the light mood, the man was arrested on a charge involving begging. In subsequent conversation the patrolman acknowledged that the charge was only speciously appropriate and mainly a pretext. Having committed

[14]When evidence is present to indicate that a serious crime has been committed, considerations of culpability acquire a position of priority. Two such arrests were observed, both involving checkpassers. The first offender was caught in *flagrante delicato*. In the second instance, the suspect attracted the attention of the patrolman because of his sickly appearance. In the ensuing conversation the man made some remarks that led the officer to place a call with the Warrant Division of his department. According to the information that was obtained by checking records, the man was a wanted checkpasser and was immediately arrested.

himself to demanding information he could not accept defeat. When this incident was discussed with another patrolman, the second officer found fault not with the fact that the arrest was made on a pretext but with the first officer's own contribution to the creation of conditions that made it unavoidable. "You see," he continued, "there is always the risk that the man is testing you and you must let him know what is what. The best among us can usually keep the upper hand in such situations without making arrests. But when it comes down to the wire, then you can't let them get away with it."

Finally, it must be mentioned that the reduction of the significance of culpability is built into the normal order of Skid-Row life, as patrolmen see it. Officers almost unfailingly say, pointing to some particular person, "I know that he knows that I know that some of the things he 'owns' are stolen, and that nothing can be done about it." In saying this, they often claim to have knowledge of such a degree of certainty as would normally be sufficient for virtually any kind of action except legal proceedings. Against this background, patrolmen adopt the view that the law is not merely imperfect and difficult to implement, but that on Skid-Row, at least, the association between delict and sanction is distinctly occasional. Thus, to implement the law naïvely, i.e., to arrest someone *merely* because he committed some minor offense, is perceived as containing elements of injustice.

Moreover, patrolmen often deal with situations in which questions of culpability are profoundly ambiguous. For example, an officer was called to help in settling a violent dispute in a hotel room. The object of the quarrel was a supposedly stolen pair of trousers. As the story unfolded in the conflicting versions of the participants, it was not possible to decide who was the complainant and who was alleged to be the thief, nor did it come to light who occupied the room in which the fracas took place, or whether the trousers were taken from the room or to the room. Though the officer did ask some questions, it seemed, and was confirmed in later conversation, that he was there not to solve the puzzle of the missing trousers but to keep the situation from getting out of hand. In the end, the exhausted participants dispersed, and this was the conclusion of the case. The patrolman maintained that no one could unravel mysteries of this sort because "these people take things from each other so often that no one could tell what 'belongs' to whom." In fact, he suggested, the terms owning, stealing, and swindling, in their strict sense, do not really belong on Skid-Row, and all efforts to distribute guilt and innocence according to some rational formula of justice are doomed to failure.

It could be said that the term "curbstone justice" that is sometimes applied to the procedures of patrolmen in Skid-Rows contains a double irony. Not only is the procedure not legally authorized, which is the intended irony in the expression, but it does not even pretend to distribute deserts. The best among the patrolmen, according to their own standards, use the law to keep Skid-Row inhabitants from sinking deeper into the misery they already experience. The worst, in terms of these same standards, exploit the practice for personal aggrandizement or gain. Leaving motives aside, however, it is easy to see that if culpability is not the salient consideration leading to an arrest in cases where it is patently obvious, then the practical patrolman may not view it as being wholly out of line to make arrests lacking in formal legal justification. Conversely, he will come to view minor offense arrests made solely because legal standards are met as poor craftsmanship.

The Background of Ad Hoc Decision-Making

When Skid-Row patrolmen are pressed to explain their reasons for minor offense arrests, they most often mention that it is done for the protection of the arrested person. This, they maintain, is the case in virtually all drunk arrests, in the majority of arrests involving begging and other nuisance offenses, and in many cases involving acts of violence. When they are asked to explain further such arrests as the one cited earlier involving the man attempting to sell the pocket knife, who was certainly not arrested for his own protection, they cite the consideration that belligerent persons constitute a much greater menace on Skid-Row than any place else in the city. The reasons for this are twofold. First, many of the inhabitants are old, feeble, and not too smart, all of which makes them relatively defenseless. Second, many of the inhabitants are involved in illegal activities and are known as persons of bad character, which does not make them credible victims or witnesses. Potential predators realize that the resources society has mobilized to minimize the risk of criminal victimization do not protect the predator himself. Thus, reciprocal exploitation constitutes a preferred risk. The high vulnerability of everybody on Skid-Row is public knowledge and causes every seemingly aggressive act to be seen as a potentially grave risk.

When, in response to all this, patrolmen are confronted with the observation that many minor offense arrests they make do not seem to involve a careful evaluation of facts before acting, they give the following explanations: First, the two reasons of protection and prevention represent a global background, and in individual cases it may sometimes not be possible to produce adequate justification on these grounds. Nor is it thought to be a problem of great moment to estimate precisely whether someone is more likely to come to grief or to cause grief when the objective is to prevent the proliferation of troubles. Second, patrolmen maintain that some of the seemingly

spur-of-the-moment decisions are actually made against a background of knowledge of facts that are not readily apparent in the
situations. Since experience not only contains this information but
also causes it to come to mind, patrolmen claim to have developed
a special sensitivity for qualities of appearances that allow an intui-
tive grasp of probable tendencies. In this context, little things are
said to have high informational value and lead to conclusions without the intervention of explicitly reasoned chains of inferences.
Third, patrolmen readily admit that they do not adhere to high
standards of adequacy of justification. They do not seek to defend the
adequacy of their method against some abstract criteria of merit.
Instead, when questioned, they assess their methods against the
background of a whole system of *ad hoc* decision-making, a system
that encompasses the courts, correction facilities, the welfare establishment, and medical services. In fact, policemen generally maintain that their own procedures not only measure up to the workings
of this system but exceed them in the attitude of carefulness.

In addition to these recognized reasons, there are two additional
background factors that play a significant part in decisions to employ
coercion. One has to do with the relevance of situational factors, and
the other with the evaluation of coercion as relatively insignificant
in the lives of the inhabitants.

There is no doubt that the nature of the circumstances often has
decisive influence on what will be done. For example, the same
patrolman who arrested the man trying to sell his pocket knife was
observed dealing with a young couple. Though the officer was
clearly angered by what he perceived as insolence and threatened
the man with arrest, he merely ordered him and his companion to
leave the street. He saw them walking away in a deliberately slow
manner and when he noticed them a while later, still standing only
a short distance away from the place of encounter, he did not respond to their presence. The difference between the two cases was
that in the first there was a crowd of amused bystanders, while the
latter case was not witnessed by anyone. In another instance, the
patrolman was directed to a hotel and found a father and son fighting
about money. The father occupied a room in the hotel and the son
occasionally shared his quarters. There were two other men present,
and they made it clear that their sympathies were with the older
man. The son was whisked off to jail without much study of the
relative merits of the conflicting claims. In yet another case, a middle-aged woman was forcefully evacuated from a bar even after the
bartender explained that her loud behavior was merely a response
to goading by some foul-mouth youth.

In all such circumstances, coercive control is exercised as a means
of coming to grips with situational exigencies. Force is used against

particular persons but is incidental to the task. An ideal of "economy of intervention" dictates in these and similar cases that the person whose presence is most likely to perpetuate the troublesome development be removed. Moreover, the decision as to who is to be removed is arrived at very quickly. Officers feel considerable pressure to act unhesitatingly, and many give accounts of situations that got out of hand because of desires to handle cases with careful consideration. However, even when there is no apparent risk of rapid proliferation of trouble, the tactic of removing one or two persons is used to control an undesirable situation. Thus, when a patrolman ran into a group of four men sharing a bottle of wine in an alley, he emptied the remaining contents of the bottle into the gutter, arrested one man —who was no more and no less drunk than the others—and let the others disperse in various directions.

The exigential nature of control is also evident in the handling of isolated drunks. Men are arrested because of where they happen to be encountered. In this, it matters not only whether a man is found in a conspicuous place or not, but also how far away he is from his domicile. The further away he is, the less likely it is that he will make it to his room, and the more likely the arrest. Sometimes drunk arrests are made mainly because the police van is available. In one case a patrolman summoned the van to pick up an arrested man. As the van was pulling away from the curb the officer stopped the driver because he sighted another drunk stumbling across the street. The second man protested saying that he "wasn't even half drunk yet." The patrolman's response was "OK, I'll owe you half a drunk." In sum, the basic routine of keeping the peace on Skid-Row involves a process of matching the resources of control with situational exigencies. The overall objective is to reduce the total amount of risk in the area. In this, practicality plays a considerably more important role than legal norms. Precisely because patrolmen see legal reasons for coercive action much more widely distributed on Skid-Row than could ever be matched by interventions, they intervene not in the interest of law enforcement but in the interest of producing relative tranquility and order on the street.

Taking the perspective of the victim of coercive measures, one could ask why he, in particular, has to bear the cost of keeping the aggregate of troubles down while others, who are equally or perhaps even more implicated, go scot-free. Patrolmen maintain that the *ad hoc* selection of persons for attention must be viewed in the light of the following consideration: Arresting a person on Skid-Row on some minor charge may save him and others a lot of trouble, but it does not work any real hardships on the arrested person. It is difficult to overestimate the Skid-Row patrolman's feeling of certainty that his coercive and disciplinary actions toward the inhabitants have but the most passing significance in their lives. Sending a man to jail on some charge that will hold him for a couple of days is seen as a matter of such slight importance to the affected person that it could hardly give rise to scruples. Thus, every indication that a coercive measure should be taken is accompanied by the realization "I might as well, for all it matters to him." Certain realities of life on Skid-Row furnish the context for this belief in the attenuated relevance of coercion in the lives of the inhabitants. Foremost among them is that the use of police authority is seen as totally unremarkable by everybody on Skid-Row. Persons who live or work there are continuously exposed to it and take its existence for granted. Shopkeepers, hotel clerks, and bartenders call patrolmen to rid themselves of unwanted and troublesome patrons. Residents expect patrolmen to arbitrate their quarrels authoritatively. Men who receive orders, whether they obey them or not, treat them as part of life as usual. Moreover, patrolmen find that disciplinary and coercive actions apparently do not affect their friendly relations with the persons against whom these actions are taken. Those who greet and chat with them are the very same men who have been disciplined, arrested, and ordered around in the past, and who expect to be thus treated again in the future. From all this, officers gather that though the people on Skid-Row seek to evade police authority, they do not really object to it. Indeed, it happens quite frequently that officers encounter men who welcome being arrested and even actively ask for it. Finally, officers point out that sending someone to jail from Skid-Row does not upset his relatives or his family life, does not cause him to miss work or lose a job, does not lead to his being reproached by friends and associates, does not lead to failure to meet commitments or protect investments, and does not conflict with any but the most passing intentions of the arrested person. Seasoned patrolmen are not oblivious to the irony of the fact that measures intended as mechanisms for distributing deserts can be used freely because these measures are relatively impotent in their effects.

Summary and Conclusions

It was the purpose of this paper to render an account of a domain of police practice that does not seem subject to any system of external control. Following the terminology suggested by Michael Banton, this practice was called keeping the peace. The procedures employed in keeping the peace are not determined by legal mandates but are, instead, responses to certain demand conditions. From among several demand conditions, we concentrated on the one produced by the concentration of certain types of persons in districts known as Skid-Row. Patrolmen maintain that the lives of the inhabitants of the area are lacking in prospective coherence. The consequent reduction in the temporal horizon of predictability constitutes the main problem of keeping the peace on Skid-Row.

Peacekeeping procedure on Skid-Row consists of three elements. Patrolmen seek to acquire a rich body of concrete knowledge about people by cultivating personal acquaintance with as many residents as possible. They tend to proceed against persons mainly on the basis of perceived risk, rather than on the basis of culpability. And they are more interested in reducing the aggregate total of troubles in the area than in evaluating individual cases according to merit.

There may seem to be a discrepancy between the Skid-Row patrolman's objective of preventing disorder and his efforts to maintain personal acquaintance with as many persons as possible. But these efforts are principally a tactical device. By knowing someone individually the patrolman reduces ambiguity, extends trust and favors, but does not grant immunity. The informality of interaction on Skid-Row always contains some indications of the hierarchical superiority of the patrolman and the reality of his potential power lurks in the background of every encounter.

Though our interest was focused initially on those police procedures that did not involve invoking the law, we found that the two cannot be separated. The reason for the connection is not given in the circumstance that the roles of the "law officer" and of the "peace officer" are enacted by the same person and thus are contiguous. According to our observations, patrolmen do not act alternatively as one or the other, with certain actions being determined by the intended objective of keeping the peace and others being determined by the duty to enforce the law. Instead, we have found that *peace-keeping occasionally acquires the external aspects of law enforcement.* This makes it specious to inquire whether or not police discretion in invoking the law conforms with the intention of some specific legal formula. The real reason behind an arrest is virtually always the actual state of particular social situations, or of the Skid-Row area in general.

We have concentrated on those procedures and considerations that Skid-Row patrolmen regard as necessary, proper, and efficient relative to the circumstances in which they are employed. In this way, we attempted to disclose the conception of the mandate to which the police feel summoned. It was entirely outside the scope of the presentation to review the merits of this conception and of the methods used to meet it. Only insofar as patrolmen themselves recognized instances and patterns of malpractice did we take note of them. Most of the criticism voiced by officers had to do with the use of undue harshness and with the indiscriminate use of arrest powers when these were based on personal feelings rather than the requirements of the situation. According to prevailing opinion, patrolmen guilty of such abuses make life unnecessarily difficult for themselves and for their co-workers. Despite disapproval of harshness, officers tend to be defensive about it. For example, one sergeant who was outspokenly critical of brutality, said that though in general brutal men create more problems than they solve, "they do a good job in some situations for which the better men have no stomach." Moreover, supervisory personnel exhibit a strong reluctance to direct their subordinates in the particulars of their work performance. According to our observations, control is exercised mainly through consultation with superiors, and directives take the form of requests rather than orders. In the background of all this is the belief that patrol work on Skid-Row requires a great deal of discretionary freedom. In the words of the same sergeant quoted above, "a good man has things worked out in his own ways on his beat and he doesn't need anybody to tell him what to do."

The virtual absence of disciplinary control and the demand for discretionary freedom are related to the idea that patrol work involves "playing by ear." For if it is true that peacekeeping cannot be systematically generalized, then, of course, it cannot be organizationally constrained. What the seasoned patrolman means, however, in saying that he "plays by ear" is that he is making his decisions while being attuned to the realities of complex situations about which he has immensely detailed knowledge. This studied aspect of peacekeeping generally is not made explicit, nor is the tyro or the outsider made aware of it. Quite to the contrary, the ability to discharge the duties associated with keeping the peace is viewed as a reflection of an innate talent of "getting along with people." Thus, the same demands are made of barely initiated officers as are made of experienced practitioners. Correspondingly, beginners tend to think that they can do as well as their more knowledgeable peers. As this leads to inevitable frustrations, they find themselves in a situation that is conducive to the development of a particular sense of "touchiness." Personal dispositions of individual officers are, of course, of great relevance. But the license of discretionary freedom and the expectation of success under conditions of autonomy, without any indication that the work of the successful craftsman is based on an acquired preparedness for the task, is ready-made for failure and malpractice. Moreover, it leads to slipshod practices of patrol that also infect the standards of the careful craftsman.

The uniformed patrol, and especially the foot patrol, has a low preferential value in the division of labor of police work. This is, in part, at least, due to the belief that "anyone could do it." In fact, this belief is thoroughly mistaken. At present, however, the recognition that the practice requires preparation, and the process of obtaining the preparation itself, is left entirely to the practitioner.

Police Encounters with Juveniles

Irving Piliavin and Scott Briar

As the first of a series of decisions made in the channeling of youth-ful offenders through the agencies concerned with juvenile justice and corrections, the disposition decisions made by police officers have potentially profound consequences for apprehended juveniles. Thus, arrest, the most severe of the dispositions available to police, may not only lead to confinement of the suspected offender but also bring him loss of social status, restriction of educational and employ-ment opportunities, and future harassment by law enforcement per-sonnel. According to some criminologists, the stigmatization resulting from police apprehension, arrest, and detention actually reinforces deviant behavior.[1] Other authorities have suggested, in fact, that this stigmatization serves as the catalytic agent initiating delinquent careers.[2] Despite their presumed significance, however, little empirical analysis has been reported regarding the factors in-fluencing, or consequences resulting from, police actions with juve-nile offenders. Furthermore, while some studies of police encounters with adult offenders have been reported, the extent to which the findings of these investigations pertain to law enforcement practices with youthful offenders is not known.

The above considerations have led the writers to undertake a lon-gitudinal study of the conditions influencing, and consequences flowing from, police actions with juveniles. In the present paper findings will be presented indicating the influence of certain factors on police actions. Research data consist primarily of notes and records based on nine months' observation of all juvenile officers in one police department.[3] The officers were observed in the course of

SOURCE: *American Journal of Sociology* 70 (September 1964): 206–14. Reprinted by permission of the author and the University of Chicago Press. Copyright © 1964 by the University of Chicago.

[1]Richard A. Cloward and Lloyd E. Ohlin, *Delinquency and Opportunity*, Glencoe, Ill.: Free Press, 1960, pp. 124–30.

[2]Frank Tannenbaum, *Crime and the Community*, New York: Columbia University Press, 1936, pp. 17–20; Howard S. Becker, *Outsiders: Studies in the Sociology of Devi-ance*, New York: Free Press of Glencoe, 1963, chaps. i and ii.

[3]Approximately thirty officers were assigned to the Juvenile Bureau in the depart-ment studied. While we had an opportunity to observe all officers in the Bureau during the study, our observations were concentrated on those who had been working in the Bureau for one or two years at least. Although two of the officers in the Juvenile Bureau were Negro, we observed these officers on only a few occasions.

their regular tours of duty.[4] While these data do not lend themselves
to quantitative assessments of reliability and validity, the candor
shown by the officers in their interviews with the investigators and
their use of officially frowned-upon practices while under observation provide some assurance that the materials presented below
accurately reflect the typical operations and attitudes of the law
enforcement personnel studied.

The setting for the research, a metropolitan police department
serving an industrial city with approximately 450,000 inhabitants,
was noted within the community it served and among law enforcement officials elsewhere for the honesty and superior quality of its
personnel. Incidents involving criminal activity or brutality by
members of the department had been extremely rare during the ten
years preceding this study; personnel standards were comparatively
high; and an extensive training program was provided to both new
and experienced personnel. Juvenile Bureau members, the primary
subjects of this investigation, differed somewhat from other members of the department in that they were responsible for delinquency prevention as well as law enforcement; that is, juvenile
officers were expected to be knowledgeable about conditions leading
to crime and delinquency and able to work with community agencies serving known or potential juvenile offenders. Accordingly, in
the assignment of personnel to the Juvenile Bureau, consideration
was given not only to an officer's devotion to and reliability in law
enforcement but also to his commitment to delinquency prevention.
Assignment to the Bureau was of advantage to policemen seeking
promotions. Consequently, many officers requested transfer to this
unit, and its personnel comprised a highly select group of officers.

In the field, juvenile officers operated essentially as patrol officers.
They cruised assigned beats and, although concerned primarily
with juvenile offenders, frequently had occasion to apprehend and
arrest adults. Confrontations between the officers and juveniles occurred in one of the following three ways, in order of increasing
frequency: (1) encounters resulting from officers' spotting officially
"wanted" youths; (2) encounters taking place at or near the scene of
offenses reported to police headquarters; and (3) encounters occur-
ring as the result of officers' directly observing youths either committing offenses or in "suspicious circumstances." However, the
probability that a confrontation would take place between officer
and juvenile, or that a particular disposition of an identified offender
would be made, was only in part determined by the knowledge that

[4]Although observations were not confined to specific days or work shifts, more
observations were made during evenings and weekends because police activity was
greatest during these periods.

an offense had occurred or that a particular juvenile had committed an offense. The bases for and utilization of non-offense-related criteria by police in accosting and disposing of juveniles are the focuses of the following discussion.

Sanctions for Discretion

In each encounter with juveniles, with the minor exception of officially "wanted" youths,[5] a central task confronting the officer was to decide what official action to take against the boys involved. In making these disposition decisions, officers could select any one of five discrete alternatives:

1. Outright release
2. Release and submission of a "field interrogation report" briefly describing the circumstances initiating the police-juvenile confrontation
3. "Official reprimand" and release to parents or guardian
4. Citation to juvenile court
5. Arrest and confinement in juvenile hall

Dispositions 3, 4, and 5 differed from the others in two basic respects. First, with rare exceptions, when an officer chose to reprimand, cite, or arrest a boy, he took the youth to the police station. Second, the reprimanded, cited, or arrested boy acquired an official police "record." That is, his name was officially recorded in Bureau files as a juvenile violator.

Analysis of the distribution of police disposition decisions about juveniles revealed that in virtually every category of offense the full range of official disposition alternatives available to officers was employed. This wide range of discretion resulted primarily from two conditions. First, it reflected the reluctance of officers to expose certain youths to the stigmatization presumed to be associated with official police action. Few juvenile officers believed that correctional agencies serving the community could effectively help delinquents. For some officers this attitude reflected a lack of confidence in rehabilitation techniques; for others, a belief that high caseloads and lack of professional training among correctional workers vitiated their efforts at treatment. All officers were agreed, however, that juvenile-justice and correctional processes were essentially concerned with apprehension and punishment rather than treatment.

---

[5]"Wanted" juveniles usually were placed under arrest or in protective custody, a practice which in effect relieved officers of the responsibility for deciding what to do with these youths.

Furthermore, all officers believed that some aspects of these processes (e.g., judicial definition of youths as delinquents and removal of delinquents from the community), as well as some of the possible consequences of these processes (e.g., intimate institutional contact with "hard-core" delinquents, as well as parental, school, and conventional peer disapproval or rejection), could reinforce what previously might have been only a tentative proclivity toward delinquent values and behavior. Consequently, when officers found reason to doubt that a youth being confronted was highly committed to deviance, they were inclined to treat him with leniency.

Second, and more important, the practice of discretion was sanctioned by police department policy. Training manuals and departmental bulletins stressed that the disposition of each juvenile offender was not to be based solely on the type of infraction he committed. Thus, while it was departmental policy to "arrest and confine all juveniles who have committed a felony or misdemeanor involving theft, sex offense, battery, possession of dangerous weapons, prowling, peeping, intoxication, incorrigibility, and disturbance of the peace," it was acknowledged that "such considerations as age, attitude, and prior criminal record might indicate that a different disposition would be more appropriate."[6] The official justification for discretion in processing juvenile offenders, based on the preventive aims of the Juvenile Bureau, was that each juvenile violator should be dealt with solely on the basis of what was best for him.[7] Unofficially, administrative legitimation of discretion was further justified on the grounds that strict enforcement practices would overcrowd court calendars and detention facilities, as well as dramatically increase juvenile crime rates—consequences to be avoided because they would expose the police department to community criticism.[8]

In practice, the official policy justifying use of discretion served as a demand that discretion be exercised. As such, it posed three problems for juvenile officers. First, it represented a departure from the traditional police practice with which the juvenile officers themselves were identified, in the sense that they were expected to justify their juvenile disposition decisions not simply by evidence proving a youth had committed a crime—grounds on which police were officially expected to base their dispositions of non-juvenile offend-

[6]Quoted from a training manual issued by the police department studied in this research.

[7]Presumably this also implied that police action with juveniles was to be determined partly by the offenders' need for correctional services.

[8]This was reported by beat officers as well as supervisory and administrative personnel of the Juvenile Bureau.

ers[9]—but in the *character* of the youth. Second, in disposing of juvenile offenders, officers were expected, in effect, to make judicial rather than ministerial decisions.[10] Third, the shift from the offense to the offender as the basis for determining the appropriate disposition substantially increased the uncertainty and ambiguity for officers in the situation of apprehension because no explicit rules existed for determining which disposition different types of youths should receive. Despite these problems, officers were constrained to base disposition decisions on the character of the apprehended youth, not only because they wanted to be fair, but because persistent failure to do so could result in judicial criticism, departmental censure, and, they believed, loss of authority with juveniles.[11]

Disposition Criteria

Assessing the character of apprehended offenders posed relatively few difficulties for officers in the case of youths who had committed serious crimes such as robbery, homicide, aggravated assault, grand theft, auto theft, rape, and arson. Officials generally regarded these juveniles as confirmed delinquents simply by virtue of their involvement in offenses of this magnitude.[12] However, the infraction committed did not always suffice to determine the appropriate disposition for some serious offenders;[13] and, in the case of minor offenders, who comprised over 90 percent of the youths against whom police took action, the violation itself generally played an insignificant role in the choice of disposition. While a number of minor offenders were seen as serious delinquents deserving arrest, many others were perceived either as "good" boys whose offenses were atypical of their customary behavior, as pawns of undesirable associates or, in any case, as boys for whom arrest was an unwarranted and possibly harmful punishment. Thus, for nearly all minor violators and for some serious delinquents, the assessment of character—the distinction between serious delinquents, "good" boys, mis-

[9]In actual practice, of course, disposition decisions regarding adult offenders also were influenced by many factors extraneous to the offense per se.

[10]For example, in dealing with adult violators, officers had no disposition alternative comparable to the reprimand-and-release category, a disposition which contained elements of punishment but did not involve mediation by the court.

[11]The concern of officers over possible loss of authority stemmed from their belief that court failure to support arrests by appropriate action would cause policemen to "lose face" in the eyes of juveniles.

[12]It is also likely that the possibility of negative publicity resulting from the failure to arrest such violators—particularly if they became involved in further serious crime—brought about strong administrative pressure for their arrest.

[13]For example, in the year preceding this research, over 30 percent of the juveniles involved in burglaries and 12 percent of the juveniles committing auto theft received dispositions other than arrest.

guided youths, and so on—and the dispositions which followed from these assessments were based on the youths' personal characteristics and not their offenses.

Despite this dependence of disposition decisions on the personal characteristics of these youths, however, police officers actually had access only to very limited information about boys at the time they had to decide what to do with them. In the field, officers typically had no data concerning the past offense records, school performance, family situation, or personal adjustment of apprehended youths.[14] Furthermore, files at police headquarters provided data only about each boy's prior offense record. Thus both the decision made in the field—whether or not to bring the boy in—and the decision made at the station—which disposition to invoke—were based largely on cues that emerged from the interaction between the officer and the youth, cues from which the officer inferred the youth's character. These cues included the youth's group affiliations, age, race, grooming, dress, and demeanor. Older juveniles, members of known delinquent gangs, Negroes, youths with well-oiled hair, black jackets, and soiled denims or jeans (the presumed uniform of "tough" boys), and boys who in their interactions with officers did not manifest what were considered to be appropriate signs of respect tended to receive the more severe dispositions. Other than prior record, the most important of the above cues was a youth's *demeanor.* In the opinion of juvenile patrolmen themselves the demeanor of apprehended juveniles was a major determinant of their decisions for 50–60 percent of the juvenile cases they processed.[15] A less subjective indication of

Severity of Police Disposition by Youth's Demeanor

Severity of Police Disposition	Youth's Demeanor		
	Cooperative	Uncooperative	Total
Arrest (most severe)	2	14	16
Citation or official reprimand	4	5	9
Informal reprimand	15	1	16
Admonish and release (least severe)	24	1	25
Total	45	21	66

[14]On occasion, officers apprehended youths whom they personally knew to be prior offenders. This did not occur frequently, however, for several reasons. First approximately 75 percent of apprehended youths had no prior official records; second, officers periodically exchanged patrol areas, thus limiting their exposure to, and knowledge about, these areas; and third, patrolmen seldom spent more than three or four years in the juvenile division.

[15]While reliable subgroup estimates were impossible to obtain through observation because of the relatively small number of incidents observed, the importance of demeanor in disposition decisions appeared to be much less significant with known prior offenders.

the association between a youth's demeanor and police disposition is provided by the table below, which presents the police dispositions for sixty-six youths whose encounters with police were observed in the course of this study. For purposes of this analysis, each youth's demeanor in the encounter was classified as either cooperative or uncooperative.[16] The results clearly reveal a marked association between youth demeanor and the severity of police dispositions.

The cues used by police to assess demeanor were fairly simple. Juveniles who were contrite about their infractions, respectful to officers, and fearful of the sanctions that might be employed against them tended to be viewed by patrolmen as basically law-abiding or at least "salvageable." For these youths it was usually assumed that informal or formal reprimand would suffice to guarantee their future conformity. In contrast, youthful offenders who were fractious, obdurate, or who appeared nonchalant in their encounters with patrolmen were likely to be viewed as "would-be tough guys" or "punks" who fully deserved the most severe sanction: arrest. The following excerpts from observation notes illustrate the importance attached to demeanor by police in making disposition decisions.

1. The interrogation of "A" (an 18-year-old upper-lower-class white male accused of statutory rape) was assigned to a police sergeant with long experience on the force. As ... we waited for the youth to arrive for questioning, the sergeant expressed his uncertainty as to what he should do with this young man. On the one hand, he could not ignore the fact that an offense had been committed; he had been informed, in fact, that the youth was prepared to confess to the offense. Nor could he overlook the continued pressure from the girl's father (an important political figure) for the police to take severe action against the youth. On the other hand, the sergeant had formed a low opinion of the girl's moral character, and he considered it unfair to charge "A" with statutory rape when the girl was a willing partner to the offense and might even have been the instigator of it. However, his sense of injustice concerning "A" was tempered by his image of the youth as a "punk," based, he explained, on information he had received that the youth belonged to a certain gang, the members of which were well known to, and disliked by, the police. Nevertheless, as we prepared to leave his office to inter-

---

[16]The data used for the classification of demeanor were the written records of observations made by the authors. The classifications were made by an independent judge not associated with this study. In classifying a youth's demeanor as cooperative or uncooperative, particular attention was paid to: (1) the youth's responses to police officers' questions and requests; (2) the respect and deference—or lack of these qualities—shown by the youth toward police officers; and (3) police officers' assessments of the youth's demeanor.

view "A," the sergeant was still in doubt as to what he should do with him.

As we walked down the corridor to the interrogation room, the sergeant was stopped by a reporter from the local newspaper. In an excited tone of voice, the reporter explained that his editor was pressing him to get further information about this case. The newspaper had printed some of the facts about the girl's disappearance, and as a consequence the girl's father was threatening suit against the paper for defamation of the girl's character. It would strengthen the newspaper's position, the reporter explained, if the police had information indicating that the girl's associates, particularly the youth the sergeant was about to interrogate, were persons of disreputable character. This stimulus seemed to resolve the sergeant's uncertainty. He told the reporter, "unofficially," that the youth was known to be an undesirable person, citing as evidence his membership in the delinquent gang. Furthermore, the sergeant added that he had evidence that this youth had been intimate with the girl over a period of many months. When the reporter asked if the police were planning to do anything to the youth, the sergeant answered that he intended to charge the youth with statutory rape.

In the interrogation, however, three points quickly emerged which profoundly affected the sergeant's judgment of the youth. First, the youth was polite and cooperative; he consistently addressed the officer as "sir," answered all questions quietly, and signed a statement implicating himself in numerous counts of statutory rape. Second, the youth's intentions toward the girl appeared to have been honorable; for example, he said that he wanted to marry her eventually. Third, the youth was not in fact a member of the gang in question. The sergeant's attitude became increasingly sympathetic, and after we left the interrogation room he announced his intention to "get 'A' off the hook," meaning that he wanted to have the charges against "A" reduced or, if possible, dropped.

2. Officers "X" and "Y" brought into the police station a 17-year-old white boy who, along with two older companions, had been found in a home having sex relations with a 15-year-old girl. The boy responded to police officers' queries slowly and with obvious disregard. It was apparent that his lack of deference toward the officers and his failure to evidence concern about his situation were irritating his questioners. Finally, one of the officers turned to me and, obviously angry, commented that in his view the boy was simply a "stud" interested only in sex, eating, and sleeping. The policemen conjectured that the boy "probably already had knocked up half a dozen girls." The boy ignored these remarks, except for an occasional impassive stare at the patrolmen. Turning to the boy, the officer remarked, "What the hell am I going to do with you?" And again the

boy simply returned the officer's gaze. The latter then said, "Well,
I guess we'll just have to put you away for a while." An arrest report
was then made out, and the boy was taken to Juvenile Hall.

Although anger and distrust frequently characterized officers' attitudes toward recalcitrant and impassive juvenile offenders, their
manner while processing these youths was typically routine, restrained, and without rancor. While the officers' restraint may have
been due in part to their desire to avoid accusation and censure it also
seemed to reflect their inurement to a frequent experience. By and
large, only their occasional "needling" or insulting of a boy gave any
hint of the underlying resentment and dislike they felt toward many
of these youths.[17]

Prejudice in Apprehension and Disposition Decisions

Compared to other youths, Negroes and boys whose appearance
matched the delinquent stereotype were more frequently stopped
and interrogated by patrolmen—often even in the absence of evidence that an offense had been committed[18]—and usually were
given more severe dispositions for the same violations. Our data
suggest, however, that these selective apprehension and disposition
practices resulted not only from the intrusion of long-held prejudices of individual police officers but also from certain job-related
experiences of law enforcement personnel. First, the tendency for
police to give more severe dispositions to Negroes and to youths
whose appearance corresponded to that which police associated with
delinquents partly reflected the fact, observed in this study, that
these youths also were much more likely than were other types of
boys to exhibit the sort of recalcitrant demeanor which police construed as a sign of the confirmed delinquent. Further, officers assumed, partly on the basis of departmental statistics, that Negroes

[17]Officers' animosity toward recalcitrant or aloof offenders appeared to stem from
two sources: moral indignation that these juveniles were self-righteous and indiffer-
ent about their transgressions, and resentment that these youths failed to accord
police the respect they believed they deserved. Since the patrolmen perceived themselves as honestly and impartially performing a vital community function, warranting respect and deference from the community at large, they attributed the lack of
respect shown them by these juveniles to the latter's immorality.

[18]The clearest evidence for this assertion is provided by the overrepresentation of
Negroes among "innocent" juveniles accosted by the police. Of the seventy-six juveniles on whom systematic data were collected, ten were exonerated and released
without suspicion. Seven of these ten "innocent" juveniles were Negro, in contrast to
the allegedly "guilty" youths, less than one-third of whom were Negro. The following
incident illustrates the operation of this bias: One officer, observing a youth walking
along the street, commented that the youth "looks suspicious" and promptly stopped
and questioned him. Asked later to explain what aroused his suspicion, the officer
explained, "He was a Negro wearing dark glasses at midnight."

and juveniles who "look tough" (e.g., who wear chinos, leather jackets, boots, etc.) commit crimes more frequently than do other types of youths.[19] In this sense, the police justified their selective treatment of these youths along epidemiological lines: that is, they were concentrating their attention on those youths whom they believed were most likely to commit delinquent acts. In the words of one highly placed official in the department:

> If you know that the bulk of your delinquent problem comes from kids who, say, are from 12 to 14 years of age, when you're out on patrol you are much more likely to be sensitive to the activities of juveniles in this age bracket than older or younger groups. This would be good law enforcement practice. The logic in our case is the same except that our delinquency problem is largely found in the Negro community and it is these youths toward whom we are sensitized.

As regards prejudice per se, eighteen of twenty-seven officers interviewed openly admitted a dislike for Negroes. However, they attributed their dislike to experiences they had as policemen with youths from this minority group. The officers reported that Negro boys were much more likely . . . to "give us a hard time," be uncooperative, and show no remorse for their transgressions. Recurrent exposure to such attitudes among Negro youth, the officers claimed, generated their antipathy toward Negroes. The following excerpt is typical of the views expressed by these officers:

> They [Negroes] have no regard for the law or for the police. They just don't seem to give a damn. Few of them are interested in school or getting ahead. The girls start having illegitimate kids before they are 16 years old, and the boys are always "out for kicks." Furthermore, many of these kids try to run you down. They say the damnedest things to you, and they seem to have absolutely no respect for you as an adult. I admit I am prejudiced now, but frankly I don't think I was when I began police work.

Implications

It is apparent from the findings presented above that the police officers studied in this research were permitted and even encouraged to exercise immense latitude in disposing of the juveniles they en-

---

[19]While police statistics did not permit an analysis of crime rates by appearance, they strongly supported officers' contentions concerning the delinquency rate among Negroes. Of all male juveniles processed by the police department in 1961, for example, 40.2 percent were Negro and 33.9 percent were white. These two groups comprised at that time, respectively, about 22.7 percent and 73.6 percent of the population in the community studied.

countered. That is, it was within the officers' discretionary authority, except in extreme limiting cases, to decide which juveniles were
to come to the attention of the courts and correctional agencies and
thereby be identified officially as delinquents. In exercising this
discretion policemen were strongly guided by the demeanor of those
who were apprehended, a practice which ultimately led, as seen
above, to certain youths (particularly Negroes[20] and boys dressed in
the style of "toughs") being treated more severely than other juveniles for comparable offenses.

But the relevance of demeanor was not limited only to police
disposition practices. Thus, for example, in conjunction with police
crime statistics the criterion of demeanor led police to concentrate
their surveillance activities to areas frequented or inhabited by
Negroes. Furthermore, these youths were accosted more often than
others by officers on patrol simply because their skin color identified
them as potential troublemakers. These discriminatory practices—
and it is important to note that they are discriminatory, even if based
on accurate statistical information—may well have self-fulfilling
consequences. It is not unlikely that frequent encounters with police, particularly those involving youths innocent of wrongdoing,
will increase the hostility of these juveniles toward law enforcement
personnel. It is also not unlikely that the frequency of such encounters will in time reduce their significance in the eyes of apprehended
juveniles, thereby leading these youths to regard them as "routine."
Such responses to police encounters, however, are those which law
enforcement personnel perceive as indicators of the serious delinquent. They thus serve to vindicate and reinforce officers' prejudices,
leading to closer surveillance of Negro districts, more frequent encounters with Negro youths, and so on, in a vicious circle. Moreover,
the consequences of this chain of events are reflected in police statistics showing a disproportionately high percentage of Negroes among
juvenile offenders, thereby providing "objective" justification for
concentrating police attention on Negro youths.

To a substantial extent, as we have implied earlier, the discretion
practiced by juvenile officers is simply an extension of the juvenile-
court philosophy, which holds that in making legal decisions regarding juveniles more weight should be given to the juvenile's
character and life situation than to his actual offending behavior.
The juvenile officer's disposition decisions—and the information he
uses as a basis for them—are more akin to the discriminations made
by probation officers and other correctional workers than they are

[20]An uncooperative demeanor was presented by more than one-third of the Negro
youths but by only one-sixth of the white youths encountered by the police in the
course of our observations.

to decisions of police officers dealing with nonjuvenile offenders. The problem is that such clinical-type decisions are not restrained by mechanisms comparable to the principles of due process and the rules of procedure governing police decisions regarding adult offenders. Consequently, prejudicial practices by police officers can escape notice more easily in their dealings with juveniles than with adults.

The observations made in this study serve to underscore the fact that the official delinquent, as distinguished from the juvenile who simply commits a delinquent act, is the product of a social judgment, in this case a judgment made by the police. He is a delinquent because someone in authority has defined him as one, often on the basis of the public face he has presented to officials rather than the kind of offense he has committed.

The Social Organization of Arrest

Donald J. Black

This article offers a set of descriptive materials on the social conditions under which policemen make arrests in routine encounters. At
this level, it is a modest increment in the expanding literature on the
law's empirical face. Scholarship on law-in-action has concentrated
upon criminal law in general and the world of the police in particular.[1] Just what, beyond the hoarding of facts, these empirical studies
will yield, however, is still unclear. Perhaps a degree of planned
change in the criminal justice system will follow, be it in legal
doctrine or in legal administration. In any event, evaluation certainly appears to be the purpose, and reform the expected outcome,
of much empirical research. This article pursues a different sort of
yield from its empirical study: a sociological theory of law.[2] The
analysis is self-consciously inattentive to policy reform or evaluation of the police; it is intentionally bloodless in tone. It examines
arrest in order to infer patterns relevant to an understanding of all
instances of legal control.

The empirical analysis queries how a number of circumstances
affect the probability of arrest. The factors considered are: the suspect's race, the legal seriousness of the alleged crime, the evidence

SOURCE: *Stanford Law Review* 23 (June 1971): 1087–1111. Copyright © 1971 by the
Board of Trustees of the Leland Stanford Junior University. Reprinted by permission
of Fred B. Rothman & Co.

NOTE: This article's findings derive from a larger research project under the direction
of Professor Albert J. Reiss, Jr., Department of Sociology and Institute of Social Science,
Yale University. The project was coordinated at the Center for Research on Social
Organization, Department of Sociology, University of Michigan. It was supported by
Grant Award 006, Office of Law Enforcement Assistance, U.S. Department of Justice,
under the Law Enforcement Assistance Act of 1965, and by grants from the National
Science Foundation and the Russell Sage Foundation.

[1] *See generally* E. Schur, *Law and Society* (1968); Skolnick, "The Sociology of Law
in America: Overview and Trends," in *Law and Society,* 4 (1965) (supplement to 13
Social Problems [1965]); Bordua and Reiss, "Law Enforcement," in *The Uses of Sociology* 275 (1967); Manning, "Observing the Police," in *Observing Deviance* (J. Douglas
ed., forthcoming). The empirical literature is so abundant and is expanding so rapidly
that these published bibliographic discussions are invariably inadequate.

[2] It should be noted that the article's approach to legal life differs quite radically
from the approach of Philip Selznick, one of the most influential American sociologists of law. Selznick's sociology of law attempts to follow the path of natural law;
my approach follows the general direction of legal positivism. In Lon Fuller's language, Selznick is willing to tolerate a confusion of the *is* and *ought,* while I am not.
L. Fuller, *The Law in Quest of Itself* 5 (1940). *See* P. Selznick, *Law and Society, and
Industrial Justice* (1969); Selznick, "The Sociology of Law," 9 *International Encyclope-
dia of the Social Sciences,* (D. L. Sills ed., 1968), 50; Selznick, "Sociology and Natural
Law," *Natural L.F.* 6 (1961), 84.

available in the field setting, the complainant's preference for police action, the social relationship between the complainant and suspect, the suspect's degree of deference toward the police, and the manner in which the police come to handle an incident, whether in response to a citizen's request or through their own initiative. The inquiry seeks to discover general principles according to which policemen routinely use or withhold their power to arrest, and thus to reveal a part of the social organization[3] of arrest.

The article begins with a skeletal discussion of the field method. Next follows a brief ethnography of routine police work designed to place arrest within its mundane context. The findings on arrest are then presented, first for encounters involving both a citizen complainant and a suspect, and second for police encounters with lone suspects. The article finally speculates about the implications of the empirical findings at the level of a general theory of legal control, the focus shifting from a sociology of the police to a sociology of law.

Field Method

The data were collected during the summer of 1966 by systematic observation of police-citizen transactions in Boston, Chicago, and Washington, D.C.[4] Thirty-six observers—persons with law, social science, and police administration backgrounds—recorded observations of encounters between uniformed patrolmen and citizens. The observers' training and supervision was, for all practical purposes, identical in the three cities. Observers accompanied patrolmen on all work shifts on all days of the week for seven weeks in each city. Proportionately more of our man-hours were devoted to times when police activity is comparatively high, namely evening shifts, and particularly weekend evenings. Hence, to a degree the sample over-represents the kinds of social disruptions that arise more on evenings and weekends than at other times. The police precincts chosen as observation sites in each city were selected to maximize scrutiny of lower socioeconomic, high crime rate, racially homogeneous residential areas. Two precincts were used in both Boston and Chicago, and four precincts were used in Washington, D.C. The Washington,

[3]As used in this article, the broad concept "social organization" refers to the supraindividual principles and mechanisms according to which social events come into being, are maintained and arranged, change, and go out of existence. Put another way, social organization refers to the descriptive grammar of social events.

[4]At this writing, the data are [about ten] years old. However, there has been little reform in routine patrol work since 1966. This is in part because the police work in question—everyday police contact with citizens—is not as amenable to planned change as other forms of police work, such as crowd or riot control, traffic regulation, or vice enforcement. Moreover, the data have value even if they no longer describe contemporary conduct, since they remain useful for developing a theory of law as a behavior system. A general theory of law has no time limits. Indeed, how fine it would be if we possessed more empirical data from legal life past.

D.C., precincts, however, were more racially integrated than were those in Boston and Chicago.

Observers recorded the data in "incident booklets," forms structurally similar to interview schedules. One booklet was used for each incident. A field situation involving police action was classified as an "incident" if it was brought to the officer's attention by the police radio system or by a citizen on the street or in the police station, or if the officer himself noticed a situation and decided that it required police attention. Also included as incidents were a handful of situations which the police noticed themselves but which they chose to ignore.

The observers did not fill out incident booklets in the presence of policemen. In fact, the line officers were told that the research was not concerned with police behavior but only with citizen behavior toward the police and the kinds of problems citizens make for the police.

The observers recorded a total of 5,713 incidents, but the base for the present analysis is only a little more than 5 percent of the total. This attrition results primarily from the general absence of opportunities for arrest in patrol work, where most of the incidents involve noncriminal situations or criminal situations for which there is no suspect. Traffic encounters also were excluded, even though technically any traffic violation presents an opportunity for arrest. Other cases were eliminated because they involved factors that could invisibly distort or otherwise confuse the analysis. The encounters excluded were those initiated by citizens who walked into a police station to ask for help (6 percent of total) or who flagged down the police on the street (5 percent). These kinds of encounters involve peculiar situational features warranting separate treatment, though even that would be difficult, given their statistically negligible number. For similar reasons encounters involving participants of mixed race and mixed social-class status[5] were also eliminated. Finally, the sample of encounters excludes suspects under 18 years of age—legal juveniles in most states—and suspects of white-collar status.[6] Thus,

[5]This means that encounters involving a complainant and suspect of different races were excluded. Similarly, the sample would not include the arrest of a black man with a white wife. However, it does not mean the exclusion of encounters where the policeman and suspect were not of the same race.

[6]Because field observers occasionally had difficulty in judging the age or social class of a citizen, they were told to use a "don't know" category whenever they felt the danger of misclassification. Two broad categories of social class, blue-collar and white-collar, were employed. Since the precincts sampled were predominantly lower class, the observers labeled the vast majority of the citizen participants blue-collar. In fact, not enough white-collar cases were available for separate analysis. The small number of adults of ambiguous social class were combined with the blue-collar cases into a sample of "predominantly blue-collar" suspects. The observers probably were reasonably accurate in classifying suspects because the police frequently interviewed suspects about their age and occupation.

it investigates arrest patterns in police encounters with predominantly blue-collar adult suspects.

Routine Police Work

In some respects, selecting arrest as a subject of study implicitly misrepresents routine police work. Too commonly, the routine is equated with the exercise of the arrest power, not only by members of the general public but by lawyers and even many policemen as well. In fact, the daily round of the patrol officer infrequently involves arrest[7] or even encounters with a criminal suspect. The most cursory observation of the policeman on the job overturns the imagery of a man who makes his living parceling citizens into jail.

Modern police departments are geared to respond to citizen calls for service; the great majority of incidents the police handle arise when a citizen telephones the police and the dispatcher sends a patrol car to deal with the situation. The officer becomes implicated in a wide range of human troubles, most not of his own choosing, and many of which have little or nothing to do with criminal law enforcement. He transports people to the hospital, writes reports of auto accidents, and arbitrates and mediates between disputants— neighbors, husbands and wives, landlords and tenants, and businessmen and customers. He takes missing-person reports, directs traffic, controls crowds at fires, writes dogbite reports, and identifies abandoned autos. He removes safety hazards from the streets, and occasionally scoops up a dead animal. Policemen disdain this kind of work, but they do it every day. Such incidents rarely result in arrest; they nevertheless comprise nearly half of the incidents uniformed patrolmen encounter in situations initiated by phone calls from citizens.[8] Policemen also spend much of their time with "juvenile trouble," a police category typically pertaining to distinctively youthful disturbances of adult peace—noisy groups of teenagers on a street corner, ball-playing in the street, trespassing or playing in deserted buildings or construction sites, and rock-throwing. These situations, too, rarely result in arrest. Some officers view handling juvenile trouble as work they do in the service of neighborhood grouches. The same may be said of ticketing parking violations in

[7]In this article, "arrest" refers only to transportation of a suspect to a police station. It does not include the application of constraint in field settings, and it does not require formal booking of a suspect with a crime. *See* W. Lafave, *Arrest: The Decision to Take a Suspect into Custody* (1965), 4.

[8]D. Black, "Police Encounters and Social Organization: An Observation Study," 51–57, Dec. 15, 1968 (unpublished dissertation in Department of Sociology, University of Michigan). *See also* Cumming, Cumming, and Edell, "Policeman as Philosopher, Guide and Friend," *Social Problems,* 12 (1965), 276.

answer to citizen complaints. All these chores necessitate much unexciting paperwork.

Somewhat less than half of the encounters arising from a citizen telephone call have to do with a crime—a felony or a misdemeanor other than juvenile trouble. Yet even criminal incidents are so constituted situationally as to preclude arrest in the majority of cases, because no suspect is present when the police arrive at the scene. In 77 percent of the felony situations and in 51 percent of the misdemeanor situations the only major citizen participant is a complainant.[9] In a handful of other cases the only citizen present is an informant or bystander. When no suspect is available in the field setting, the typical official outcome is a crime report, the basic document from which official crime statistics are constructed and the operational prerequisite of further investigation by the detective division.

The minority of citizen-initiated crime encounters where a suspect is present when the police arrive is the appropriate base for a study of arrest. In the great majority of these suspect encounters a citizen complainant also takes part in the situational interaction, so any study of routine arrest must consider the complainant's role as well as those of the police officer and the suspect.[10]

Through their own discretionary authority, policemen occasionally initiate encounters that may be called *proactive* police work, as opposed to the *reactive,* citizen-initiated work that consumes the greater part of the average patrol officer's day.[11] On an evening shift (traditionally 4 P.M. to midnight) a typical workload for a patrol car is six radio-dispatched encounters and one proactive encounter. The ratio of proactive encounters varies enormously by shift, day of week, patrol beat or territory, and number of cars on duty. An extremely busy weekend night could involve 20 dispatches to a single car. Under these rushed conditions the officers might not initiate any encounters on their own. At another time in another area a patrol car might receive no dispatches, but the officers might initiate as many as eight or ten encounters on the street. During the observa-

[9]D. Black, *supra* note 8, at 94.

[10]In fact, of all the felony cases the police handle in response to a citizen request by telephone, including cases where only a complainant, informant, or bystander is present in the situation, a mere 3 percent involve a police transaction with a lone suspect. D. Black, *supra* note 8, at 94.

[11]The concepts "reactive" and "proactive" derive from the origins of individual action, the former referring to actions originating in the environment, the latter to those originating within the actor. *See* Murray "Toward a Classification of Interactions," in *Toward a General Theory of Action* (1967), 434.

tion study only 13 percent of incidents came to police attention without the assistance of citizens.[12] Still, most officers as well as citizens probably think of proactive policing as the form that epitomizes the police function.

The police-initiated encounter is a bald confrontation between state and citizen. Hardly ever does a citizen complainant take part in a proactive field encounter and then only if a policeman were to discover an incident of personal victimization or if a complainant were to step forth subsequent to the officer's initial encounter with a suspect. Moreover, the array of incidents policemen handle—their operational jurisdiction—is quite different when they have the discretion to select situations for attention compared to what it is when that discretion is lodged in citizens. In reactive police work they are servants of the public, with one consequence being that the social troubles they oversee often have little if anything to do with the criminal law. Arrest is usually a situational impossibility. In proactive policing the officer is more a public guardian and the operational jurisdiction is a police choice; the only limits are in law and in departmental policy. In proactive police work, arrest is totally a matter of the officer's own making. Yet the reality of proactive police work has an ironic quality about it. The organization of crime in time and space deprives policemen on free patrol of legally serious arrests. Most felonies occur in off-street settings and must be detected by citizens. Even those that occur in a visible public place usually escape the policemen's ken. When the police have an opportunity to initiate an encounter, the occasion is more likely than not a traffic violation. Traffic violations comprise the majority of proactive encounters, and most of the remainder concern minor "disturbances of the peace."[13] In short, where the police role is most starkly aggressive in form, the substance is drably trivial, and legally trivial incidents provide practically all of the grist for arrest in proactive police operations.

Perhaps a study of arrest flatters the legal significance of the everyday police encounter. Still, even though arrest situations are uncommon in routine policing, invocation of the criminal process accounts for more formal-legal cases, more court trials and sanctions, more public controversies and conflicts than any other mechanism

[12]This proportion is based upon the total sample of 5,713 incidents.

[13]Much proactive patrol work involves a drunken or disorderly person. Typically, however, arrest occurs in these cases only when the citizen is uncooperative; ordinarily the policeman begins his encounter by giving an order such as "Move on," "Take off," or "Take it easy." Arrest is an outcome of interaction rather than a simple and direct response of an officer to what he observes as an official witness.

in the legal system. As a major occasion of legal control, then, arrest cries out for empirical study.[14]

Complainant and Suspect

The police encounter involving both a suspect and a complainant is a microcosm of a total legal control system. In it are personified the state, the alleged threat to social order, and the citizenry. The complainant is to a police encounter what an interest group is to a legislature or a plaintiff to a civil lawsuit. His presence makes a dramatic difference in police encounters, particularly if he assumes the role of situational lobbyist. This section will show, *inter alia,* that the fate of suspects rests nearly as much with complainants as it does with police officers themselves.

Of the 176 encounters involving both a complainant and a suspect a little over one-third were alleged to be felonies; the remainder were misdemeanors of one or another variety. Not surprisingly, the police make arrests more often in felony than in misdemeanor situations, but the difference is not as wide as might be expected. An arrest occurs in 58 percent of the felony encounters and in 44 percent of the misdemeanor encounters. The police, then, release roughly half of the persons they suspect of crimes. This strikingly low arrest rate requires explanation.[15]

[14]Earlier observational studies have neglected patterns of arrest in the everyday work of uniformed patrolmen. Emphasis has instead been placed upon detective work, vice enforcement, policing of juveniles, and other comparatively marginal aspects of police control. *See* J. Skolnick, *Justice Without Trial* (1966) (patterns of arrest in vice enforcement); Bittner, "The Police on Skid-Row: A Study of Peace Keeping" *Am. Soc. Rev.,* 32 (1967), 699; Black and Reiss, "Police Control of Juveniles" *Am. Soc. Rev.,* 63 (1970); Piliavin and Briar, "Police Encounters with Juveniles," *Am. J. Soc.,* 70 (1964), 206. Several observational studies emphasizing other dimensions of police work are also directly relevant. *See* L. Tiffany, D. McIntyre, and D. Rotenberg, *Detection of Crime* (1967); Reiss and Black, "Interrogation and the Criminal Process," *Annals of the Am. Academy of Pol. & Soc. Sci.,* 374 (1967), 47; Project, "Interrogations in New Haven: The Impact of Miranda," *Yale L.J.,* 76 (1967), 519. There also have been a number of studies based upon official arrest statistics. *See* N. Goldman, *The Differential Selection of Juvenile Offenders for Court Appearance* (1963); J. Wilson, *Varieties of Police Behavior* (1968); Green, "Race, Social Status, and Criminal Arrest," *Am. Soc. Rev.,* 35 (1970), 476; Terry, "The Screening of Juvenile Offenders," *J. Crim. L.C. & P.S.,* 58 (1967), 173. For a more speculative discussion *see* Goldstein, "Police Discretion Not to Invoke the Criminal Process: Low-Visibility Decisions in the Administration of Justice," *Yale L.J.,* 69 (1960), 543. See generally *W. LaFave, supra* note 7.

[15]At this point a word should be said about the explanatory strategy to be followed in the analysis of data. The article's approach is radically behavioral or, more specifically, supramotivational, in that it seeks out supraindividual conditions with which the probability of arrest varies. Implicit in this strategy is a conception of arrest as a social event rather than as an individual event. The mental processes of the police and the citizens whose outward behavior our observers recorded are not important to this analysis. At this point the sole object is to delineate aspects of the social context of arrest as a variety of legal intervention.

Evidence

Factors other than the kind of evidence available to an officer in the field setting affect the probability of arrests, for even exceptionally clear situational evidence of criminal liability does not guarantee that arrest will follow a police encounter.

One of two major forms of evidence ordinarily is present when the police confront a suspect in the presence of a complainant: Either the police arrive at the setting in time to witness the offense, or a citizen —usually the complainant himself—gives testimony against the suspect. Only rarely is some other kind of evidence available, such as a physical clue on the premises or on the suspect's person. On the other hand, in only three of the complainant-suspect encounters was situational evidence entirely absent. In these few cases the police acted upon what they knew from the original complaint as it was relayed to them by radio dispatch and upon what they heard about the crime from the complainant, but they had no other information apparent in the field situation linking the suspect to the alleged crime.

In a great majority of felony situations the best evidence accessible to the police is citizen testimony, whereas in misdemeanor situations the police generally witness the offense themselves. These evidentiary circumstances are roughly equivalent as far as the law of arrest is concerned, since the requirements for a misdemeanor arrest without a formal warrant are more stringent than are those for a felony arrest. In most jurisdictions the police must observe the offense or acquire a signed complaint before they may arrest a misdemeanor suspect in the field. In felony situations, however, they need only have "probable cause" or "reasonable grounds" to believe the suspect is guilty. Thus, though the evidence usually is stronger in misdemeanor than in felony situations, the law in effect compensates the police by giving them more power in the felony situations where they would otherwise be at a disadvantage. Correspondingly the law of arrest undermines the advantage felons in the aggregate would otherwise enjoy.

Table 1 indicates that the police do not use all the legal power they possess. They arrest only slightly over one-half of the felony suspects against whom testimonial evidence is present in the field encounter, although "probable cause" can be assumed to have been satisfied in nearly every such incident. Furthermore, during the observation study the police released two of the six felony suspects they observed in allegedly felonious activity. These two cases are noteworthy even though based upon a sample several times smaller than the other samples. In misdemeanor situations the arrest rate is about two-thirds when the police observe the offense, while it drops to about one-third when the only evidence comes from a citizen's

Table 1.   Arrest Rates in Citizen-Initiated Encounters
According to Type of Crime and Major Situational Evidence

Crime	Evidence	Total Number of Incidents	Arrest Rate in Percent
Felony	Police Witness[a]	6	(4)[b]
	Citizen Testimony	45	56
	Other Evidence	1	(0)
	No Evidence	0	(0)
Misdemeanor	Police Witness[a]	52	65
	Citizen Testimony	39	31
	Other Evidence	0	(0)
	No Evidence	3	(0)
All Crimes[c]	Police Witness[a]	58	66
	Citizen Testimony	84	44
	Other Evidence	1	(0)
	No Evidence	3	(0)

[a] This category includes all cases in which the police witness evidence was supplemented by other types of evidence.

[b] Arrest rate figures in parentheses in this and later tables are used whenever the total number of incidents is statistically too small to justify making a generalized assertion of arrest rate.

[c] This excludes 30 cases for which the observer did not ascertain the character of the evidence. Thus the total is 146 cases.

testimony. An evidentiary legal perspective alone, therefore, cannot account for differentials in police arrest practices. On the other hand, evidence is not irrelevant to arrest differentials. In none of the three cases where no evidence was available did the police make an arrest, and where the legal standing of the police was at best precarious—misdemeanor situations with citizen testimonial evidence—the arrest rate was relatively low.

The Complainant's Preference

While complainants frequently are present when policemen fail to invoke the law against suspects who are highly vulnerable to arrest, the complainants do not necessarily resent police leniency. In 24 percent of the misdemeanor situations and in 21 percent of the felony situations the complainant expresses to the police a preference for clemency toward the suspect.[16] The complainant manifests a preference for an arrest in 34 percent of the misdemeanors and in 48 percent of the felonies. In the remainder of encounters the com-

[16] In such cases a complainant's preference is clear from his response to the question posed by the police. When police did not solicit the complainant's opinion, the observer classified the complainant's preference according to the audible or visible clues available to him. Some complainants made explicit demands upon the police; others appeared more confused and made no attempt to influence the outcome.

plainant's preference is unclear; frequently the complainant's outward behavior is passive, especially in misdemeanor situations.

The findings in Table 2 indicate that police arrest practices, in both felony and misdemeanor situations, sharply reflect the complainant's preferences, whether they be compassionate or vindictive. In felony situations where a citizen's testimony links a suspect to the crime, arrest results in about three-fourths of the cases in which the complainant specifies a preference for that outcome. When the complainant prefers no arrest, the police go against his wishes in only about one-tenth of the cases. Passive or unexpressive complainants see the police arrest suspects in a little under two-thirds of the situations where the police have a complainant's testimonial evidence. Thus, when the complainant leaves the decision to arrest wholly in police hands, the police are by no means reluctant to arrest the felony suspect. They become strikingly reluctant only when a complainant exerts pressure on the suspect's behalf.

The findings for misdemeanor situations likewise show police compliance with the complainant's preference and also demonstrate the relevance of situational evidence to the suspect's fate. Encounters where the complainant outwardly prefers arrest and where the police observe the offense itself have an extremely high probability of arrest, 95 percent, a proportion somewhat higher than that for felony situations involving testimonial evidence alone. When the major situational evidence is citizen testimony against a misdemeanor suspect, the proportion drops to 70 percent. On the other hand, even when the police observe the offense, the arrest rate drops to less than one-fifth in those encounters where the complainant outwardly prefers leniency for his adversary. Plainly, therefore, the complainant's preference is a more powerful situational factor than evidence, though the two operate jointly. As might be expected, evidence is particularly consequential when the complainant expresses no clear preference for police action, and in those cases the suspect is almost twice as likely to be arrested when the police observe the offense as when the major evidence is the complainant's or another citizen's testimony. As noted above, however, the complainant does make his preference clear in the majority of encounters, and that preference appears to be strongly associated with the arrest rate.

Relational Distance

When police enter into an encounter involving both a complainant and a suspect they find themselves not only in a narrow legal conflict but also in a conflict between citizen adversaries within a social relationship—one between family members, acquaintances, neighbors, friends, business associates, or total strangers. The data in Table 3 suggest that police arrest practices vary

Table 2. Arrest Rates in Citizen-Initiated Encounters According to
Type of Crime, Major Situational Evidence, and Complainant's Preference

Felony				Misdemeanor			
Evidence	Complainant's Preference	Total Number of Incidents	Arrest Rate in Percent	Evidence	Complainant's Preference	Total Number of Incidents	Arrest Rate in Percent
Police Witness	Arrest	2	(1)	Police Witness	Arrest	21	95
	Unclear	4	(3)		Unclear	23	52
	No Arrest	0	(0)		No Arrest	11	18
Citizen Testimony	Arrest	23	74	Citizen Testimony	Arrest	10	70
	Unclear	11	64		Unclear	15	27
	No Arrest	11	9		No Arrest	11	9
All Felonies[a]	Arrest	25	72	All Misdemeanors[b]	Arrest	31	87
	Unclear	15	67		Unclear	38	42
	No Arrest	11	9		No Arrest	22	14

[a] Excludes one case of "other evidence" and seven cases in which the observer did not ascertain the evidence.
[b] Excludes three cases of "no evidence" and 23 cases where the type of evidence was not ascertained.

Table 3. Arrest Rates in Citizen-Initiated Encounters According to
Type of Crime, Relational Tie Between Complainant and Suspect, and Complainant's Preference

	Felony			Misdemeanor		
Relational Tie	Complainant's Preference	Total Number of Incidents	Arrest Rate in Percent	Complainant's Preference	Total Number of Incidents	Arrest Rate in Percent
Family Members	Prefers Arrest	20	55	Prefers Arrest	15	80
	Preference Unclear	8	(6)	Preference Unclear	13	38
	Prefers No Arrest	10	0	Prefers No Arrest	8	(0)
Friends, Neighbors, Acquaintances	Prefers Arrest	5	(4)	Prefers Arrest	11	64
	Preference Unclear	8	(6)	Preference Unclear	15	40
	Prefers No Arrest	0	(0)	Prefers No Arrest	20	5
Strangers	Prefers Arrest	3	(3)	Prefers Arrest	15	87
	Preference Unclear	2	(2)	Preference Unclear	15	47
	Prefers No Arrest	3	(2)	Prefers No Arrest	5	(0)
All Family Members		38	45		36	47
All Friends, Neighbors, Acquaintances		13	77		46	30
All Strangers		8	(7)		35	57

with the relational nature of complainant-suspect conflicts. The probability of arrest is highest when the citizen adversaries have the most distant social relation to one another, *i.e.,* when they are strangers. The felony cases especially reveal that arrest becomes more probable as the relational distance increases: Forty-five percent of suspects are arrested in a family member relationship, 77 percent in a friends, neighbors, acquaintances relationship, and 7 out of 8 or 88 percent in a stranger relationship.[17] In the misdemeanor cases the pattern is not so consistent. Although the likelihood of arrest is still highest in conflicts between strangers, the lowest likelihood is in situations involving friends, neighbors, or acquaintances. When the complainant's preference is unclear, or when he prefers no arrest, no difference of any significance is discernible across the categories of relational distance; the type of social conflict embodied in the police encounter visibly affects arrest probability only when the complainant presses the police to make an arrest.

Race, Respect, and the Complainant

Table 4 demonstrates that police arrest blacks at a higher rate than whites. But no evidence supports the view that the police discriminate against blacks. Rather, the race differential seems to be a function of the relatively higher rate at which black suspects display disrespect toward the police. When the arrest rate for respectful black suspects is compared to that for respectful whites, no difference is apparent. Before examining this last finding in detail, however, the importance of citizen respect in itself should be established.

Considering felony and misdemeanor situations together, the arrest rate for differential suspects is 40 percent of 10 cases. For civil

Table 4.   Arrest Rates in Citizen-Initiated Encounters
According to Type of Crime and Race of Suspect

Crime	Race	Total Number of Incidents	Arrest Rate in Percent
Felony	Black	48	60
	White	11	45
Misdemeanor	Black	75	47
	White	42	38
All Crimes	Black	123	52
	White	53	39

[17]Little confidence can be placed in findings based on less than ten cases. Nevertheless, the article occasionally mentions such findings when they are strikingly consistent with patterns seen in the larger samples. In no instances, however, do broader generalizations rest upon these inadequate statistical bases.

suspects it is effectively the same at 42 percent of 71 cases, but it is 70 percent of 37 cases for antagonistic or disrespectful suspects.[18] Unquestionably, the suspect who refuses to defer to police authority takes a gamble with his freedom. This pattern persists in felony and misdemeanor situations when they are examined separately, but the small samples that result from dividing the data by type of crime prevents any more refined comparison than between civil and disrespectful levels of deference. The police make an arrest in 40 percent of the 25 felony encounters in which the suspect is civil, as compared to 69 percent of the 16 felony encounters in which he is disrespectful. In misdemeanor situations the corresponding proportions are 43 percent of 46 cases and 71 percent of 21 cases. In the aggregate of cases, the police are more likely to arrest a misdemeanor suspect who is disrespectful toward them than a felony suspect who is civil. In this sense the police enforce their authority more severely than they enforce the law.

The complainant's preference can erode the impact of the suspect's degree of respect somewhat, but when complainant's preference is held constant, the pattern remains, as Table 5 shows. When the complainant expresses a preference for arrest of his adversary, the police comply more readily if the suspect is disrespectful rather than civil toward them. Table 5 also reveals that, when the complainant desires an arrest and the suspect is civil, the probability of arrest for black and white suspects is almost exactly equal, but black suspects are disrespectful toward the police more often than are whites, a pattern that operates to increase disproportionately the overall black arrest rate.

When the complainant's preference is unclear the degree of deference of the suspect is especially consequential. The police arrest civil suspects in 32 percent of these cases, while they arrest disrespectful suspects in 83 percent of the cases. This difference is far wider than where the complainant expresses a preference for arrest (68 percent and 75 percent). Especially when the complainant is passive, the suspect carries his fate in his own hands. Under these circumstances blacks more than whites tend, to their own disadvantage, to be disrespectful toward the police.

The small sample of cases rules out a complete analysis of the encounters in which the complainant favors clemency for his adver-

---

[18]The observers classified a suspect's degree of deference on the basis of whatever clues they could cull from his behavior. The observers undoubtedly made classificatory errors from time to time since some suspects, particularly some disrespectful suspects, could be extremely subtle in their communicative demeanor. Some, for example, were exceedingly deferential as a way of ridiculing the police. In the great majority of cases, however, the classifications accurately described the outward behavior to which the police were relating. Of course, the suspects' *feelings* were not necessarily reflected in their behavior.

Table 5. Arrest Rates in Citizen-Initiated Encounters According to Complainant's Preference, Suspect's Race, and Degree of Deference

Complainant Prefers Arrest

Race	Suspect's Deference	Total Number of Incidents	Arrest Rate in Percent
Black	Very Deferential	2	(2)
	Civil	19	68
	Antagonistic	12	83
White	Very Deferential	1	(1)
	Civil	15	67
	Antagonistic	4	(2)
Both Races[a]	Very Deferential	3	(3)
	Civil	34	68
	Antagonistic	16	75

Complainant's Preference Is Unclear

Race	Suspect's Deference	Total Number of Incidents	Arrest Rate in Percent
Black	Very Deferential	2	(0)
	Civil	18	33
	Antagonistic	15	93
White	Very Deferential	1	(1)
	Civil	7	(2)
	Antagonistic	3	(1)
Both Races[b]	Very Deferential	3	(1)
	Civil	25	32
	Antagonistic	18	83

Complainant Prefers No Arrest

Race	Suspect's Deference	Total Number of Incidents	Arrest Rate in Percent
Black	Very Deferential	3	(0)
	Civil	13	23
	Antagonistic	4	(1)
White	Very Deferential	1	(0)
	Civil	6	(1)
	Antagonistic	1	(0)
Both Races[c]	Very Deferential	4	(0)
	Civil	19	21
	Antagonistic	5	(1)

[a] Excludes 16 cases for which the suspect's degree of deference was not ascertained.
[b] Excludes 15 cases for which the suspect's degree of deference was not ascertained.
[c] Excludes 18 cases for which the suspect's degree of deference was not ascertained.

sary. The cases are only adequate for establishing that a civil suspect is less likely to be arrested under these conditions than when the complainant prefers arrest or expresses no preference. Although statistically negligible, it is noteworthy that four of the five disrespectful suspects were released by the police under these conditions. The evidence suggests that complainants have voices sufficiently persuasive in routine police encounters to save disrespectful suspects from arrest.

Encounters without Complainants

Police transactions with lone suspects comprise a minority of the encounters with adults, but they nevertheless carry a special significance to a description of police work. There is no complainant available to deflect the outcome, so the encounter is all between the polity and the accused. This kind of situation often arises when citizens call the police but refuse to identify themselves or when they identify themselves but fail to materialize when the police arrive. In these cases the police handle incidents, usually in public places, as the servants of unknown masters. Only rarely do the police themselves detect and act upon crime situations with no prompting from a concerned citizen. This section treats separately the citizen-initiated and the police-initiated encounters. With no complainant participating, the analysis contains fewer variables. Absent are the complainant's preference and the relational distance between complainant and suspect. Because the police rarely encounter felony suspects without the help of a complaining witness, the legal seriousness of the lone suspect's offense is likewise invariable: Nearly all police-initiated encounters involve misdemeanors. Finally, the situational evidence in the vast majority of lone-suspect encounters is a police officer's claim that he witnessed an offense. The size of the sample is too small to allow separate analysis of encounters resting upon other kinds of evidence or those apparently based only upon diffuse police suspicion. The analysis, therefore, is confined to the effect on arrest rates of suspect's race, the suspect's degree of respect for the police, and the type of police mobilization—i.e., whether a citizen or the police initiated the encounter.

Race, Respect, and the Lone Suspect

In 67 situations the police witnessed a misdemeanor after being called to the scene by a citizen's telephone request. They arrested a suspect in 49 percent of these cases. In another 45 situations the police witnessed a misdemeanor and entered into an encounter with a suspect wholly upon their own initiative. In these police-initiated encounters the arrest rate was somewhat higher—62 percent. Hence, the police seem a bit more severe when they act completely upon their own authority than when they respond to citizens' calls. Conversely, when a citizen calls the police but avoids the field situation, the officers match the citizen's seeming indifference with their own.

Table 6 shows the arrest rates for blacks and whites in citizen- and police-initiated encounters where no complainant participated. Under both types of mobilization the police arrested blacks at a higher rate, though in police-initiated encounters the difference is statistically negligible, given the sample size. However, just as in encounters involving complainants, the race difference disappeared in lone-suspect encounters when the suspect's level of respect for the police was held constant, as Table 7 shows.

In citizen-initiated encounters black suspects disproportionately show disrespect for the police, and the police reply with a high arrest rate—83 percent. They arrest only 36 percent of the civil black suspects, a rate comparable to that for civil white suspects, 29 percent (a difference of just one case of the 14 in the sample). Considering both races together in citizen-initiated encounters, disrespectful conduct toward the police clearly is highly determinative for a suspect whose illegal behavior is witnessed by the police. A display of respect for the officers, on the other hand, can overcome the suspect's evidentiary jeopardy.

Arrest practices differ to a degree in encounters the police initiate. While again arrest rates for civil blacks and civil whites are the same, no significant difference emerges between the vulnerability of civil suspects and that of suspects disrepectful toward the police. In other words, neither the race nor suspect's degree of respect has predictive effect on arrest rates in police-initiated encounters with misdemeanor suspects. The absence of variance in arrest rates for disrespectful and civil suspects is the major difference between police-initiated and citizen-initiated encounters. Moreover, it is the major anomaly in the findings presented in this article, one that

Table 6.   Arrest Rates in Police Encounters with Suspects in
Police-Witnessed Misdemeanor Situations Without Complainant Participation
According to Type of Mobilization and Suspect's Race

Type of Mobilization	Race	Total Number of Incidents	Arrest Rate in Percent
Citizen-Initiated	Black	43	58
	White	24	33
Police-Initiated	Black	28	64
	White	17	59
All Citizen-Initiated Encounters		67	49
All Police-Initiated Encounters		45	62

Table 7. Arrest Rates in Police Encounters with Suspects in Police-Witnessed Misdemeanor Situations Without Complainant Participation According to Type of Mobilization, Suspect's Race, and Degree of Deference

	Citizen-Initiated Encounters				Police-Initiated Encounters		
Race	Suspect's Deference	Total Number of Incidents	Arrest Rate in Percent	Race	Suspect's Deference	Total Number of Incidents	Arrest Rate in Percent
Black	Very Deferential	5	(0)	Black	Very Deferential	2	(1)
	Civil	14	36		Civil	13	69
	Antagonistic	18	83		Antagonistic	10	70
White	Very Deferential	3	(1)	White	Very Deferential	1	(0)
	Civil	14	29		Civil	10	70
	Antagonistic	5	(3)		Antagonistic	6	(3)
Both Races[a]	Very Deferential	8	(1)	Both Races[b]	Very Deferential	3	(1)
	Civil	28	32		Civil	23	70
	Antagonistic	23	78		Antagonistic	16	62

[a] Excludes 8 cases for which the suspect's degree of deference was not ascertained.
[b] Excludes 3 cases for which the suspect's degree of deference was not ascertained.

might disappear if the sample of police-initiated encounters were larger.

Generalizations

This section restates the major findings of this study in the form of empirical generalizations, which should provide a manageable profile of police behavior in routine situations where arrest is a possibility. When appropriate, inferences are drawn from these materials to more abstract propositions at the level of a general theory of legal control. Arrest patterns may reveal broad principles according to which legal policy is defined, legal resources mobilized, and dispositions made.[19]

Mobilization

Most arrest situations arise through citizen rather than police initiative. In this sense, the criminal law is invoked in a manner not unlike that of private law systems that are mobilized through a reactive process, depending upon the enterprise of citizen claimants in pursuit of their own interests. In criminal law as in other areas of public law, although the state has formal, proactive authority to bring legal actions, the average criminal matter is the product of a citizen complaint.

One implication of this pattern is that most criminal cases pass through a moral filter in the citizen population before the state assumes its enforcement role. A major portion of the responsibility for criminal-law enforcement is kept out of police hands. Much like courts in the realm of private law, the police operate as moral servants of the citizenry. A further implication of this pattern of reactive policing is that the deterrence function of the criminal process, to an important degree, depends upon citizen willingness to mobilize the criminal law, just as the deterrence function of private law depends so much upon citizen plaintiffs.[20] Sanctions cannot deter illegal behavior if the law lies dormant because of an inefficient

[19]These three functional foci of legal control—prescription, mobilization, and disposition—correspond roughly to the legislative, executive, and judicial dimensions of government, though they are useful in the analysis of subsystems of legal control as well as total systems. For instance, the police can be regarded as the major mobilization subsystem of the criminal justice system. Yet the police subsystem itself can be approached as a total system involving prescription, mobilization, and disposition subsystems. *Cf.* H. Lasswell, *The Decision Process* (1956), 2.

[20]Contemporary literature on deterrence is devoted primarily to the role of sanctions in criminal law. *See, e.g.,* Andenaes, "The General Preventive Effects of Punishment," *U. Pa. L. Rev.,* 144 (1966), 949. But *see* R. Von Jhering, *The Struggle for Law* (1879).

mobilization process.[21] In this sense all legal systems rely to a great extent upon private citizens.

Complainants

Arrest practices sharply reflect the preferences of citizen complainants, particularly when the desire is for leniency and also, though less frequently, when the complainant demands arrest. The police are an instrument of the complainant, then, in two ways: Generally they handle what the complainant wants them to handle and they handle the matter in the way the complainant prescribes.

Often students of the police comment that a community has the kind of police it wants, as if the community outlines the police function by some sort of *de facto* legislative process.[22] That view is vague, if not mistaken. Instead, the police serve an atomized mass of complainants far more than they serve an organized community. The greater part of the police workload is case-by-case, isolated contacts between individual policemen and individual complainants. In this sense the police serve a phantom master who dwells throughout the population, who is everywhere but nowhere at once. Because of this fact, the police are at once an easy yet elusive target for criticism. Their field work evades planned change, but as shifts occur in the desires of the atomized citizenry who call and direct the police, changes ripple into policemen's routine behavior.

The pattern of police compliance with complainants gives police work a radically democratic character. The result is not, however, uniform standards of justice, since the moral standards of complainants doubtlessly vary to some extent across the population. Indeed, by complying with complainants the police in effect perpetuate the moral diversity they encounter in the citizen mass.[23] In this

[21]Roscoe Pound concludes that the contingent nature of legal mobilization is one of the major obstacles to the effectiveness of law as a social engineering device. *See* Pound, "The Limits of Effective Legal Action," *Int'l J. Ethics,* 27 (1917), 150. *See also* H. Jones, *The Efficacy of Law* (1969), 21–26; Bohannan, "The Differing Realms of the Law," in *The Ethnography of Law* 33 (1965) [Supplement to *Am. Anthropologist,* 67 (1965), 33].

[22]*See, e.g.,* P. Slater, *The Pursuit of Loneliness: American Culture at the Breaking Point* (1970), 49.

[23]This generalization does not apply to proactive police operations such as vice control or street harassment, which seldom involve a citizen complainant. By definition, street harassment is the selective and abrasive attention directed at people who are, at best, marginally liable to arrest—for example, a police command to "move on" to a group of unconventional youths. Proactive policing may involve an attack on particular moral subcultures. *Compare* J. Clebert, *The Gypsies* (1963), 87–119, *with* Brown, "The Condemnation and Persecution of Hippies," *Trans-Action,* Sept. 1969 at 33, *and* W. Hagan, *Indian Police and Judges* (1966).

respect again, a public law system bears similarity to systems of private law.[24] Both types seem organized, visibly and invisibly, so as to give priority to the demands of their dispersed citizens. Whoever may prescribe the law and however the law is applied, many sovereigns call the law to action.[25] Public law systems are peculiar in that their formal organization allows them to initiate and pursue cases without complainants as sponsors. Still, the reality of public law systems such as the police belies their formal appearance. The citizenry continually undermines uniformity in public as well as private law enforcement. Perhaps democratic organization invariably jeopardizes uniformity in the application of legal controls.[26]

Leniency

The police are lenient in their routine arrest practices; they use their arrest power less often than the law would allow. Legal leniency, however, is hardly peculiar to the police. Especially in the private law sector[27] and also in other areas of public law,[28] the official process for redress of grievances is invoked less often than illegality is detected. Citizens and public officials display reluctance to wield legal power in immediate response to illegality, and a soci-

[24]*See* Pashukanis, "The General Theory of Law and Marxism" in *Soviet Legal Philosophy* III (H. Babb transl. 1951).

[25]This is true historically as well; legal systems usually have made the citizen complainant the *sine qua non* of legal mobilization, except under circumstances posing a direct threat to political order. A well-known example was the Roman legal process, where even extreme forms of personal violence required the initiative of a complainant before government sanctions were imposed. *See generally* A. Lintott, *Violence in Republican Rome* (1968). A theory of legal control should treat as problematic the capacity and willingness of governments to initiate cases and sanction violators in the absence of an aggrieved citizen demanding justice. *See generally* S. Ranulf, *Moral Indignation and Middle Class Psychology: A Sociological Study* (1938).

[26]The norm of universalism reflected in systems of public law in advanced societies is a norm of impersonalism: The police are expected to enforce the law impersonally. But by giving complainants a strong role in the determination of outcomes, the police personalize the criminal law. This pattern allows fellow family members and friends to mobilize the police to handle their disputes with little danger that the police will impose standards foreign to their relationships. At the level of disputes between strangers, however, the same pattern of police compliance with complainants can, given moral diversity, result in a form of discriminatory enforcement. A law enforcement process that takes no account of the degree of intimacy between complainant and suspect may also upset the peculiar balance of close social relationships. *See* Kawashima, "Dispute Resolution in Contemporary Japan," *Law in Japan: The Legal Order in a Changing Society* (A. von Mehren ed., 1964), 41.

[27]*See, e.g.,* Macaulay, "Non-Contractual Relations in Business: A Preliminary Study," *Am. Soc. Rev.,* 28 (1963), 55.

[28]*See, e.g.,* M. Mileski, "Policing Slum Landlords: An Observation Study of Administrative Control," June 14, 1971 (unpublished dissertation in Department of Sociology, Yale University).

ology of law must treat as problematic the fact that legal cases arise at all.

Evidence

Evidence is an important factor in arrest. The stronger the evidence in the field situation, the more likely is an arrest. When the police themselves witness a criminal offense they are more likely to arrest the suspect than when they only hear about the offense from a third party. Rarely do the police confront persons as suspects without some evidence; even more rarely are arrests unsupported by evidence. The importance of situational evidence hardly constitutes a major advance in knowledge. Evidence has a role in every legal process. It is the definition of evidence, not whether evidence is required, that differs across legal systems. It should be emphasized that even when the evidence against a suspect is very strong, the police frequently take action short of arrest. Evidence alone, then, is a necessary but not a sufficient basis for predicting invocation of the law.

Seriousness

The probability of arrest is higher in legally serious crime situations than in those of a relatively minor nature. This finding certainly is not unexpected, but it has theoretical significance. The police levy arrest as a sanction to correspond with the defined seriousness of the criminal event in much the same fashion as legislators and judges allocate punishments. The formal legal conception of arrest contrasts sharply with this practice by holding that arrest follows upon detection of any criminal act without distinguishing among levels of legal seriousness. Assuming the offender population is aware that arrest represents legislation and adjudication by police officers, arrest practices should contribute to deterrence of serious crime, for the perpetrator whose act is detected risks a greater likelihood of arrest as well as more severe punishment. The higher risk of arrest, once the suspect confronts the police, may help to offset the low probability of detection for some of the more serious crimes.[29]

Intimacy

The greater the relational distance between a complainant and a suspect, the greater is the likelihood of arrest. When a complainant demands the arrest of a suspect the police are most apt to comply if

[29] *See* Black, "Production of Crime Rates," *Am. Soc. Rev.*, 35 (1970), 733 , 735 (remarks on detection differentials in police work).

the adversaries are strangers. Arrest is less likely if they are friends, neighbors, or acquaintances, and it is least likely if they are family members. Policemen also write official crime reports according to the same differential.[30] Relational distance likewise appears to be a major factor in the probability of litigation in contract disputes[31] and other private law contexts.[32] One may generalize that in all legal affairs relational distance between the adversaries affects the probability of formal litigation. If the generalization is true, it teaches that legal control may have comparatively little to do with the maintenance of order between and among intimates.

Yet the findings on relational distance in police arrest practices may merely reflect the fact that legal control operates only when sublegal control is unavailable.[33] The greater the relational distance, the less is the likelihood that sublegal mechanisms of control will operate. This proposition even seems a useful principle for understanding the increasing salience of legal control in social evolution.[34] Over time the drift of history delivers proportionately more and

---

[30]Black, *supra* note 29, at 740. Jerome Hall hypothesizes that relational distance influences the probability of criminal prosecution. J. Hall, *Theft, Law and Society*, (2d ed. 1952), 318.

[31]Macaulay, *supra* note 27, at 56.

[32]For example, in Japan disputes that arise across rather than within communities are more likely to result in litigation. *See* Kawashima, *supra* note 26, at 45. In American Chinatowns disputes that arise between Chinese and non-Chinese are far more likely to result in litigation than disputes between Chinese. *See* Grace, "Justice, Chinese Style," *Case & Com.*, Jan–Feb., 1970, at 50. The same is true of disputes between gypsies and non-gypsies as compared to disputes between gypsies. *See* J. Clebert, *supra* note 23, at 90. Likewise, in the United States in the first half of the nineteenth century, crimes committed between Indians generally were left to the tribes. *See* F. Prucha, *American Indian Policy in the Formative Years: The Indian Trade and Intercourse Acts* (1962), 188–212. In medieval England the same sort of pattern obtained in the legal condition of the Jews. Ordinary English rules applied to legal dealings between Jews and the King and between Jews and Christians, but disputes between Jew and Jew were heard in Jewish tribunals and decided under Jewish law. *See* F. Pollock and F. Maitland, *The History of English Law* (2d ed. 1898), 468–75.

[33]*See* L. Peattie, *The View From the Barrio* (1968), 54–62 (for a stark illustration of this pattern). *See generally* R. Pound, *Social Control Through Law* (1942), 18–25; S. Van Der Sprenkel, *Legal Institutions in Manchu China: A Sociological Analysis* (1962); Cohen, "Chinese Mediation on the Eve of Modernization," *Calif. L. Rev.*, 54 (1966), 1201; Nader, "An Analysis of Zapotec Law Cases," *Ethnology*, 3 (1964), 404; Nader and Metzger, "Conflict Resolution in Two Mexican Communities," *Am. Anthropolgist*, 65 (1963), 584; Schwartz, "Social Factors in the Development of Legal Control: A Case Study of Two Settlements," *Yale L.J.*, 63 (1954), 471; notes 26, 30–31 *supra*.

[34]It is at this level that Pound posits his thesis concerning the priority of sublegal control. R. Pound, *supra* note 33, at 33. *See also* Fuller, "Two Principles of Human Association," *Nomos*, 11 (1969), 3; Selznick, "Legal Institutions and Social Controls," *Vand. L. Rev.*, 17 (1963), 79.

more strangers who need the law to hold them together and apart. Law seems to bespeak an absence of community, and law grows ever more prominent as the dissolution of community proceeds.[35]

Disrespect

The probability of arrest increases when a suspect is disrespectful toward the police. The same pattern appears in youth officer behavior,[36] patrol officer encounters with juveniles,[37] and in the use of illegal violence by the police.[38] Even disrespectful complainants receive a penalty of sorts from the police, as their complaints are less likely to receive official recognition.[39] In form, disrespect in a police encounter is much the same as "contempt" in a courtroom hearing. It is a rebellion against the processing system. Unlike the judge, however, the policeman has no special legal weapons in his arsenal for dealing with citizens who refuse to defer to his authority at a verbal or otherwise symbolic level. Perhaps as the legal system further differentiates, a crime of "contempt of police" will emerge. From a radically behavioral standpoint, indeed, this crime has already emerged; the question is when it will be formalized in the written law.

All legal control systems, not only the police and the judiciary, defend their own authority with energy and dispatch. To question or assault the legitimacy of a legal control process is to invite legal invocation, a sanction, or a more serious sanction, whatever is at issue in a given confrontation. Law seems to lash out at every revolt against its own integrity. Accordingly, it might be useful to consider disrespect toward a policeman to be a minor form of civil disorder, or revolution the highest form of disrespect.

Discrimination

No evidence exists to show that the police discriminate on the basis of race. The police arrest blacks at a comparatively high rate, but the difference between the races appears to result primarily from the greater rate at which blacks show disrespect for the police. The behavioral difference thus lies with the citizen participants, not the

[35] *See* F. Tonnies, *Community and Society* (C. Loomis trans. 1957), 202.

[36] Piliavin and Briar, *supra* note 14, at 210.

[37] Black and Reiss, "Police Control of Juveniles," *supra* note 14, at 74–75.

[38] P. Chevigny, *Police Power: Police Abuses in New York City,* (1969), 51–83; Reiss, "Police Brutality—Answers to Key Questions," *Trans-Action,* July–Aug. 1968, at 18; Westley, "Violence and the Police," *Am. L. Soc.,* 59 (1954), 34.

[39] Black, *supra* note 29, at 742–44.

police.[40] This finding conflicts with some ideological conceptions of police work, but it is supported by the findings of several studies based upon direct observation of the police.[41] These findings should be taken as a caveat that in general improper or illegal behavior toward blacks does not in itself constitute evidence of discrimination toward blacks. A finding of discrimination or of nondiscrimination requires a comparative analysis of behavior toward each race with other variables such as level of respect held constant. No study of citizen opinions or perceptions[42] or of official statistics[43] can hold these variables constant.

In closing this section it is important to note that the findings on racial discrimination by the police should not remotely suggest that law is oblivious to social rank. On the contrary, broader patterns in the form and substance of legal control seem at any one time to reflect and to perpetuate existing systems of social stratification. That the degradation of arrest is reserved primarily for the kinds of illegality committed by lower status citizens exemplifies this broader tendency of the law in action.

Concluding Remarks

A major commitment of this article is to dislodge the discussion from its grounding in empirical findings and to raise the degree of abstraction to the level of general theory. Statements at this level

[40]Of course, "discrimination" can be defined to include any *de facto* unequal treatment, regardless of its causes. *See* L. Mayhew, *Law and Equal Opportunity,* (1968), 59–60. The evidence in the article simply indicates that blacks are treated differently not because they are blacks, but because they manifest other behavioral patterns, such as disrespect for the police, more frequently than whites. The question of why blacks disproportionately show disrespect for the police cannot be addressed with the observational data. We could speculate, for example, that in anticipation of harsh treatment blacks often behave disrespectfully toward the police, thereby setting in motion a pattern that confirms their expectations.

Despite the article's finding of nondiscrimination the police officers observed did reveal considerable prejudice in their attitudes toward blacks. *See generally* Black and Reiss, "Patterns of Behavior in Police and Citizen Transactions," in 2 President's Commission on Law Enforcement and Administration of Justice, *Studies in Crime and Law Enforcement in Major Metropolitan Areas,* 132–39. *See also* Deutscher, "Words and Deeds: Social Science and Social Policy," *Social Problems,* 13 (1966), 235.

[41]*See generally* W. Lafave, *supra* note 7; J. Skolnick, *supra* note 14, at 83–88; L. Tiffany, D. McIntyre, and D. Rottenberg, *supra* note 14; Piliavin and Briar, *supra* note 14 (despite innuendos to the contrary); Project, *supra* note 14, at 1645, n.9. These studies do not report evidence of discrimination or fail altogether to mention race as an analytically important variable.

[42]*E.g.,* Werthman and Piliavin, "Gang Members and the Police," in *The Police: Six Sociological Essays* 56 (D. Bordua ed. 1967).

[43]*See* N. Goldman, *supra* note 14, at 45; J. Wilson, *supra* note 14, at 113; Green, *supra* note 14, at 481.

ignore the boundaries and distinctions that ordinarily contain and constrain generalization about law as a social phenomenon. The various subsystems of law—criminal law, torts, contracts, constitutional law, family law, property law, criminal procedure, administrative law—are assumed to contain common elements. As if this aim were too faint-hearted, a general theory of legal control also seeks to discover patterns present in several functional dimensions of law: prescription, mobilization, and disposition; or, respectively, the articulation of legal policy, the engagement of legal cases by legal organizations, and the situational resolution of legal disputes. This sort of sociology of law shares with jurisprudence the inclusiveness of its subject matter. Each discipline acts upon a longing for a universal understanding of law. For each, the past shares the relevance of the present, and other legal systems illustrate our own. Unlike jurisprudence, however, sociology of law abjures problems of a normative character; unlike sociology of law, jurisprudence bypasses the ordeal of concrete description.

A closing note should state what the article has not done. Arrest might be examined from a number of other perspectives that have their own vocabulary suited to their own special kind of discourse. For example, arrest may usefully be conceived as one stage in an elaborate processing network, an assembly line of inputs and outputs. This technocratic metaphor has been popular in recent studies of the criminal justice system. Another perspective might see every arrest as a political event. When and how the arrest power is used says much about the nature of a political system and the quality of life within it. Then, too, arrest is part of a job. It is a role performance of a bureaucratic functionary. Police work may be contemplated as it arises from its rich occupational subculture with standards and values that policemen share and enforce among their peers. And every arrest is enveloped by the police bureaucracy. Not surprisingly, therefore, the arrest practices of individual officers are under some degree of surveillance from their superiors as well as their peers. Finally, a study of arrest can inform and benefit from the sociology of face-to-face interaction. The police encounter is a small group with its own morphology, its own dynamics. What happens in an encounter may have less to do with crime and law than with the demands of situational order, with social etiquette or the pressures of group size or spatial configuration. An arrest may be the only means available to a policeman bent on restoring order to a field situation, yet other times it is the surest way to undermine order by making a situation disintegrate.

Some encouragement may be taken from the development of social science to the point where a subject such as arrest can occasion so many diverse perspectives. Diversity of this degree, nevertheless, casts a film of arbitrariness over whatever theoretical framework is chosen. Although the many perspectives available to a study of arrest surely mirror the empirical nature of arrest itself, its theoretical identity is precarious and unstable. Here it is sanction and justice; there input, coercion, expectation, job, criterion, or gesture. Any single theoretical view of arrest is inevitably incomplete.

Investigating Criminal Homicides
Police Work in Reporting and Solving Murders

W. Clinton Terry III And David F. Luckenbill

The study of criminal homicide has proceeded along three general lines. First, it has focused on explanations of individual conduct. One form of this type of explanation is psychodynamic theory. This approach explains a person's violent actions on the basis of disorders in his personality structure, including deficient superego development (Brearley, 1932:95–96; Mead, 1968), internalization of aggressive norms (Duncan et al., 1958), and faulty ego development (Bromberg, 1951; Menninger et al., 1960; Smith 1965). Another form of individualistic explanation makes use of interaction theory, an approach that stresses the emerging definition of the situation as favorable to criminal homicide (Toch, 1969:183–95; Banitt et al., 1970; Shoham et al., 1973; Clinard and Quinney, 1973:40–42).

Second, research has focused on variations in the rates of criminal homicide, explaining it in terms of structural and cultural factors. Included in this category are theories emphasizing the external constraints of social position in situations of frustration (Henry and Short, 1954) and adherence to the norms of a "subculture of violence" in situations of conflict (Wolfgang and Ferracutti, 1967).

Third, research has focused on the model characteristics of offenders, victims, and murder scenes. This research shows, for example, that criminal homicides are typically committed by young, male, urban ghetto dwellers of the lower socioeconomic and racially disadvantaged classes; hence they are more frequent in larger rather than smaller cities and suburbs (Bullock, 1955; Wolfgang, 1958; Pokorny, 1965; Mulvihill and Tumin, 1969: 53–96, 206–40; Hepburn and Voss, 1970).

These three directions of research into criminal homicide all deal in one fashion or another with the notion of constraint. Each points to underlying yet objectively observable features of social or psychic structures that influence or constrain social action. Furthermore, adherents of each explanation use or cite as proof police, prosecution, court, and correctional documents and records.

It may be objected, however, that the cases contained in these official documents are unrepresentative of the "actual" universe of criminal homicide (cf. Brearley, 1932:10, 12–15, 200–3; Wolfgang, 1958:284–94). Some events classified as accidents, suicides, missing

SOURCE: Previously unpublished. Printed by permission of the authors.

persons, or deaths due to natural causes may in fact be cleverly disguised murders.[1] A further objection may be that research based on these documents treats them as mere compilations of unambiguous events, although several recent investigations suggest that official documents are more representative of the interpretive activities by which organizational members find meaning in an event and fit it to a particular category of understanding (Kitsuse and Cicourel, 1963; Bittner, 1965, Sudnow, 1965; Sacks, 1972:280–94; Garfinkel, 1967: 11–18, 186–208; Cicourel, 1968:112–23, 330; Zimmerman, 1969, 1970; Sanders and Daudistel, 1974; Daudistel and Sanders, 1974; Sanders, 1974).

It is our intention here to describe the organizational activities involved in interpreting cases of criminal homicide, activities that underlie the production of official records and statistics. In so doing, we will trace the stages of investigation, beginning with a patrolperson's response to the scene of the crime, through the summoning of detectives from the major crime detail of the county sheriff's office, to the final disposition of the case. We will also point to the investigative distinction made between "walk-through" and "whodunit" cases, which effects the treatment of evidence and the establishment of foul play.

Method of Investigation

This study was conducted in a California county sheriff's office.[2] Ideally, our approach lends itself to participant observation, but there were no homicides being investigated at the time we began the study. Moreover, as we were to learn, part of the investigation of any homicide is "sealing off the crime scene" from outside interference and contamination by inquisitive sociologists, among others. Consequently, when later in our investigation a case did occur, we had to be content with watching its development through the display of evidence and reconstruction of events that occur within the confines of the sheriff's office. Because of the care with which cases are documented, this apparent limitation proved to be less of a hindrance to our observation of the interpretive practices of criminal homicide investigations than one might suppose.

Except for one current case, our material is drawn from reports filed by the detectives of the major crimes detail during the years 1970–74 and from interviews with the investigating personnel. We

[1]The case of Carl Coppolino, reported by F. Lee Bailey in *The Defense Never Rests,* New York: Stein and Day, 1971, 187–230, illustrates the difficulty of detecting alleged "clever murders."

[2]This same sheriff's office is the focus of several other investigations and reports. Cf. Sanders and Daudistel, 1974; Daudistel and Sanders, 1974; Sanders, 1974.

were also drawn to some older cases that had become "legend" within the department. We organized our notes according to the natural occurrence of an investigation, from the initial offense report to the final disposition of the case.

Patrol Response and "Securing the Scene"

Investigations of deaths and homicides[3] are most often citizen-activated. When the sheriff's department is notified that a death has occurred, a deputy sheriff–coroner[4] is dispatched to the scene. The responding officer's first duty is to inspect the scene and determine the victim's physical condition. If he or she is still alive, the officer administers first aid and calls an ambulance. If the person is dead and death appears to be of natural causes, a mortuary is called. If the cause of death is uncertain the field supervisor is consulted. If the death appears to be a homicide, detectives of the major crimes detail are called to the scene. In the meantime the patrol officer secures the crime scene, an action that is critical to the subsequent investigation. Failure to do so could destroy leads to the identity of an as-yet-unknown offender, cause evidence to be inadmissible in a court of law, and even make it impossible to reconstruct the events surrounding the murder. The members of this sheriff's office are acutely aware of the importance of securing the scene of a crime because of the consequences of their failure to do so in the Rodriquez-Eaton case twelve years ago.

The Rodriguez-Eaton Case[5]

> Late one afternoon, a high school couple was found murdered in a shack near an isolated beach. Both had been shot repeatedly with a .22 caliber weapon. The bathing suit of the woman had been cut off. An attempt had been made to burn the shack. Reconstruction of the crime indicated that this couple had been lying on the beach when the unknown assailant had attacked them. As the victims fled from the beach, this person continued to shoot at them as he pursued them into the adjacent brush. Having downed them, he dragged them to the shack and there piled the bodies one above the other.

[3]"Homicide" is the death of a human being at the hands of another, whether intentional or unintentional, criminal or noncriminal. Every homicide is the subject of police investigation, but only criminal homicide is subject to punishment by the state.

[4]In this department, all deputy sheriffs, whether they work patrol, burglary, or major crimes, are also deputy coroners. There is, however, one man who has the major responsibility for investigating natural deaths, which falls within the jurisdictional requirements of the coroner's function.

[5]The names of the persons in this and the cases that follow are fictitious.

Because darkness overtook the intitial investigation, fire department lighting equipment was brought in, a move that altered the original crime scene. Preserved in the files of this case, for example, is a revealing photograph of that night. In it five men, including the sheriff, are standing next to the shack where the bodies were discovered. Visible on the ground are seven or eight cigarette butts, and several other smoldering cigarettes are clamped between the fingers of the men in the picture.

This twelve-year-old case, which remains unsolved, has become a classic example for the department of what not to do; it separates old styles of investigation from the new. "In recent years the importance of physical evidence and the crime scene has been pounded into everyone's head," we were told. "If you have a whodunit and a crime scene, then you are going to have to work that to death. And if things [like the events described above] happen, then you are going to lose valuable evidence, maybe even lose the lead thread, the one little piece of physical evidence that can put the whole banana together."

The new approach is apparent in the cases we studied. In the Akkaba case, for instance, Akkaba killed two men whom he had lured to his hotel room. Securing this crime scene was relatively simple, essentially keeping people from entering the room where the victims had been shot and the patio area, where the suspect had seated himself to await the arrival of police. Since Akkaba had acted alone and the area was naturally isolated, not many persons happened by to trespass into this potential danger spot.

In the Casper case presented later, on the other hand, an eighteen-year-old male was slain in a wooded park. This area was geographically large and therefore less easily controllable. Consequently, a group of curious onlookers quickly assembled, drifting in and out of the scene before the sheriff's deputies arrived. Nevertheless, officers responding to the call cordoned off the immediate site of the slaying, monitored the main roads of the camp grounds, and ascertained the identity of the principal witnesses.

Styles of Investigation: "Whodunit" and "Walk-Through"

Detectives categorize investigations of criminal homicide as "whodunits" or "walk-throughs,"[6] designations that are more than

[6]W. B. Sanders (1974:276) also mentions that detectives distinguish between walk-throughs and whodunits. His handling of this dichotomy is, however, different from ours, particularly in terms of the relationship between walk-through and whodunit cases and the treatment of evidence.

simple descriptive categories; they represent practiced and organizationally sanctioned styles of investigation.

A whodunit investigation is concerned with identifying the victim, determining the events leading up to and surrounding the death, and locating persons having knowledge of or involvement in the events. If investigators are unable to establish the identity of the victim, it generally follows that the events of the case, including the persons involved, remain unknown. Even if investigators develop strong suspicions about a possible suspect and are able to place this person in the vicinity of the crime, without identifying the victim it is impossible to establish that the suspect knew or had any reason to kill him.

The Jane Doe Case[7]

A group of hunters found a partially decomposed female body lying down the embankment of a road. The victim's wrists were bound, her throat was slit, and she had been stabbed repeatedly. Questioning local residents, checking missing-persons lists, and examining all other possible leads, such as places where she might have purchased her clothes, turned up no clues as to her identity. A nationwide check of dentists also turned up negative, except for the suggestion that some of her dental work had possibly been done in Europe.

Failing here, the investigators attempted to locate possible suspects by matching the MOs of known offenders and the identification of people near the scene at the estimated time of death. One possible suspect was located. He had been charged with the murder of his roommate and the theft of his car. This suspect also was known to carry a sheathed knife. Soil samples taken from the stolen car and the suspect's boots matched the scene of the murder as well as other locations.

To date this case is unsolved.

For the body in a criminal homicide to remain unidentified is the exception rather than the rule. A more typical whodunit case is the murder of Barbara Whitmore.

The Barbara Whitmore Case

The nude body of a 21-year-old woman was discovered by another woman, who was horseback riding. The body had been tossed from a car at a road intersection in an isolated rural area

[7]Jane Doe is the name given all cases involving unknown female victims; John Doe is the male counterpart of Jane Doe. When identification is established, the label is dropped.

and had apparently been there for several days. The victim had died of multiple stab wounds. Leads to her identification were established by checking missing-persons lists. Positive identification was made by the victim's dentist and through fingerprints.

The investigation, which is still going on, is now able to establish who knew the victim and who might have had reason to kill her.

In walk-throughs, in contrast to whodunits, the offender generally confesses his actions. Consequently, the identities of the victim and offender are known, as are the circumstances leading to and surrounding the homicide.

The Akkaba Case

Akkaba lured two fellow Middle Eastern men to his hotel room. After some casual conversation, he pulled a 9mm Luger from a copy of *Who's Who in the West,* which he had hollowed out prior to their arrival in order to conceal the weapon, and shot each man four times. He then took a Browning automatic pistol from his top dresser drawer and shot each man twice in the head. He phoned the hotel switchboard operator, informing her that she should notify the sheriff's office. By the time the sheriff's deputies arrived, he had put on a white trench coat and beret and seated himself on the patio to await their arrival.

Many persons had heard the shots. Several of them spoke cautiously with Akkaba while he sat on the patio. He even asked one of these persons to get him a glass of water, which was done. Akkaba maintained throughout that "I did what had to be done, and I killed them."

Categorizing Events

All cases, both whodunits and walk-throughs, require a label in order to satisfy the organization's record-keeping needs. Logically speaking, the death of a person may be categorized as resulting from natural causes, suicide, accidental causes (for example, unintentionally self-caused deaths such as falling down a flight of stairs), or homicide. The actual label affixed to the individual case, however, such as "death by gunshot," "possible homicide," or "possible suicide," is more descriptive. As we shall see, these designations are the important indicators of the case's complexity and difficulty.

How to label a case is often decided after considerable investigative work. Much of the basic case data are collected during the first twelve to twenty-four hours, during which the crime scene is secured, witnesses are interviewed, and leads are explored. When an appropriate label is determined, it is affixed to both the initial offense report and all subsequent reports. Although this process appears to give detectives considerable discretion in determining the future course of the investigation, their decisions are made in full view of their organizational superiors.

Decisions as to how to label a case cut across the distinction between a whodunit and walk-through. A person who confesses to killing another human being admits having committed a homicide. But, as we shall see shortly, this homicide may be labeled either criminal or noncriminal—that is, justifiable or accidental—depending on the outcome of the investigation initiated by the confession. It is true, nonetheless that walk-throughs, by their very nature, are homicides, whereas whodunits may be instances of suicide or accidental death, death from natural cause, as well as homicide.

Cases that defy immediate classification receive such labels as "death by unknown means," "possible suicide," "possible homicide," or even "probable homicide." These labels are understood to be temporary designations, indicating the expectation that at some point in the not-too-distant future the case will be reclassified. The following death, for example, was labeled a "possible suicide."

The Donna Berry Case

Detectives entered the scene of an apparent suicide. They found a "suicide note" written in the victim's own hand; her relatives and a close friend related that she had been very depressed the previous few weeks over her family affairs; the room was locked from the inside; she was found slumped on her bed with a pump-action shotgun wedged between her legs. The victim was dead, the top of her head splattered against the ceiling.

Closer examination of the scene gave investigators cause to consider the possibility that there had been another person who either assisted in the suicide or killed the victim. Of primary importance in this regard was the observation that the breach of the pump-action shotgun was open and the shell casing was in the wastebasket on the other side of the room.

By testing the victim's shotgun as the victim would have had to use it in order to have shot herself—that is, with the gun stock on the ground and light pressure applied to the slide—it was discovered that a shell would indeed eject from the chamber. That the casing landed in the wastebasket was held to be pure happenstance. Consequently, the case's designation changed from "possible suicide" to "suicide."

Establishing Foul Play:
Criminal or Noncriminal Homicide?

If investigators are certain they are dealing with a homicide, their first concern is to determine whether the homicide is criminal or noncriminal. The legal elements and degrees of criminal involvement are specified in the penal code. Murder (187 Calif. P.C.), for example, is the unlawful killing of a human being with malice aforethought. "Manslaughter" (192 Calif. P.C.), in contrast, is the unlawful killing of a human being without malice aforethought. These distinctions per se, however, do not play a fundamental role in investigative work. Their determination is felt to be the work of the district attorney and the courts.

The *modus operandi* in investigating homicides is to treat all questionable cases as if they were murder, with the intention of eliminating the element of foul play. In other words, designation "murder" is used as a generic label for all cases exhibiting the possibility of foul play. A murder in which the elements of foul play are missing is an instance of noncriminal homicide.

In some cases, foul play is readily apparent. A bludgeon slaying, because of its manifest brutality is clearly an instance of foul play, as are cases involving multiple gunshot or knife wounds. In other cases, however, foul play is more difficult to determine.

The Robb Case

> At approximately six in the morning, the victim arose and started to make coffee. He returned to the living room, where he had been sleeping on the couch. Shortly thereafter, an argument occurred between the victim and his wife over a banking matter. He became quite hostile and argumentative. His wife recounts that he "came swinging at me," but she was not struck. She asked him to calm down, but he continued toward her. She backed out of the kitchen and proceeded down the hall to the bedroom. Reaching the dresser, she pulled a .38 caliber revolver out of the drawer. She pointed the gun at her husband and it went off.
>
> After the shot, the victim asked, "Why did you do that?" He turned and walked down the hall to the kitchen. She followed. He tried to sit down, but fell backwards through the door onto the porch. Mrs. Robb then drove to the house of friends. She told them what happened, and they phoned the sheriff's department.

Since foul play could not be ruled out on the basis of Mrs. Robb's testimony alone, she was arrested on a charge of murder. As it turned out, the district attorney, in consultation with detectives, decided that there was insufficient evidence for criminal prosecution.

If a case is classified as other than a criminal homicide, it has already become sufficiently clear that there was no foul play. Mrs. Robb's case, however, was insufficently clear at the outset because there were no witnesses to the shooting. In the Casper case, however, there were many persons who could corroborate the sequence of events.

The Casper Case

About four in the morning, four youths entered the public camping grounds of a national forest. They had been drinking and decided they would scavenge for food left at picnic tables and campsites. The victim attempted to steal Casper's ice chest. A woman in an adjacent tent saw the incident and awakened Casper, who, with shotgun in hand, yelled at the victim to stop where he was and bring the ice chest back. He fired one round in the air, whereupon the victim dropped the chest and ran.

The victim returned to his friends and told them of the incident. He then decided to return to the campsite in order to scare Casper, who in the meantime had returned to his tent. The victim approached Casper's tent. Casper again came out with his shotgun. Both men exchanged threats. The victim told Casper that he knew karate and appraoched him making karate gestures. The gun discharged when the victim, in his alcoholic uncertainty, brushed Casper's arm.

Because many persons had heard the two separate shotgun blasts and because others could verify parts of Casper's account, the detectives decided to label the incident "death by gunshot." As one detective told us, "I didn't want to call it murder, I didn't want to call it manslaughter, I didn't want to call it anything, because there just wasn't enough evidence to say it was criminal."

As the last two illustrations indicate, what foul play means cannot be specified in so many words. Nevertheless, it is assumed that its specific meaning in any given case would be interpreted in the same fashion by any competent detective. By attending to the concrete features of particular situations, to their otherwise normal appearances (Goffman, 1971), detectives develop a sensitivity to foul play, "because things are not just quite right." As one detective put it, "it is common sense and experience."

The Development and Documentation of Evidence

The way evidence is interpreted points to the existence of foul play, if any, thus confirming or denying that certain events are instances of criminal homicide. The fact that cases are divisible into whodunits and walk-throughs indicates that this distinction itself affects how a case is worked.

Detectives working whodunit cases have to develop their leads as to suspects from information about the victim or from information developed in analyzing the physical evidence. In working the physical evidence, the crime location receives meticulous attention. Empty shell casings are carefully collected and labeled; bullets are dug from walls, floors, or trees; weapons such as knives and guns as well as lengths of pipe, bloodied rocks and tree limbs, tire irons, and icepicks are handled gingerly and marked for future identification; cigarette and cigar butts are examined and put into plastic bags, as are pieces of torn clothing, cut rope, and other objects found at the crime scene.

Objects that are normally present at the scene of a crime but are noted missing are also vital to the investigation. A missing car, wallet, money, or credit cards suggests robbery as the principal reason for the murder. A missing finger from the victim's hand or a missing lock of hair or a photo cut from the victim's driver's license suggests that the offender was "crazy" and took such an item as a memento of the occasion. These missing items, when found in the possession of a suspect, not only confirm the detectives' suspicions but also place the suspect at the scene of the crime.[8]

Although information garnered from the physical evidence is important, the information gathered about the victim is of greater importance. For example, being able to probe the victim's personal habits and associations allows investigators to locate his whereabouts and contacts immediately before the murder. The Malby investigation is a good case in point.

The Malby Case

A young woman was hitchhiking late at night. One of the persons who picked her up shot her many times with a .22 caliber weapon. She was then dumped onto the road, apparently near where she had been picked up. Shortly thereafter, another driver discovered her body and rushed her to the hospital. All she said before she died was, "He shot me, he shot me" and, in response to a deputy sheriff's question as to who shot her, "Go to hell."

By placing a notice in the paper asking for leads, interviewing the dead girl's roommate and friends about her activities that night, and

---

[8]This contrasts with the basic strategy for investigating apparent suicides, as in the Donna Berry case, which involves eliminating the possibility of any other person's being present at the time of death.

questioning people in the neighborhoods through which she had traveled, detectives were able to account for all but five minutes of her time. They were also able to obtain a description of the possible murderer's car.

If one knows the victim's family or acquaintances, another dimension is added to the investigation—namely examination of the verbal evidence produced by talking with these persons. Of course, the most important type of verbal evidence is an eyewitness account. Lacking this, however, the investigators of a whodunit attempt to construct a portrait of the victim's personality and lifestyle from these interviews. This "portrait" allows the investigators to evaluate the statements of persons known by the victim and, consequently, their status as suspects.

In the Norman case, for example, Martin became a suspect when his account of the victim's intentions and actions failed to match the intentions and actions detectives had come to expect from the information they had gained in interviewing Norman's closer friends and family. It seemed far-fetched that Norman would turn his boat over to Martin and go off on a smuggling venture.

The Norman Case

Charles Norman had worked hard and sold many of his material possessions in order to buy a boat. While this boat was moored at a marina, Charles met Martin. Some weeks later, the two men departed on a scuba-diving trip for several days, each taking his own boat. Three days later, Martin returned to a neighboring marina with Norman's boat in tow. The same day, Martin filed a change of ownership, transferring title of Norman's boat to himself. Martin later sold the boat.

Norman's disappearance was reported to the police by relatives. The case was designated a "missing person." An investigation of the victim's activities prior to disappearance determined that Norman had last been seen by Martin, who was brought in for questioning.

Martin related the following story of Norman's disappearance. "While [Norman] and I were sailing in separate boats off the California coast, we came upon a large yacht. Tying up to this yacht, we met the captain and crew, who were members of a large dope-smuggling ring. The smugglers offered Norman a piece of the action in exchange for a small investment. He agreed. He asked me to take his boat, sell it, and hold the money until he could get in touch with me. Norman remained aboard the yacht, and I took both boats back to port and sold Norman's."

Inconsistencies in verbal statements and testimonies also provide sufficient reason for detectives to suspect the source. In the Norman case, for example, Martin stated when first contacted that he had *not* invested in the dope-smuggling operation. The next day, however, he admitted having been "burned" by losing his investiment in the venture. When asked if he had ever seen the captain of the mysterious yacht, he first said he had not. Yet the next day he confessed seeing the captain near the victim's boat when it was docked.

A person also becomes a suspect when it is discovered that he has lied. In the Norman case, once again, Martin had told detectives that he had waited several weeks before transferring the ownership of Norman's boat to himself. An examination of the Department of Motor Vehicles' records, however, indicated that this transfer had occurred on the same day that Martin returned to port. Martin had also told detectives the name of the smugglers' yacht. In checking the whereabouts of this boat, it was discovered that the vessel was some 300 miles from where Martin had said it was. Finally, he also claimed that he had placed $5,000 in $20 bills in a standard-size envelope, later mailing it to a Mexican address, where the victim was supposedly staying (as related in a mysterious letter that had been shoved under the suspect's door). Yet, when detectives attempted to place the same amount of money in the same denominations in a standard-size envelope, it would not fit.

Another important factor in locating suspects is a person's emotional response to being questioned. Undue nervousness or uncooperativeness are taken as signs of guilt or criminal involvement. Martin was so nervous and sweated so profusely when asked for a sample of his handwriting that he could hardly hold a pen in his hand.

As soon as a whodunit case has developed strong leads pointing to the culpability of a certain suspect, the same investigative practices used to delve into the personal life of the victim are used to investigate the suspect's life.

Investigations in cases where there is no body but a strong possibility that a certain suspect has killed a missing person begin with investigation of this suspect's motives and opportunities for committing the suspected act. Thus information about the suspect's background, temperament, and prior record, including his MO, and his whereabouts and activities at the time of the murder is assembled. The realm of factual information, at first limited to the physical evidence of the crime scene and victim's body, is enlarged by the addition of this information about the suspect.

The working of walk-through cases differs markedly from the working of whodunits. As a matter of practical accomplishment, the case is already solved. Hence, the focus of the investigation is upon the offender rather than the victim. The goal of this type of investigation is the documentation of the offender's reconstruction of events and his reasons for doing it.

The line between gathering evidence and documenting it is a thin one. It is not a question of one procedure being more thorough than the other. The scene of the Akkaba case, for example, was microscopically examined and documented. Photographs were taken of the entire room, the hallway, the patio, and the victims' bodies. Wooden dowels were placed in the bullet holes in the floor and walls and photographed in order to record the bullets' trajectory. Close-up photos were made of a bullet that had lodged in the floor. The autopsy was also extensively photographed, with probes placed in the wounds in order to determine the angles of the bullets' entry and exit.

Sections of carpet and wall where bullets had entered were removed and seized as evidence. The weapons used and the spent shell casings, as well as Akkaba's copy of *Who's Who in the West,* were also taken, as were several pieces of broken and bloodied furniture. In short, everything relevant to the case was seized, not as evidence from which leads could be developed, but as evidence supporting the occurrence of already known events.[9]

There is also no difference in principle between walk-throughs and whodunits in the examination of verbal evidence. In the Casper case, for example, detectives interviewed most of the persons at the camp grounds. They also established a profile of the victim, which indicated his violent nature when drunk. They learned, for example, that his mother had had him arrested because of his uncontrollable actions while intoxicated. Although there were differences between Casper's story and the accounts given by the victim's friends, the information detectives gathered about Casper and the victim, including eyewitness support of Casper's reconstruction of events, in general corroborated Casper's story.

Only when the documentation of evidence turns up gross discrepancies does the character of the case change. Minor inconsistencies in the physical and verbal information, as in the Casper case, are seldom treated as leads to be attended to. In the Robb case, to cite another example, Mrs. Robb told the court-appointed psychiatrist that she had awakened in the morning, made coffee, and backed down the hallway away from the bedroom, but, remembering that the revolver was in the bedroom, changed direction and remained in the bedroom after the victim was shot. All these points directly contradicted her first account. These inconsistencies were not attended to because of the overwhelming consensus among the couple's acquaintances that the husband was "no good" and had beaten her in the past. These sentiments supported her insistence that she had acted out of fear for her own physical well-being.

[9]This case was perhaps more thoroughly documented than is normally the case because of the international repercussions of the double murder.

Discussion

It is evident from the cases we have considered that police investigations of homicides often involve feast-or-famine situations. On the one hand, detectives may find themselves sorting through myriad confusing, often conflicting, details. On the other hand, they may find themselves working the slimmest of leads, grasping at each and every piece of information that promises in some fashion to help them break the case. To see these investigations merely as the mechanical result of responding to the scene of a crime, following through on leads, and apprehending offenders overlooks the manifold complexities and uncertainties surrounding every investigation.

Regardless of the varied circumstances under which investigators work, generally they succeed in sorting out and interpreting events. They do this not as individuals but as competent organizational members, in constant interaction and communication with other organizational personnel, performing routine, rational tasks (Garfinkel, 1967, 1968).

Part of every routine investigation is keeping track of its progress. All officers fill out reports describing events and information they experienced in the course of carrying out their assigned tasks. These reports, together with the coroner's report, psychiatric report, offender's arrest record, photographs, copies of letters and Teletypes, and any other relevant case material, are gathered together and placed in a folder under an appropriate case label.

Often all we know about these records is the final disposition of the case as presented in the department's yearly statistical report. Nevertheless, these official statistics and accompanying explanations are often viewed as the raw data that point to an objective and underlying reality. Little or no attention is given to the manner by which these case materials are collected and given meaning. This is a serious shortcoming.

Detectives investigating homicides are not neutral observers of unambiguous events. They are active agents. Their activities determine whether a set of events will be placed within the criminal-homicide column or seen as instances of suicide or natural death.

It is true that certain homicides, unlike other types of violent offenses, are unequivocally criminal. The discovery of a person killed by violent means is quickly understood by all observers as a case of murder. Regardless of the subsequent investigation, these cases will remain tallied in the criminal-homicide column.

Other cases, however, are more ambiguous. Despite the obviousness of a violent death, it may be difficult to determine either the existence of foul play or the presence of a second party. The case of

Donna Berry, for example, where a spent shotgun shell was found in the wastebasket, could well have been labeled a "possible homicide" rather than a "possible suicide," thus becoming another criminal murder statistic. The Robb case, in which a wife shot her husband during a domestic altercation, might have remained a "murder" had not the investigators discovered that Mrs. Robb had just cause to fear her husband.

The Norman case, where the victim is alleged to have embarked on a smuggling venture, represents yet another problematic type of case in that it might have remained a "missing persons" rather than a criminal homicide had Martin been able to tell a smooth, articulate story.

The Norman case raises another salient observation about criminal-homicide statistics. There is a real possibility that they fail to include cases that are initially reported to the police as missing persons. Unless there is reason to suspect foul play, a missing-persons report does not become a part of the major crime detail's workload.

To assume, therefore, that statistical data accurately represent the universe of criminal homicides overlooks both the ambiguous and perplexed, albeit reasonable, nature of investigations and the probable inaccuracy in the reports of homicides. In the light of these difficulties, the thought must at least be entertained that official documents reflect only those homicides that are readily visible and capable of being investigated. Thus, murders committed by urban ghetto dwellers of the lower socioeconomic and racially disadvantaged classes are heavily overrepresented in the official statistics.

References

Bannit, Riuka, Shoshana Katznebon, and Shlomit Streit. 1970. The Situational Aspects of Violence: A Research Model. In *Israel Studies in Criminology,* vol. 1., ed. Shlomo Shoham. Tel-Aviv: Gomeh.

Bittner, Egon. 1965. The Concept of Organization. *Social Research* 32:239–55.

———. 1970. The Functions of the Police in Modern Society. Rockville, Md.: National Institute of Mental Health.

Brearley, H. C. 1932. *Homicide in the United States.* Montclair, N.J.: Patterson Smith.

Bromberg, Walter. 1951. A Psychological Study of Murder. *International Journal of Psychoanalysis* 32:117–27.

Bullock, Henry. 1955. Urban Homicide in Theory and Fact. *Journal of Criminal Law, Criminology, and Police Science* 45 (January-February): 565–75.

Chodorkoff, Bernold, and Seymond Baxter. 1969. Psychodynamic and Psychoanalytic Theories of Violence. In Mulvihill and Tumin, op. cit., vol. 13.

Cicourel, Aaron V. 1968. *The Social Organization of Juvenile Justice.* New York: Wiley.

Clinard, Marshall, and Richard Quinney. 1973. *Criminal Behavior Systems: A Typology.* New York: Holt, Rinehart and Winston.

Daudistel, Howard C., and William B. Sanders. 1974. Police Discretion in Application of the Law. et al. 3, no. 3:26–40.

Duncan, Glen M., Shervert H. Frazier, Edward M. Litan, Adelaide M. Johnson, and Alfred J. Barron. 1958. Etiological Factors in First Degree Murder. *Journal of the American Medical Association* 168 (November):1755–58.

Garfinkel, Harold. 1967. *Studies in Ethnomethodology.* Englewood Cliffs, N.J.: Prentice-Hall.

———. 1968. The Origins of the Term "Ethnomethodology." In *Proceedings of the Purdue Symposium on Ethnomethodology,* ed. Richard J. Hill and Kathleen S. Crittenden, pp. 5–11. Institute Monograph Series no. 1, Institute for the Study of Social Change, Purdue University.

Goffman, Erving. 1971. Normal Appearances. In *Relations in Public.* New York: Harper & Row.

Henry, Andrew, and James F. Short, Jr. 1954. *Suicide and Homicide: Some Economic, Sociological, and Psychological Aspects of Agression.* New York: Free Press.

Hepburn, John, and Harwin Voss. 1970. Patterns of Criminal Homicide: A Comparison of Chicago and Philadelphia. *Criminology* (May):21–45.

Kitsuse, John, and Aaron V. Cicourel. A Note on the Use of Official Statistics. *Social Problems* 11 (Fall):131–39.

Mead, Margaret. 1968. Cultural Factors in the Cause and Prevention of Pathological Homicide. In *Homicidal Threats,* ed. John M. MacDonald, pp. 73–87. Springfield, Ill.: Charles C Thomas.

Megargee, John. 1969. The Psychology of Violence. In Mulvihill and Tumin, op. cit.

Menninger, Karl, et al. 1960. Murder without Apparent Motive: A Study in Personality Disorganization. *American Journal of Psychiatry* 117 (July):48–53.

Mulvihill, Donald, and Melvin Tumin. 1969. *Crimes of Violence: Report to the National Commission on the Causes and Prevention of Violence,* vols. 11, 12, 13. Washington, D.C.: U.S. Government Printing Office.

Pokorny, Alex D. 1965. A Comparison of Homicides in Two Cities. *Journal of Criminal Law, Criminology, and Police Science* 56, no. 4.

Sacks, Harvey. 1972. Notes on Police Assessment of Moral Character. In *Studies in Social Interaction,* ed. David Sudnow, pp. 280–93. New York: Free Press.

Sanders, William B. 1974. Detective Story: A Study of Criminal Investigations. Ph.D. dissertation, University of California, Santa Barbara.

Sanders, William B., and Howard C. Daudistel. Detective Work: Patterns of Criminal Investigations. In *The Sociologist as Detective,* ed. William B. Sanders, pp. 166–83. New York: Praeger.

Shoham, Shlomo, et al. 1973. The Cycles of Interaction in Violence. In *Israel Studies in Criminology,* ed. Shlomo Shoham, pp. 69–87. Jerusalem: Jerusalem Academic Press.

Smith, Sydney. 1965. The Adolescent Murderer: A Psychodynamic Interpretation. *Archives of General Psychiatry* 13 (October):310–19.

Sudnow, David. 1965. Normal Crimes: Sociological Features of the Penal Code in a Public Defender Office. *Social Problems* 12 (Winter):255–76.

Toch, Hans. 1969. *Violent Men: An Inquiry into the Psychology of Violence.* Chicago: Aldine.

Wolfgang, Marvin E. 1958. *Patterns of Criminal Homicide.* Philadelphia: University of Pennsylvania Press.

Wolfgang, Marvin E., and Franco Ferracutti. 1967. *The Subculture of Violence: Towards an Integrated Theory in Criminology.* London: Tavistock.

Zimmerman, Don H. 1969. Tasks and Troubles: The Practical Basis of Work Activities in a Public Assistance Organization. In *Explorations in Sociology and Counseling,* ed. D. A. Hansen. Boston: Houghton Mifflin.

———. 1970. The Practicalities of Rule Use. In *Understanding Everyday Life: Toward the Reconstruction of Sociological Knowledge,* ed. Jack D. Douglas, pp. 221–38. Chicago: Aldine.

Police Discretion in Application of the Law

Howard C. Daudistel and William B. Sanders

Over the past few years, social scientific research dealing with decision-making in the criminal justice system, particularly discretionary legal pronouncements by law enforcement officials, have become a significant feature of the criminological literature. For example, Clarence Schrag (1971) lists twenty publications explicitly dealing with police discretion. An examination of the sociological literature on criminal justice reveals an overwhelming concern with the informal practices that are used in place of the strictly legal ones by officials in the criminal justice system.

For sociologists, the notability of discretion is that it consists of legal phenomena that cannot be accounted for in terms of legally established procedures. Simply stated, there is nothing in jurisprudence that allows for or accounts for variations in the application of the law. The law does provide sanctions for nonenforcement by police, district attorneys, judges and other sworn officials (LaFave, 1965). But these sanctions are not regularly employed for the control of routine discretionary acts, so the nonapplication (or even application) of the sanctions only provides another set of cases requiring sociological analysis.

Besides identifying organizational and political elements that effect legal decisions, sociologists have been interested in the role of custom as a source for interpreting behaviors as legal or illegal. For example, the influence of custom on the policeman's decision whether to arrest has been viewed in terms of racial prejudice. Additionally, La Fave (1965) more than anyone else, has shown that custom provides police with an understanding of what is considered proper and improper when deliberating whether to charge a suspect with a crime. The routine practice of ignoring "blue laws" by police, for instance, is accounted for by a change in customs regarding religion.

Although not all discretion-related studies have been done by sociologists, most exhibit a general sociological orientation to the criminal justice system and the decision-making processes within it. That is, most, if not all, investigations implicitly or explicitly search for a normative scheme that can be used to explain the observed patterns of behavior exhibited by the members of various legal agen-

SOURCE: *et al.* 3, no. 3 (1974): 26–40. Reprinted by permission.

cies. In the tradition of Durkheim, patterns of police discretion (rates of arrest and types of arrests per specific population) are taken to be the observable phenomena of study that are produced by members' compliance to normative orders. Patterns of legal decisions that are made by police officers are seen as objective phenomena that are the result of normative systems which are exterior to them, constraining and independent of individual psychologies. James Q. Wilson (1968), for example, showed that a policeman's use of the law varied in terms of departmental policy and community structure. Departments in communities with partisan political structures were observed to have styles of enforcement that produced fewer arrests for almost all types of law violations than did departments characterized by "legalistic" styles found in communities experiencing a "reform" or "good-government" political atmosphere.

In sociology this perspective on police discretion can, for analytical purposes, be catalogued as an instance of what Thomas Wilson labeled the "normative paradigm" (Wilson, 1970). This "paradigm" characterizes much of the past and current work in sociology, and is indicated in the sociologists' reliance on normative orders to account for the production of social structure, i.e., repetitive and typical patterns of concerted action. These normative orders are assumed to instruct the actor on how to act within certain social situations. Not only are systems of rules, norms, values and roles assumed to account for rates of concerted action, they offer a schema of motives that also account for the reasons why members act as they do within particular situations.

A problem arises when the normative paradigm is preserved by the observer even though the subject's behavior does not conform to the formally recognized system of rules, the uncritical reliance on rules as devices of social order is not significantly altered when researchers discover that members in fact do not act in accordance with the rules. Such discoveries are not devastating to the normative paradigm because the theorist usually accounts for such witnessed activities in terms of a set of *informal* rules. He thereby preserves the normative character of the action. For example, Goldstein (1967) claims that because discretionary power is essential, but not adequately prescribed by law, the policeman is left to function according to *informal* standards that are based on the officers' ideas about the gravity of certain situations and the character of suspects. In fact, it is Goldstein's contention that the relative order observed in the majority of police-citizen contacts is due to this informal system of rules. Consequently, violation of them is a serious matter and frequently results, according to Goldstein, in citizens' charges of "harsh treatment."

The Interpretive Paradigm

An alternative model, developed around problems encountered in analyses grounded in the normative paradigm, is labeled by Wilson (1970) as the "interpretive paradigm":

> The conception of interaction as an interpretive process ... differs sharply from the normative paradigm. Turner (1962:23), for instance, directly contrasts the normative role model with the concept of role taking: "The idea of role taking shifts emphasis away from the simple process of enacting a prescribed role to devising a performance on the basis of an imputed other role. The actor is not the occupant of a status for which there is a neat set of rules—a culture or set of norms—but a person who must act in the perspective supplied in part by his relationship to others whose actions reflect roles he must identify" [Wilson, 1970:700].

Central to this view is the concept of "definition of the situation." "Group life is [seen to be] built up out of social interaction, out of constructed meanings in action in which individuals jointly engage" (Psathas, 1973:6). Actors define a situation in one way or another and act in terms of that definition. For example, Reiss (1971) specifically claims that citizens play an active role in legal discretionary decisions made by police officers. The following excerpt is illustrative of a theoretical grounding in the interpretive paradigm:

> We see, then, that it is incumbent upon a police officer to enter upon a variety of social stages, encounter the actors, determine their roles, and figure out the plot. Often, before they can act, the police must uncover the "plot" and identify the roles and behavior of the actors. This is true even in emergency situations where an officer is expected to assess the situation [and] almost immediately make judgments as to what he must do [Reiss, 1971:45].[1]

Now, it is not the claim here that Reiss's work represents an excellent example of interpretive sociology. Rather, the excerpt simply points to what an analyst using the interpretive paradigm would take as problematic. In terms of rules, Reiss's example implicitly indicates that it is not so much that actors follow or violate them; rather that actors together define situations and act in terms of those definitions. Nevertheless, it must be remembered that the interpretive paradigm maintains the concept of the norm: "Acting units,

[1]Implicit in this statement is the recognition that the documentary method of interpretation is a members' method for coming to an understanding of situations (cf. Garfinkel, 1967).

whether individuals or groups, act in relation to defined situations. Included in their definitions are such 'objects' as norms, values, organizations, roles, and expectations" (Psathas, 1973:6).

Having mutually defined a situation, actors are, as in the normative paradigm, expected to act in accordance with the situationally relevant rules, expectations, or codes of conduct. However, the interpretive paradigm goes on to make it essential that a definition of the situation and consequent rule use be seen as a processual event subject to continuous revision by members. Therefore, a definition of a situation is not something that is simply discovered after a certain amount of interpretive work—it is always subject to retrospective redefinition and altered expectations.

Going beyond the Normative and Interpretive Paradigms

Our concern here is for the contextual nature of laws. Through an examination of decision-making situations it will be shown that (a) interpretive work is essential when police officers categorize encountered scenes in accordance with the law and (b) the ideal that legal codes are specific or objective is just that, an ideal. Additionally, we suggest that "informal" rules, as a set of discretionary prescriptions outlined either by a member or by an observer, do not resolve the problematic character of decision-making in law enforcement. Our claim is *not* that informal rules are insignificant. It is that rules of any sort, including laws, do not have stable uses and their plurisituational character is an ongoing accomplishment by actors.

The Ethnomethodological Perspective

In contrast to the normative and interpretive conceptions of what constitutes the proper province of sociological inquiry, the problem for ethnomethodology is the study of *how* members of society manage to sustain the attitude that they are living in an ordered world that is independent of their attending to it. Importantly, the methods that members use to accomplish a sense of order are the phenomena that ethnomethodologists hold as analyzable by way of members' talk. For example, their descriptions of scenes and accounts of their behavior can be used as data, pointing to the methods members use to organize the world:

> The ethnomethodologist is *not* concerned with providing causal explanations of observably regular, patterned, repetitive actions by some kind of analyses of the actors point of view. He is concerned with how members of society go about the task of *seeing, describing,* and *explaining* order in the world in which they live [Zimmerman and Wieder, 1970:289].

Thus, in addition to viewing members' accounts as descriptions of interaction, ethnomethodologists maintain that the major importance of accounts resides in the fact that reportable patterns of behavior (e.g., rates of criminality) exist through them. Because the uses of rules and laws are specific kinds of accounts, they are seen by the ethnomethodologist as requiring use of interpretive procedures that allow those rules to be used by the members as instructions (to themselves and others) for viewing behavior as sanctionable. Importantly, interpretive procedures are not practices that have the same properties as rules. Aaron Cicourel comments:

> Interpretive procedures in everyday life and scientific research, however, are not "rules" in the sense of general policies or practices like operational definitions or legal and extralegal norms, where a sense of "right" and "wrong" pre- or proscriptive norm or practice is at issue. Instead they are constitutive of all inquiry yet exhibit empirically defensible properties that "advise" the member with a sense of social structure (1970:146).

In sum, the interpretive procedures are a set of members' methods that are essential if rules, laws, and policies are to be seen as relevant by participants.

Of particular importance to our research are the ethnomethodological contentions (a) that the plurisituationality of rules is a situated accomplishment, (b) that rules and the behavior that ethnomethodology refers to are reflexively related, each elaborating and "specifying" the other, and (c) that members cannot determine how to interact within a particular setting by consulting a rule that will give them specific criteria indicating what encountered situations definitely fall within the province of that rule.

The Interpretive Work of Crime Identification

During our field research that was conducted in a county sheriff's office, we discovered that in every instance in which the Penal Code was utilized, there was evidence that this use was not achieved by a literal matching of Penal Code sections (via a set of definitive criterial attributes or elements) with encountered situations. On the contrary, the situation encountered by the police officer assigned to investigate a case either was *made* to fit one or more of the Penal Code categories or that situation was not officially reported as a criminal matter at all.

For instance, a vast amount of theoretical work is necessary if a setting is to be identified as one that indicates that a crime took place.

Even when a suspect and his actions are known, the officer is still confronted with the task of making that particular social action fit the provided Penal Code sections. For example, in the Penal Code of California (1972) there is a crime numbered "415" and entitled "Disturbing the Peace." Even though police officers were observed to use the "415" category and rarely expressed its use as being of major difficulty, their application of it involved unnoticed (by officers) interpretive work that articulated particulars of alleged criminal events to elements provided by the law. An indicator of these interpretive processes is roughly provided by cases in which "415" was used to characterize husband-wife disputes, despite the fact that there is nothing in the Penal Code section "415" that mentions husbands or wives.

In effect, as Wieder (1970:134) found in his study of names or titles, we found that circumstances elaborate the "elements" of a crime and the "elements" of the crime elaborate the particular features of the circumstances. In other words, the relevance of a law is specifically determined on the occasions in which the law is used.

Any policeman writing an official report for the law enforcement agency we studied has an opportunity to account for his categorization of a particular behavior as an instance of crime. When an officer documents an offense, arrest or incident, he fills in spaces in the report form which ask him to specify the elements of the crime and to classify the reported event in accordance with the Penal Code. Following this, the report form requests, among other things, the victim's name and address, day and time crime occurred, person who discovered crime, location of property or victim at time of offense, point of entry, method used to gain entrance, weapons used, and possible suspects. Finally, there is a request that the officer "summarize the details relating to the crime." This is a major portion of the form, generally referred to as the "narrative section" to be used for the summary. This narrative section provides a context through which an officer and others may interpret the officers' categorization of the crime. The "narrative section" was seen by officials as a lot of extra work but unavoidable if the categorization of the crime was to be fully accounted for, i.e., seen as reasonable and rational.

Although a reading of some crime reports indicates that the classification of the behavior was clearly a reasonable one, the narrative account provided an alternative context through which the same particulars reported in the structured document could be seen as *not* indicative of an actual crime. Commonly, the elements of a "real" crime could be found in the check list indicating that a particular crime was committed. However, the context provided by the added narrative suggested that the listing of these same elements indicated that *no* crime had actually taken place.

For instance, a report on a series of incidents classified by patrol officers as a "burglary" and an "assault with a deadly weapon" was forwarded as a matter of routine to detective investigators. The report was given a case number that routed it to a file containing numerous reports involving similar incidents taking place in one family over a brief period of time. Detectives assigned to do something with this file said the new report was only one of a series of family complaints asserting that a "madman was harassing them." The report indicated that while the daughter-in-law (who lived at her in-laws' address) was "cleaning up" the bathroom, a man suddenly came from behind and grasped her, placed his hand over her mouth and slipped a rope over her head, then around her neck, and began to choke her. She was reportedly found by her mother-in-law lying in the bathroom with "blue skin color and purple lips."

All this suggested that the report was a genuine account of a crime. But the officer who wrote it attached a narrative account that was successful in providing a context for seeing that the crime was a "phony." He said many other reports of harassment made by this family had led to numerous police "stake-outs" of the house, but no one was ever seen around the home, even at the time when an alleged attack took place. Then the officer analyzed certain of the particulars of the incident, establishing what he took to be "evidence" that a crime could not have taken place as reported, e.g., rope could not be placed around neck while suspect kept hand over her mouth, report that victim had purple lips and blue skin was inconsistent with slight irritation on the neck, and report that suspect ripped the screen door of the house and broke the frame violently was an action which must have been noisy, but victim did not pay attention to it.

These particulars could have been left unstated (as they were in the official crime report) as minor details that are interesting but irrelevant, because alone they do not deny the possibility that an actual crime took place. Certainly, other reports of violent crimes were received by detectives and treated as valid even though certain details seemed "odd" or "unlikely." But in this case, it was the determination that all the reports relating to this family represented a series of crimes that "just don't happen this way." They provided a background through which the specific crimes of "assault with a deadly weapon" and "burglary" could be seen as "not really there."

More generally, a literal reading of the law does not specify what "really constitutes" the elements of a certain crime. As Thomas Wilson (1970:75) has noted, the police officer's classification of "behavior of an actor on a given occasion . . . as an instance of a particular type of [criminal] action is not based on a limited set of specifiable features of the behavior and the occasion but, rather, depends on the indefinite context seen as relevant by the observer, a context that gets its meaning partly through the very action it is being used to interpret." In short, the elements of a crime are "essentially vague" (Garfinkel, 1967) in a manner such that they can be represented in a scene and then again not be represented in the self-same setting.

This vague, contextual nature of a crime's elements was illustrated for us by a case involving a group of juveniles who took a can of spray paint from a vandal and sprayed him with it. A detective said he was going to tell the juveniles that they could be charged with robbery, a serious felony. However, he said that although "technically" he could point out the elements of a robbery—the suspects used force to obtain something that was possessed by the victim— "it really wasn't a robbery" and "he knew it" (Sanders, 1974).

All this suggests that any investigator who says he can, for example, understand the meaning of a "211 P.C." (robbery) only by strict literal reliance upon the elements—(1) person, (2) taking another's possessions, (3) from his person or immediate presence, (4) against his will, (5) by means of force or fear—has eliminated the possibility that he will discover an actual "245 P.C." The policeman's knowledge of the elements of the code is more than can be told in so many words.[2] Because members experience all scenes and objects, including rules, in an indexical fashion, to recognize the significance of any set of instructions, members must engage in interpretative practices "in order to recognize what the instructions are definitely talking about" (Garfinkel, 1967:22). Given this feature of members' perception, statutory codes are necessarily dependent on the various particulars that comprise the context in which they are used.

The interpetive work of "properly employing" Penal Code categories consists primarily of those practices that Garfinkel (1967:20) has labeled "ad hoc considerations," which include the "et cetera" feature of rules and the practices of "let it pass," "unless" and "factum valet." Use of "ad hoc" practices enables officers to claim that they legitimately coded crimes "in accordance with necessary and sufficient criteria" (Garfinkel, 1967:22) prescribed by the crime elements attached to particular Penal Code categories. It is only through "et cetera" that these elements can maintain their status as objective features of Penal Codes. The elements carry an "open structure" (Cicourel, 1970) that "provides for unknown contingencies that may arise such that owing to new practical circumstances" (Garfinkel, 1967:73) the elements of the crime as described by the Penal Code can be reread to find what they really have meant all along (Garfinkel, 1967:73).

---

[2]Michael Polanyi (1958) discusses the importance of unarticulated personal knowledge, claiming that we "know more than we can say."

This "et cetera" nature of Penal Code categories became evident when we asked officers to list what constitutes a "415" ("Disturbing the Peace"). One officer constructed the following listing of particular behaviors that are not specified by the code: (1) loud parties, (2) moocher "panhandler", (3) domestic disturbance, (4) neighbors' argument, (5) street racing, (6) motorcycles racing, and (7) fights.

Apparent reasonableness is itself generated on an ad hoc basis. As a police officer prepares a structured crime report, he anticipates that others will (if necessary) wait for "narrative details" which will enable them to construct the meaning and rationality of his crime classifications, e.g., as a burglary or robbery. Likewise as readers of structured reports, other policemen are willing to let equivocal features "pass," anticipating that further information will be discovered in the account, or will be provided by others in the organization who will make such equivocalities understandable.

Investigating Crimes That Are Significant

Further evidence of the "open-ended" character of rules is offered by detectives' evaluations of crime complaints received from citizens and reported by patrol officers. Only some of these crime cases are "worked" (investigated). The crimes the detectives consider "significant" enough to be investigated were worked. But the significance of a crime was observed to be judged in various ways including: (a) actual or potential physical or "social" harm, (b) victim's loss (was it great, will it be impossible to recover, e.g., a six pack of beer), (c) whether "leads" were available (Sanders and Daudistel, 1974:173).

Obviously, these criteria for deciding whether or not investigation will be instigated have an indexical character, as do all other rules. Such informal policies or unofficial rules for determining what cases will be investigated do not eliminate the need for interpretive work. Proper use of informal rules necessarily involves the same "ad hoc-ing" practices that characterize the use of formal rules. Among the detectives we studied, the informal rule, generally stated, is that all significant cases shall be investigated. But the following two examples illustrate how the sense of adhering to this informal rule was preserved even though detectives did not regularly investigate cases that others in the organization characterized as "significant."

In the first case, detectives received a report identifying what the patrol officer took to be an "attempted murder." Naturally, according to detectives, "attempted murder" is a significant crime. But we noted that a detective was not assigned to work the case. When a detective sergeant was questioned, he replied, simply, that it was not a "good case" of "attempted murder," but rather "some kids screwing around." The official patrol report stated that some hikers (victims) were walking in an open area when someone shot a rifle in their direction. The report claimed that while the victims hid behind a rock the shots continued to be fired, not allowing the victims to move from behind their cover (intent to commit deadly harm). As formulated by the patrol report, these features of the event could be seen to match the elements necessary for the act to constitute an "attempted murder." However, in a context formulated by an experienced detective, the same features were analyzed within the context of "kids screwing around," rather than in a context that would make them representative of the elements of the crime "attempted murder." Such a reformulation of the event was not seen as a deviation from the informal policy of investigating "significant crimes," but in fact, in accordance with it.[3]

The second case also involved a crime reported as "attempted murder." The patrol report stated that a man had threatened to kill his wife and had performed acts which could possibly have been lethal. When a detective read the report he characterized it as nothing but a "glorified domestic" (a family argument usually categorized as a "415," Sanders and Daudistel, 1974:169). Again the characterization of the event as something other than what it was reported to be was based on a reformulation of the reported features supplied in the document.

Strictly speaking, there is no way of determining "what really happened" in a crime scene by literally consulting a set of descriptive features that are purported to describe it. Both cases illustrate the important point that an event's character is not a thing that exists independently of the account of it. Cases formulated by patrol officers as requiring investigative work were formulated to be something else by the detectives. *For the members* (detectives) the sense of following the rules was preserved. The accounts of what happened were indexical, meaning that the specific sense of what transpired was embedded in the context provided for the interpretation of the legal criteria as well as the features of the behavior. Neither the patrolman's interpretations nor the detectives' interpretations were necessarily different from what actually took place.

[3]Zimmerman's (1970) study of receptionists' assignment of intake interviews in a social work agency shows that much the same type of behavior was observed. Zimmerman (1970:233) comments: " . . . it would seem that the notion of action-in-accord-with-a-rule is not a matter of compliance or noncompliance per se, but of the various ways in which persons satisfy themselves and others concerning what is or is not 'reasonable' compliance in particular situations. Reference to rules might then be seen as a common sense method of accounting for, or making available for talk, the orderly features of everyday activities, thereby *making out* these activities as orderly in some fashion."

The accomplishment of a sense of what happened can be seen as an instance of the use of the "documentary method of interpretation," (Garfinkel, 1967). Each particular in an account of an event is sensible in terms of some unstated underlying pattern, while at the same time the underlying pattern is elaborated by the particular. This is to say, the indexical particular and underlying pattern are mutually elaborating. The particular points to, or is a document of, the underlying pattern; the underlying pattern is an interpretive scheme which gives a specific sense to the particular. Thus, by accounting for a reported attempted murder as a "glorified domestic," the detective suggested an underlying pattern where no one "really" intended homicide, thus transforming the sense of the reported particulars to something other than the original report of attempted murder. In this way crimes are formulated to be of one sort or another, and depending on the formulation of the case as one type or another, the subsequent events in the case can be understood. Any account specifying a legal action is not a literal reading of the law or the act. Rather it is an ongoing accomplishment by members who, through their accounting practices, make their accounts what they come to be treated as being.

Conclusion and Implications

We have shown that decision-making processes in law enforcement are not fully described by the sociologist who identifies a formal or informal normative system as an explanation of the patterns of criminal arrest. This is not to say that such identifications are useless. Our point is that other phenomena are relevant, too.

Our study suggests that analyses of discretion in the criminal justice system should be at least partly based on investigation into the methods that criminal justice personnel use to accomplish reasonable and rational use of the law. Such study necessarily involves examination of how members identify and label encountered scenes, and how they label accounts of scenes reported by others.

Describing our study as one dealing with discretion is not done without difficulty. Typically, the use of the term "discretion" in the application of the law denotes a process in which criminal justice officials purposely discriminate between those individuals who should be officially processed in various ways, and those who should not. Under our theoretical orientation this behavior remains of interest. However, our analysis is expanded to include interpretive practices that are not used by officials as a "matter of choice." The assumption that coding of various events is done via explicit and "objective" sets of laws and rules that prescribe the necessary and sufficient criteria for proper coding is a glossing over of the interpretive practices that are essential to the accomplishment of the coding. Not only are interpretive practices essential, but the very assumption that one's coding has been done "according to the rules" is dependent on "ad hoc" considerations.

References

Cicourel, Aaron. 1970. The Acquisition of Social Structure: Toward a Developmental Sociology of Language and Meaning. In *Understanding Everyday Life*, ed. J. Douglas. Chicago: Aldine.

Daudistel, Howard C. 1971. Cop Talk: An Investigation of the Police Radio Code. Master's thesis, Department of Sociology, University of California, Santa Barbara.

Garfinkel, Harold. 1967. *Studies in Ethnomethodology*. Englewood Cliffs, N.J.: Prentice-Hall.

Garfinkel, Harold, and Harvey Sacks. 1970. On Formal Structures of Practical Actions. In *Theoretical Sociology: Perspectives and Development*, ed. J. C. McKinney and E. A. Tiryakian. New York: Appleton-Century-Crofts.

Goldstein, Herman. 1967. Administrative Problems in Controlling the Exercise of Police Authority. *Journal of Criminal Law, Criminology, and Police Science* 53, no. 2.

LaFave, Wayne R. 1965. *Arrest: The Decision to Take a Suspect into Custody.* Boston: Little, Brown.

Polanyi, Michael. 1958. *Personal Knowledge: Toward a Post-Critical Philosophy.* New York: Harper, Torchbooks.

Psathas, George, ed. 1973. *Phenomenological Sociology: Issues and Applications.* New York: Wiley.

Reiss, Albert. 1971. *The Police and the Public.* New Haven: Yale University Press.

Sanders, William B. 1974. Detective Story: A Study of Criminal Investigations. Ph.D. dissertation, University of California, Santa Barbara.

Sanders, William B., and Howard C. Daudistel. 1974. Detective Work: Patterns of Criminal Investigations. In *The Sociologist as Detective: An Introduction to Research Methods,* ed. William B. Sanders. New York: Praeger.

Schrag, Clarence. 1971. *Crime and Justice: American Style.* Rockville, Md.: National Institute of Mental Health, Center for Studies of Crime and Delinquency.

Wilson, James Q. 1968. *Varieties of Police Behavior.* Cambridge: Harvard University Press.

Wilson, Thomas. 1970. Concepts of Interaction and Forms of Sociological Explanation. *American Sociological Review* 35:697–710.

Wieder, D. Lawrence. 1970. On Meaning by Rule. In *Understanding Everyday Life,* ed. J. Douglas. Chicago: Aldine.

Younger, Evelle, ed. 1972. *Penal Code of California: Peace Officers Abridged Edition.* Sacramento, Calif.: Department of General Services, Documents Section.

Zimmerman, Don H. 1970. The Practicalities of Rule Use. In *Understanding Everyday Life,* ed. J. Douglas. Chicago: Aldine.

Zimmerman, Don H., and D. Lawrence Wieder. 1970. Ethnomethodology and the Problem of Order: Comment on Denzin. In *Understanding Everyday Life,* ed. J. Douglas. Chicago: Aldine.

3
Negotiating Prosecution and Defense

In part 2 we learned that many decisions must be made before an offender is moved to the next stage in the criminal justice system. A citizen must report the crime to the police, the police must respond or initiate action themselves when they see criminal conduct, they must interpret the situation as one that requires arrest rather than some informal disposition, and detectives must document the actual occurrence of a crime in order to convince others in the system that a crime has in fact been committed. Because there are so many critical stages through which a case must pass, not everyone who has actually committed a crime is processed by the criminal justice system. It has been shown, for example, that even the initial input by citizens probably represents only a small percentage of the criminal acts that have been committed against them. Phillip Ennis (1967) found that the respondents in his crime survey called the police only 50 percent of the times when they felt a crime had been committed. Even when citizens do report crimes, only a small number of their complaints lead to arrest, and an even smaller number are ultimately resolved by the criminal courts. For example, *The Uniform Crime Reports of the United States* indicates that a total of 2,368,400 burglaries were reported (or discovered) by the police in 1971. In only 450,000 of those reported burglaries was someone arrested for the crime, and only 9.5 percent of these cases went to trial and ended in conviction (Newman, 1975:11–12).

The five articles in this part deal specifically with the social organization of prosecution and defense in the criminal justice system. Like the other authors represented in this book, the authors here are interested in understanding how decisions about criminal cases are made and whether such decisions reflect the intent of the criminal law or some informal normative system that has developed within the legal bureaucracy.

David Sudnow explores the charge-reduction process and shows how decisions are made by public defenders. As we have noted, at least 80 percent of the arrests made by the police are not resolved by criminal trials, but by a plea of guilty to a lesser charge, agreed upon by the prosecutor and defense attorney. By persuading their clients to plead guilty to a less serious charge, attorneys are able to spend relatively little time on their cases. Obviously, a quickly formulated agreement between defense and prosecution is easier than a trial before a judge or jury or both. Knowing that most cases are resolved in this manner, Sudnow attempted to determine the guidelines used by the defense attorneys. An examination of the penal code did not reveal these guidelines, but a study of the interaction between the public defender and the accused did suggest certain informal rules. Sudnow determined that the fundamental step in the defense attorney's decision-making process is the formulation of an act as a "normal" crime.

On the basis of commonly held but vaguely specified conceptions of what typical crimes are like, the public defender and the prosecutor are able to make sense of the unique criminal acts they must deal with. Once this is done, a routine charge reduction will be offered to those who have committed a "normal crime." For example, if the public defender can establish that a particular case is a "burglary just like any other," a typical reduction would be "petty theft." This reduction of charges is interesting because it is neither situationally nor necessarily included in burglary. But, according to Sudnow, petty theft is used because it "constitutes a reasonable lesser alternative to burglary as the sentence for petty theft will range between six months and one year in the county jail and burglary regularly does not carry higher than two years in the state prison." Once a particular crime is categorized as a typical one, the appropriate reduction seems obvious to the attorneys. This typification process enables the attorneys to agree quickly on the charge that should be brought, even though this charge may not be related statutorially to the actual crime that was committed. Agreement is further facilitated by the close occupational ties between the public defender and the prosecutor. Not only do they work together on a day-to-day basis, but they share a concern about caseloads and the quick processing of defendants as well.

Although the problem he discusses has received much consideration by social scientists and legal scholars, Sudnow's analysis is unique in showing that the informal rules regulating plea bargaining are enforced only after the accused's actions are interpreted as a "normal" crime. From Sudnow's work we can see that the informal policies that establish charge reductions are much less important than the interpretive work done by attorneys when they analyze crimes. If they see a crime as a typical one, it will be treated as such, and usually a deal will be made. If a crime is viewed as bizarre and extremely different from others, a routine recipe for charge reduction will not seem appropriate.

Abraham Blumberg examined the criminal court and found that various new roles, rules, and goals have developed in its highly bureaucratized state. The informal norms that regulate the conduct of judges, attorneys, and administrative personnel are distinctly different from the formal prescriptions of the law. According to Blumberg, the behavior of courtroom personnel is oriented to the goal of rapid and efficient processing of cases rather than observance of the due-process requirements established to protect the interests of defendants. In fact, the informal concern with getting clients out of the courts has become so important that it takes precedence over the question of their guilt or innocence.

Blumberg dramatically illustrates the consequences of the bureaucratization of justice by focusing on the contrast between the actual behavior of the defense attorney and the role he is supposed to play. The ideal defense attorney represents his client's interests and acts as an advocate in his defense. But, Blumberg shows, the defense attorney is in fact much more concerned about his own interests. Furthermore, even if an attorney wishes to act as an advocate, his function in the court cannot be characterized as an advocate role. Prosecutors and defense attorneys are allies to a much greater extent than they are adversaries in the battle for justice.

Interestingly, Blumberg differs from Sudnow in that he does not portray the private defense attorney as an outsider to the criminal-court bureaucracy. The private attorney may be less concerned about caseloads than the public defender, but he is equally interested in processing cases quickly. This interest in "efficiency" bonds the interests of the private attorney to those of the judge, prosecutor, and public defender. In effect, the private attorney is concerned with avoiding trial, as is the public defender and prosecutor, but he has the unique concern of obtaining payment of his fees. Blumberg shows that these two interests of the private attorney are often satisfied with the aid of others in the court.

Martin Mayer's article gives us an inside look at the operation of the office of New York County's District Attorney. The late Frank Hogan ran his office in a highly efficient manner. Even though he rarely saw many of his underlings, his policies were enforced by his bureau chiefs, and he was kept informed by his daily examination of incoming mail. Those who worked on his staff were selected according to their competency and were systematically socialized into the bureaucracy he had created.

Hogan's office was clearly engaged in the administration of justice. As Mayer indicates: "As far as serious crimes are concerned, Hogan's office determines whether accused people are guilty or not." Effective screening of cases meant that little time was wasted and few cases ended in defeat. In fact, Hogan's office was so effective that it often gave defense attorneys full disclosure of the evidence held against a client without forcing the attorneys to go through time-consuming legal proceedings to get it. Indeed, with confidence and courtesy, Frank Hogan ran a kind of ministry of justice.

Jonathan Casper's article gives us the opportunity to see how defendants feel about defense attorneys and "bargain justice." Casper interviewing defendants found they had received the services of a public defender, and each had pleaded guilty to criminal charges rather than going to trial.

The first defendant felt that he had been "double-crossed" by the public defender. He claimed that he was innocent and that he had been pressured to plead guilty by an attorney who, he felt, was not really interested in his case. Furthermore he was upset because his plea resulted in a prison sentence that was much longer than he expected. For this man the informal system of justice was not a bargain.

The next defendant was pleased with the outcome of his case. Although he too expressed a distrust of the attorneys, he did not feel that he had received a harsh sentence. In fact, he believed that by "dragging out" the case he had "made out like a bandit." This defendant recognized that plea bargains are used by the courts to expedite the processing of cases. Because the court personnel are ruled by bureaucratic concerns rather than strictly legal procedures, a defendant who stalls and takes too much time can force them to give him a drastically reduced sentence in exchange for a guilty plea, which gets the defendant out of the court calendar.

Both cases show that the most crucial decision-making in the criminal justice system does not follow the formal requirements of the law. They also show how the case overload in the courts can be to the defendant's advantage or disadvantage. In one case, attorneys pressured the defendant to "cop a plea" even though he felt he was innocent. This got him out of the system, but it left him with a deal that he did not feel was fair. In the other case, the defendant turned the tables on the court officers: He pressured them into reducing his sentence and giving him a deal he felt was more than satisfactory.

Richard Mendes and John Wold take us into the courtroom and show us how the cases brought to it daily are handled by the attorneys. Like the other authors in this part, Mendes and Wold have discovered that an informal concern for the rapid processing of cases motivates the court officers to offer the accused a reduced charge in exchange for a guilty plea. Their article is unique because it emphasizes the routine character of charge reduction. They do not utilize the concept of "normal crimes," but it appears that as long as there is nothing unusual about a defendant's criminal record or the crime he committed, a "normal reduction" will result. Such reductions have become so standardized that an experienced observer of the court can predict accurately the type of deal that will be offered to particular types of defendants. For example, someone charged with being under the influence of narcotics who has not been arrested for that crime within the past year will be allowed to plead guilty to the less serious crime of violating Section 4143 of the California Business and Professions Code, which deals with possession of a hypodermic needle and syringe. He may pay a fifty-dollar fine or serve five days in jail and agree to be placed on unsupervised probation.

In the court Mendes and Wold studied, the informal normative system had become so explicit that for all practical purposes it *was* the formal rule system. If all those who have been charged with the same crime and have no previous criminal record are treated in the same fashion, the routine outcome of cases is not so individualized as many social scientists have assumed. The Mendes and Wold findings once again indicate that the adversary nature of the court is only an ideal not achieved in practice. Even when cases are resolved by plea bargaining, there is no adversary quality to the negotiations. In effect, the court operates under a set of rules that has developed informally but has nevertheless standardized the adjudication of most types of cases.

References

Ennis, Phillip. 1967. Crimes, Victims, and the Police. *Transaction.*
Newman, Donald J. 1975. *Introduction to Criminal Justice.* Philadelphia: J. B. Lippincott.

Normal Crimes
Sociological Features of the Penal Code in a Public Defender Office
David Sudnow

Two stances toward the utility of official classificatory schema for criminological research have been debated for years. One position, which might be termed that of the "revisionist" school, has it that the categories of the criminal law, e.g., "burglary," "petty theft," "homicide," etc., are not "homogeneous in respect to causation."[1] From an inspection of penal code descriptions of crimes, it is argued that the way persons seem to be assembled under the auspices of criminal law procedure is such as to produce classes of criminals who are, at least on theoretical grounds, as dissimilar in their social backgrounds and styles of activity as they are similar. The entries in the penal code, this school argues, require revision if sociological use is to be made of categories of crime and a classificatory scheme of etiological relevance is to be developed. Common attempts at such revision have included notions such as *"white collar* crime," and *"systematic* check forger," these conceptions constituting attempts to institute sociologically meaningful specifications which the operations of criminal law procedure and statutory legislation "fail" to achieve.

The other major perspective toward the sociologist's use of official categories and the criminal statistics compiled under their heading derives less from a concern with etiologically useful schema than from an interest in understanding the actual operations of the administrative legal system. Here, the categories of the criminal law

SOURCE: *Social Problems* 12 (Winter 1965): 255–76. Reprinted by permission of the author and the Society for the Study of Social Problems.

NOTE: This investigation is based on field observations of a Public Defender Office in a metropolitan California community. The research was conducted while the author was associated with the Center for the Study of Law and Society, University of California, Berkeley. I am grateful to the Center for financial support. Erving Goffman, Sheldon Messinger, Harvey Sacks, and Emanuel Schegloff contributed valuable suggestions and criticisms to an earlier draft.

[1]D. R. Cressey, "Criminological Research and the Definition of Crimes," *American Journal of Sociology,* 61, no. 6 (1951): 548. See also, J. Hall, *Theft, Law and Society,* second edition, Indianapolis: Bobbs-Merrill, 1952; and E. Sutherland, *Principles of Criminology,* revised, New York: Lippincott, 1947, p. 218. An extensive review of "typological developments" is available in D. C. Gibbons and D. L. Garrity, "Some Suggestions for the Development of Etiological and Treatment Theory in Criminology," *Social Forces,* 38, no. 1 (1959).

are not regarded as useful or not, as objects to be either adopted, adapted, or ignored; rather, they are seen as constituting the basic conceptual equipment with which such people as judges, lawyers, policemen, and probation workers organize their everyday activities. The study of the actual use of official classification systems by actually employed administrative personnel regards the penal code as data, to be preserved intact; its use, both in organizing the work of legal representation, accusation, adjudication, and prognostication, and in compiling tallies of legal occurrences, is to be examined as one would examine any social activity. By sociologically regarding, rather than criticizing, rates of statistics and the categories employed to assemble them, one learns, it is promised, about the "rate producing agencies" and the assembling process.[2]

While the former perspective, the "revisionist" position, has yielded several fruitful products, the latter stance (commonly identified with what is rather loosely known as the "labeling" perspective), has been on the whole more promissory than productive, more programmatic than empirical. The present report will examine the operations of a Public Defender system in an effort to assess the warrant for the continued theoretical and empirical development of the position argued by Kitsuse and Cicourel. It will address the question: what of import for the sociological analysis of legal administration can be learned by describing the actual way the penal code is employed in the daily activities of legal representation? First, I shall consider the "guilty plea" as a way of handling criminal cases, focusing on some features of the penal code as a description of a population of defendants. Then I shall describe the Public Defender operation with special attention to the way defendants are represented. The place of the guilty plea and penal code in this representation will be examined. Lastly, I shall briefly analyze the fashion in which the Public Defender (P.D.) prepares and conducts a "defense." The latter section will attempt to indicate the connection between certain prominent organizational features of the Public Defender system and the penal code's place in the routine operation of that system.

Guilty Pleas, Inclusion, and Normal Crimes

It is a commonly noted fact about the criminal court system generally that the greatest proportion of cases are "settled" by a guilty

[2]The most thorough statement of this position, borrowing from the writings of Harold Garfinkel, can be found in the recent critical article by J. I. Kitsuse and A. V. Cicourel, "A Note on the Official Use of Statistics," *Social Problems* 11, no. 2 (Fall 1963): 131–39.

plea.[3] In the county from which the following material is drawn, over 80 percent of all cases "never go to trial." To describe the method of obtaining a guilty plea disposition, essential for the discussion to follow, I must distinguish between what shall be termed "necessarily-included-lesser-offenses" and "situationally-included-lesser-offenses." Of two offenses designated in the penal code, the lesser is considered to be that for which the length of required incarceration is the shorter period of time. *Inclusion* refers to the relation between two or more offenses. The "necessarily-included-lesser-offense" is a strictly legal notion:

> Whether a lesser offense is included in the crime charged is a question of law to be determined solely from the definition and corpus delicti of the offense charged and of the lesser offense. ... If all the elements of the corpus delicti of a lesser crime can be found in a list of all the elements of the offense charged, then only is the lesser included in the greater.[4]

Stated alternatively: "The test in this state of necessarily included offenses is simply that where an offense cannot be committed without necessarily committing another offense, the latter is a necessarily included offense."[5]

The implied negative is put: could Smith have committed A and not B? If the answer is yes, then B is not necessarily included in A. If the answer is no, B is necessarily included. While in a given case a battery might be committed in the course of a robbery, battery is not necessarily included in robbery. Petty theft is necessarily included in robbery but not in burglary. Burglary primarily involves the "intent" to acquire another's goods illegally (e.g., by breaking and entering); the consummation of the act need not occur for burglary to be committed. Theft, like robbery, requires that some item be stolen.

I shall call *lesser* offenses that are not necessarily but "only" *actually* included, "situationally-included-lesser-offenses." By statutory definition, necessarily included offenses are "actually" included. By actual here, I refer to the "way it occurs as a course of action." In the instance of necessary inclusion, the "way it occurs" is irrelevant. With situational inclusion, the "way it occurs" is definitive. In the

---

[3]See D. J. Newman, "Pleading Guilty for Considerations," *J. Crim. L. C. and P. S.* 46. Also, M. Schwartz, *Cases and Materials on Professional Responsibility and the Administration of Criminal Justice,* San Francisco: Matthew Bender and Co., 1961, esp. pp. 79–105.

[4]C. W. Fricke, *California Criminal Law,* Los Angeles: The Legal Book Store, 1961, p. 41.

[5]*People* v. *Creer,* 30 Cal. 2d, 589.

former case, no particular course of action is referred to. In the latter, the scene and progress of the criminal activity would be analyzed.

The issue of necessary inclusion has special relevance for two procedural matters:

A. A man cannot be charged and/or convicted of two or more crimes any one of which is necessarily included in the others, unless the several crimes occur on separate occasions.

(If a murder occurs, the defendant cannot be charged and/or convicted of both "homicide" and "intent to commit a murder," the latter of which is necessarily included in first degree murder. If, however, a defendant "intends to commit a homicide" against one person and commits a "homicide" against another, both offenses may be properly charged. While it is an extremely complex question as to the scope and definition of "in the course of," in most instances the rule is easily applied.)

B. The judge cannot instruct the jury to consider as alternative crimes of which to find a defendant guilty, crimes that are not necessarily included in the charged crime or crimes.

If a man is charged with "statutory rape" the judge may instruct the jury to consider as a possible alternative conviction "contributing to the delinquency of a minor," as this offense is necessarily included in "statutory rape." He cannot however suggest that the alternative "intent to commit murder" be considered and the jury cannot find the defendant guilty of this latter crime, unless it is charged as a distinct offense in the complaint.

It is crucial to note that these restrictions apply only to (a) the relation between several charged offenses in a formal allegation, and (b) the alternatives allowable in a jury instruction. At any time before a case "goes to trial," alterations in the charging complaint may be made by the district attorney. The issue of necessary inclusion has no required bearing on (a) what offense(s) will be charged initially by the prosecutor, (b) what the relation is between the charge initially made and "what happened," or (c) what modifications may be made after the initial charge and the relation between initially charged offenses and those charged in modified complaints. It is this latter operation, the modification of the complaint, that is central to the guilty plea disposition.

Complaint alterations are made when a defendant agrees to plead guilty to an offense and thereby avoid a trial. The alteration occurs in the context of a "deal" consisting of an offer from the district attorney to alter the original charge in such a fashion that a lighter sentence will be incurred with a guilty plea than would be the case if the defendant were sentenced on the original charge. In return for this manipulation, the defendant agrees to plead guilty. The arrangement is proposed in the following format: "if you plead guilty to this new lesser offense, you will get less time in prison than if you plead not guilty to the original, greater charge and lose the trial." The decision must then be made whether or not the chances of obtaining complete acquittal at trial are great enough to warrant the risk of a loss and higher sentence if found guilty on the original charge. As we shall see below, it is a major job of the Public Defender, who mediates between the district attorney and the defendant, to convince his "client" that the chances of acquittal are too slight to warrant this risk.

If a man is charged with "drunkenness" and the Public Defender and Public Prosecutor (hereafter P.D. and D.A.) prefer not to have a trial, they seek to have the defendant agree to plead guilty. While it is occasionally possible, particularly with first offenders, for the P.D. to convince the defendant to plead guilty to the originally charged offense, most often it is felt that some "exchange" or "consideration" should be offered, i.e., a lesser offense charged.

To what offense can "drunkenness" be reduced? There is no statutorily designated crime that is necessarily included in the crime of "drunkenness." That is, if any of the statutorily required components of drunk behavior (its corpus delicti) are absent, there remains no offense of which the resultant description is a definition. For drunkenness there is, however, an offense that while not necessarily included is "typically-situationally-included," i.e., "typically" occurs as a feature of the way drunk persons are seen to behave—"disturbing the peace." The range of possible sentences is such that, of the two offenses, "disturbing the peace" cannot call for as long a prison sentence as "drunkenness." If, in the course of going on a binge, a person does so in such a fashion that "disturbing the peace" may be employed to describe some of his behavior, it would be considered an alternative offense to offer in return for a guilty plea. A central question for the following analysis will be: in what fashion would he have to behave so that disturbing the peace would be considered a suitable reduction?

If a man is charged with "molesting a minor," there are not any necessarily included lesser offenses with which to charge him. Yet an alternative charge—"loitering around a schoolyard"—is often used as a reduction. As above, and central to our analysis the question is: what would the defendant's behavior be such that "loitering around a schoolyard" would constitute an appropriate alternative?

If a person is charged with "burglary," "petty theft" is not necessarily included. Routinely, however, "petty theft" is employed for reducing the charge of burglary. Again, we shall ask: what is the relation between burglary and petty theft and the *manner in which the former occurs* that warrants this reduction?

Offenses are regularly reduced to other offenses the latter of which are not necessarily or situationally included in the former. As I have already said the determination of whether or not offense X was situationally included in Y involves an analysis of the course of action that constitutes the criminal behavior. I must now turn to examine this mode of behavioral analysis.

When encountering a defendant who is charged with "assault with a deadly weapon," the P.D. asks: "What can this offense be reduced to so as to arrange for a guilty plea?" As the reduction is only to be proposed by the P.D. and accepted or not by the D.A., his question becomes "What reduction will be allowable?" (As shall be seen below, the P.D. and D.A. have institutionalized a common orientation to allowable reductions.) The method of reduction involves, as a general feature, the fact that the particular case in question is scrutinized to decide its membership in a class of similar cases. But *the penal code does not provide the reference for deciding the correspondence between the instant event and the general case; that is, it does not define the classes of offense types.* To decide, for purposes of finding a suitable reduction, if the instant case involves a "burglary," reference is not made to the statutory definition of "burglary." To decide what the situationally included offenses are in the instant case, the instant case is not analyzed as a *statutorily* referable course of action; rather, reference is made to a *nonstatutorily* conceived class, burglary, and offenses that are typically situationally included in it, taken as a class of behavioral events. Stated again: in searching an instant case to decide what to *reduce it to,* there is no analysis of the statutorily referable elements of the instant case; instead, its membership in a class of events, the features of which cannot be described by the penal code, must be decided. An example will be useful. If a defendant is charged with burglary and the P.D. is concerned to propose a reduction to a lesser offense, he might search the elements of the burglary at hand to decide what other offenses were committed. The other offenses he might "discover" would be of two sorts: those necessarily and those situationally included. In attempting to decide those other offenses situationally included in the instant event, the instant event might be analyzed as a statutorily referable course of action. Or, as is the case with the P.D., the instant case might be analyzed to decide if it is a "burglary" in common with other "burglaries" conceived of in terms other than those provided by the statute.

Burglaries are routinely reduced to petty theft. If we were to analyze the way burglaries typically occur, petty theft is neither situationally nor necessarily included; when a burglary is committed, money or other goods are seldom illegally removed from some person's body. If we therefore analyzed burglaries, employing the penal code as our reference, and then searched the P.D.'s records to see how burglaries are reduced in the guilty plea, we could not establish a rule that would describe the transformation between the burglary cases statutorily described and the reductions routinely made (i.e., to "petty theft"). The rule must be sought elsewhere, in the character of the nonstatutorily defined class of "burglaries," which I shall term *normal burglaries*.

Normal Crimes

In the course of routinely encountering persons charged with "petty theft," "burglary," "assault with a deadly weapon," "rape," "possession of marijuana," etc., the Public Defender gains knowledge of the typical manner in which offenses of given classes are committed, the social characteristics of the persons who regularly commit them, the features of the settings in which they occur, the types of victims often involved, and the like. He learns to speak knowledgeably of "burglars," "petty thieves," "drunks," "rapists," "narcos," etc., and to attribute to them personal biographies, modes of usual criminal activity, criminal histories, psychological characteristics, and social backgrounds. The following characterizations are illustrative:

> Most ADWs (assault with deadly weapon) start with fights over some girl.
> These sex fiends (child molestation cases) usually hang around parks or schoolyards. But we often get fathers charged with these crimes. Usually the old man is out of work and stays at home when the wife goes to work and he plays around with his little daughter or something. A lot of these cases start when there is some marital trouble and the woman gets mad.
> I don't know why most of them don't rob the big stores. They usually break into some cheap department store and steal some crummy item like a $9.95 record player you know.
> Kids who start taking this stuff (narcotics) usually start out when some buddy gives them a cigarette and they smoke it for kicks. For some reason they always get caught in their cars, for speeding or something.

They can anticipate that point when persons are likely to get into trouble:

> Dope addicts do O.K. until they lose a job or something and get back on the streets and, you know, meet the old boys. Someone tells them where to get some and there they are.

In the springtime, that's when we get all these sex crimes. You know, these kids play out in the schoolyard all day and these old men sit around and watch them jumping up and down. They get their ideas.

The P.D. learns that some kinds of offenders are likely to repeat the same offense while others are not repeat violators or, if they do commit crimes frequently, the crimes vary from occasion to occasion:

You almost never see a check man get caught for anything but checks—only an occasional drunk charge.

Burglars are usually multiple offenders, most times just burglaries or petty thefts.

Petty thefts get started for almost anything—joy riding, drinking, all kinds of little things.

These narcos are usually through after the second violation or so. After the first time some stop, but when they start on the heavy stuff, they've had it.

I shall call *normal crimes* those occurrences whose typical features, e.g., the ways they usually occur and the characteristics of persons who commit them (as well as the typical victims and typical scenes), are known and attended to by the P.D. For any of a series of offense types the P.D. can provide some form of proverbial characterization. For example, *burglary* is seen as involving regular violators, no weapons, low-priced items, little property damage, lower-class establishments, largely Negro defendants, independent operators, and a nonprofessional orientation to the crime. *Child molesting* is seen as typically entailing middle-aged strangers or lower-class middle-aged fathers (few women), no actual physical penetration or severe tissue damage, mild fondling, petting, and stimulation, bad marriage circumstances, multiple offenders with the same offense repeatedly committed, a child complainant, via the mother, etc. *Narcotics* defendants are usually Negroes, not syndicated, persons who start by using small stuff, hostile with police officers, caught by some form of entrapment technique, etc. *Petty thefts* are about 50–50 Negro-white, unplanned offenses, generally committed on lower-class persons and don't get much money, don't often employ weapons, don't make living from thievery, usually younger defendants with long juvenile assaultive records, etc. *Drunkenness* offenders are lower-class white and Negro, get drunk on wine and beer, have long histories of repeated drunkenness, don't hold down jobs, are usually arrested on the streets, seldom violate other penal code sections, etc.

Some general features of the normal crime as a way of attending to a category of persons and events may be mentioned:

1. The focus, in these characterizations, is not on particular individuals, but offense types. If asked "What are burglars like?" or "How are burglaries committed?" the P.D. does not feel obliged to refer to particular burglars and burglaries as the material for his answer.

2. The features attributed to offenders and offenses are often not of import for the statutory conception. In burglary, it is "irrelevant" for the statutory determination whether or not much damage was done to the premises (except where, for example, explosives were employed and a new statute could be invoked). Whether a defendant breaks a window or not, destroys property within the house or not, etc., does not affect his statutory classification as a burglar. While for robbery the presence or absence of a weapon sets the degree, whether the weapon is a machine gun or pocket knife is "immaterial." Whether the residence or business establishment in a burglary is located in a higher income area of the city is of no issue for the code requirements. And, generally, the defendant's race, class position, criminal history (in most offenses), personal attributes, and particular style of committing offenses are features specifically not definitive of crimes under the auspices of the penal code. For deciding "Is this a 'burglary' case I have before me," however, the P.D.'s reference to this range of nonstatutorily referable personal and social attributes, modes of operation, etc., is crucial for the arrangement of a guilty plea bargain.

3. The features attributed to offenders and offenses are, in their content, specific to the community in which the P.D. works. In other communities and historical periods the lists would presumably differ. Narcotics violators in certain areas, for example, are syndicated in dope rackets or engage in systematic robbery as professional criminals, features which are not commonly encountered (or, at least, evidence for which is not systematically sought) in this community. Burglary in some cities will more often occur at large industrial plants, banking establishments, warehouses, etc. The P.D. refers to the population of defendants in the county as "our defendants" and qualifies his prototypical portrayals and knowledge of the typically operative social structures, "for our county." An older P.D., remembering the "old days," commented: "We used to have a lot more rapes than we do now, and they used to be much more violent. Things are duller now in. . . ."

4. Offenses whose normal features are readily attended to are those which are routinely encountered in the courtroom. This feature is related to the last point. For embezzlement, bank robbery, gambling, prostitution, murder, arson, and some other uncommon offenses, the P.D. cannot readily supply anecdotal and proverbial characterizations. While there is some change in the frequencies of

offense-type convictions over time, certain offenses are continually more common and others remain stably infrequent. The troubles created for the P.D. when offenses whose features are not readily known occur, and whose typicality is not easily constructed, will be discussed in some detail below.

5. Offenses are ecologically specified and attended to as normal or not according to the locales within which they are committed. The P.D. learns that burglaries usually occur in such and such areas of the city, petty thefts around this or that park, ADWs in these bars. Ecological patterns are seen as related to socioeconomic variables and these in turn to typical modes of criminal and noncriminal activities. Knowing where an offense took place is thus, for the P.D., knowledge of the likely persons involved, the kind of scene in which the offense occurred, and the pattern of activity characteristic of such a place:

> Almost all of our ADWs are in the same half a dozen bars. These places are Negro bars where laborers come after hanging around the union halls trying to get some work. Nobody has any money and they drink too much. Tempers are high and almost anything can start happening.

6. One further important feature can be noted at this point. Its elaboration will be the task of a later section. As shall be seen, the P.D. office consists of a staff of twelve full-time attorneys. Knowledge of the properties of offense types of offenders, i.e., their normal, typical, or familiar attributes, constitutes the mark of any given attorney's competence. A major task in socializing the new P.D. deputy attorney consists in teaching him to recognize these attributes and to come to do so naturally. The achievement of competence as a P.D. is signaled by the gradual acquisition of professional command not simply of local penal code peculiarities and courtroom folklore, but, as importantly, of relevant features of the social structure and criminological wisdom. His grasp of that knowledge over the course of time is a key indication of his expertise. Below, in our brief account of some relevant organizational properties of the P.D. system, we shall have occasion to reemphasize the competence-attesting aspects of the attorney's proper use of established sociological knowledge. Let us return to the mechanics of the guilty plea procedure as an example of the operation of the notion of normal crimes.

Over the course of their interaction and repeated "bargaining" discussions, the P.D. and D.A. have developed a set of unstated recipes for reducing original charges to lesser offenses. These recipes are specifically appropriate for use in instances of normal crimes and in such instances alone. "Typical" burglaries are reduced to petty theft, "typical" ADWs to simple assault, "typical" child molestation to loitering around a schoolyard, etc. The character of these recipes deserves attention.

The specific content of any reduction, i.e., what particular offense class X offenses will be reduced to, is such that the reduced offense may bear no obvious relation (neither situationally nor necessarily included) to the originally charged offense. The reduction of burglary to petty theft is an example. The important relation between the reduced offense and the original charge is such that the reduction from one to the other is considered "reasonable." At this point we shall only state what seems to be the general principle involved in deciding this reasonableness. The underlying premises cannot be explored at the present time, as that would involve a political analysis beyond the scope of the present report.

Both P.D. and D.A. are concerned to obtain a guilty plea wherever possible and thereby avoid a trial. At the same time, each party is concerned that the defendant "receive his due." The reduction of offense X to Y must be of such a character that the new sentence will depart from the anticipated sentence for the original charge to such a degree that the defendant is likely to plead guilty to the new charge and, at the same time, not so great that the defendant does not "get his due."

In a homicide, while battery is a necessarily included offense, it will not be considered as a possible reduction. For a conviction of second degree murder a defendant could receive a life sentence in the penitentiary. For a battery conviction he would spend no more than six months in the county jail. In a homicide, however, "felony manslaughter," or "assault with a deadly weapon," whatever their relation to homicide as regards inclusion, would more closely approximate the sentence outcome that could be expected on a trial conviction of second degree murder. These alternatives would be considered. For burglary, a typically situationally included offense might be "disturbing the peace," "breaking and entering" or "destroying public property." "Petty theft," however, constitutes a reasonable lesser alternative to burglary as the sentence for petty theft will often range between six months and one year in the county jail and burglary regularly does not carry higher than two years in the state prison. "Disturbing the peace" would be a thirty-day sentence offense.

While the present purposes make the exposition of this calculus unnecessary, it can be noted and stressed that the particular content of the reduction does not necessarily correspond to a relation between the original and altered charge that could be described in either the terms of necessary or situational inclusion. Whatever the relation between the original and reduced charge, its essential feature resides in the spread between sentence likelihoods and the reasonableness of that spread, i.e., the balance it strikes between the defendant "getting his due" and at the same time "getting something less than he might so that he will plead guilty."

The procedure we want to clarify now, at the risk of some repetition, is the manner in which an instant case is examined to decide its membership in a class of "crimes such as this" (the category *normal crimes*). Let us start with an obvious case, burglary. As the typical reduction for burglary is petty theft and as petty theft is neither situationally nor necessarily included in burglary, the examination of the instant case is clearly not undertaken to decide whether petty theft is an appropriate statutory description. The concern is to establish the relation between the instant burglary and the normal category "burglaries" and, having decided a "sufficient correspondence," to now employ petty theft as the proposed reduction.

In scrutinizing the present burglary case, the P.D. seeks to establish that "this is a burglary just like any other." If that correspondence is not established, regardless of whether or not petty theft in fact was a feature of the way the crime was enacted, the reduction to petty theft would not be proposed. *The propriety of proposing petty theft as a reduction does not derive from its in-fact-existence in the present case, but is warranted or not by the relation of the present burglary to "burglaries," normally conceived.*

In a case of "child molestation" (officially called "lewd conduct with a minor"), the concern is to decide if this is a "typical child molestation case." While "loitering around a schoolyard" is frequently a feature of the way such crimes are instigated, establishing that the present defendant *did in fact loiter around a schoolyard* is secondary to the more general question: "Is this a typical child molestation case?" What appears as a contradiction must be clarified by examining the status of "loitering around a schoolyard" as a typical feature of such child molestations. The typical character of "child molesting cases" does not stand or fall on the fact that "loitering around a schoolyard" is a feature of the way they are in fact committed. It is *not* that "loitering around a schoolyard" as a *statutorily referable behavior sequence* is part of typical "child molesting cases" but that "loitering around a schoolyard" as a *socially distinct mode of committing child molestations typifies the way such offenses are enacted.* "Strictly speaking," i.e., under the auspices of the statutory corpus delicti, "loitering around a schoolyard," requires *loitering, around,* a *schoolyard;* if one loiters around a ball park or a public recreation area, he "cannot," within a proper reading of the statute, be charged with loitering around a *schoolyard.* Yet "loitering around a schoolyard," as a feature of the typical way such offenses as child molestations are committed, has the status not of a description of the way in *fact* (*fact*, statutorily decided) it occurred or typically occurs, but "the-kind-of-social-activity-typically-associated-with-such-of-fenses." It is not its statutorily conceived features but its socially relevant attributes that gives "loitering around a schoolyard" its status as a feature of the class "normal child molestations." Whether the defendant loitered around a schoolyard or a ball park, and whether he loitered or "was passing by," "loitering around a schoolyard" as a reduction will be made if the defendant's activity was such that "he was hanging around some public place or another" and "was the kind of guy who hangs around schoolyards." As a component of the class of normal child molestation cases (of the variety where the victim is a stranger), "loitering around a school-yard" typifies a mode of committing such offenses, the class of "such persons who do such things as hang around schoolyards and the like." A large variety of actual offenses could thus be nonetheless reduced to "loitering" if, as kinds of social activity, "loitering," conceived of as typifying a way of life, pattern of daily activity, social psychological circumstances, etc., characterized the conduct of the defendant. The young P.D. who would object "You can't reduce it to 'loitering'—he didn't really 'loiter,' " would be reprimanded: "Fella, you don't know how to use that term; he might as well have 'loitered' —it's the same kind of case as the others."

Having outlined the formal mechanics of the guilty plea disposition, I shall now turn to depict the routine of representation that the categories of crime, imbued with elaborate knowledge of the delinquent social structure, provide for. This will entail a brief examination of pertinent organizational features of the P.D. system.

Public "Defense"

Recently, in many communities, the burden of securing counsel has been taken from the defendant.[6] As the accused is, by law, entitled to the aid of counsel, and as his pocketbook is often empty, numerous cities have felt obliged to establish a public defender system. There has been little resistance to this development by private attorneys among whom it is widely felt that the less time they need spend in the criminal courts, where practice is least prestigeful and lucrative, the better.[7]

[6]For general histories of indigent defender systems in the United States, see The Association of the Bar of the City of New York, *Equal Justice for the Accused,* Garden City, New York: 1959; and E. A. Brownell, *Legal Aid in the United States,* Rochester, New York: The Lawyers Cooperative Publishing Company, 1951.

[7]The experience of the Public Defender system is distinctly different in this regard from that of the Legal Aid Societies, which, I am told, have continually met very strong opposition to their establishment by local bar associations.

Whatever the reasons for its development, we now find, in many urban places, a public defender occupying a place alongside judge and prosecutor as a regular court employee. In the county studied, the P.D. mans a daily station, like the public prosecutor, and "defends" all who come before him. He appears in court when court begins and his "clientele," composed without regard for his preferences, consists of that residual category of persons who cannot afford to bring their own spokesmen to court. In this county, the "residual" category approximates 65 percent of the total number of criminal cases. In a given year, the twelve attorneys who comprise the P.D. office "represent" about 3,000 defendants in the municipal and superior courts of the county.

While the courtroom encounters of private attorneys are brief, businesslike, and circumscribed, interactionally and temporally, by the particular cases that bring them there, the P.D. attends to the courtroom as his regular work place and conveys in his demeanor his place as a member of its core personnel.

While private attorneys come and leave court with their clients (who are generally "on bail"), the P.D. arrives in court each morning at nine, takes his station at the defense table, and deposits there the batch of files that he will refer to during the day. When, during morning "calendar,"[8] a private attorney's case is called, the P.D. steps back from the defense table, leaving his belongings in place there, and temporarily relinquishes his station. No private attorney has enough defendants in a given court on a given day to claim a right to make a desk of the defense table. If the P.D. needs some information from his central office, he uses the clerk's telephone, a privilege that few private lawyers feel at home enough to take. In the course of calendar work, a lawyer will often have occasion to request a delay or "continuance" of several days until the next stage of his client's proceedings. The private attorney addresses the prosecutor via the judge to request such an alteration; the P.D. talks directly over to the D.A.:

PRIVATE ATTORNEY: If the prosecutor finds it convenient, your Honor, my client would prefer to have his preliminary hearing on Monday, the 24th.
JUDGE: Is that date suitable to the district attorney?
PROSECUTOR: Yes, your Honor.
P.A.: Thank you, your Honor.
P.D.: Bob (D.A.), how about moving Smith's prelim up to the 16th?
PROS.: Well, Jim, we've got Jones on that afternoon.

[8]"Calendar part" consists of that portion of the court day, typically in the mornings, when all matters other than trials are heard, e.g., arraignments, motions, continuances, sentencing, probation reports, etc.

P.D.: Let's see, how's the 22d?
PROS.: That's fine, Jim, the 22d.

If, during the course of a proceeding, the P.D. has some minor matter
to tend to with the D.A., he uses the time when a private attorney
is addressing the bench to walk over to the prosecutor's table and
whisper his requests, suggestions or questions. The P.D. uses the
prosecutor's master calendar to check on an upcoming court date; so
does the D.A. with the P.D.'s. The D.A. and P.D. are on a first name
basis and throughout the course of a routine day interact as a team
of co-workers.

While the central focus of the private attorney's attention is his
client, the courtroom and affairs of court constitute the locus of
involvements for the P.D. The public defender and public prosecutor, each representatives of their respective offices, jointly handle the
greatest bulk of the court's daily activity.

The P.D. office, rather than assign its attorneys to clients, employs
the arrangement of stationing attorneys in different courts to "represent" all those who come before that station. As defendants are
moved about from courtroom to courtroom throughout the course of
their proceedings (both from municipal to superior courtrooms for
felony cases, and from one municipal courtroom to another when
there is a specialization of courts, e.g., jury, nonjury, arraignment,
etc.), the P.D. sees defendants only at those places in their paths
when they appear in the court he is manning. A given defendant
may be "represented" by one P.D. at arraignment, another at preliminary hearing, a third at trial, and a fourth when sentenced.

At the first interview with a client (initial interviews occur in the
jail where attorneys go, *en masse,* to "pick up new defendants" in the
afternoons) a file is prepared on the defendant. In each file is recorded
the charge brought against the defendant and, among other things,
his next court date. Each evening attorneys return new files to the
central office where secretaries prepare court books for each courtroom that list the defendants due to appear in a given court on a
given day. In the mornings, attorneys take the court books from the
office and remove from the central file the files of those defendants
due to appear in "their court" that day.

There is little communication between P.D. and client. After the
first interview, the defendant's encounters with the P.D. are primarily in court. Only under special circumstances (to be discussed below) are there contacts between lawyers and defendants in the jail
before and after appearances in court. The bulk of "preparation for
court" (either trials or nontrial matters) occurs at the first interview.
The attorney on station, the "attending attorney," is thus a stranger
to "his client," and vice versa. Over the course of his proceedings, a

defendant will have several attorneys (in one instance a man was "represented" by eight P.D.s on a charge of simple assault). Defendants who come to court find a lawyer they don't know conducting their trials, entering their motions, making their pleas, and the rest. Often there is no introduction of P.D. to defendant; defendants are prepared to expect a strange face: "Don't be surprised when you see another P.D. in court with you on Tuesday. You just do what he tells you to. He'll know all about your case."

P.D.s seldom talk about particular defendants among themselves. When they converse about trials, the facts of cases, etc., they do so not so much for briefing, e.g., "This is what I think you should do when you 'get him,' " but rather as small talk, as "What have you got going today." The P.D. does not rely on the information about a case he received from a previous attending attorney in order to know how to manage his "representation." Rather, the file is relied upon to furnish all the information essential for making an "appearance." These appearances range from morning calendar work (e.g., arraignments, motions, continuances, etc.) to trials on offenses from drunkenness to assault with a deadly weapon. In the course of a routine day, the P.D. will receive his batch of files in the morning and, seeing them for the first time that day, conduct numerous trials, preliminary hearings, calendar appearances, sentencing proceedings, etc. They do not study files overnight. Attorneys will often only look over a file a half hour or so before the jury trial begins.

The First Interview

As the first interview is often the only interview and as the file prepared there is central for the continuing "representation" of the defendant by other attorneys, it is important to examine these interviews and the file's contents. From the outset, the P.D. attends to establishing the typical character of the case before him and thereby instituting routinely employed reduction arrangements. The defendant's appearance, e.g., his race, demeanor, age, style of talk, way of attending to the occasion of his incarceration, etc., provides the P.D. with an initial sense of his place in the social structure. Knowing only that the defendant is charged with section 459 (burglary) of the penal code, the P.D. employs his conception of typical burglars against which the character of the present defendant is assessed.

> He had me fooled for a while. With that accent of his and those Parliaments he was smoking I thought something was strange. It turned out to be just another burglary. You heard him tell about New York and the way he had a hold on him there that he was running away from. I just guess N.Y. is a funny place,

you can never tell what kinds of people get involved in crimes there.

The initial fact of the defendant's "putting in a request to see the P.D." establishes his lower position in the class structure of the community: "We just never get wealthier people here. They usually don't stay in jail overnight and then they call a private attorney. The P.D. gets everything at the bottom of the pile."

Searching over the criminal history (past convictions and arrests) the defendant provides when preliminary fact sheet data are recorded in the file, the P.D. gets a sense of the man's typical pattern of criminal activity. It is not the particular offenses for which he is charged that are crucial, but the constellation of prior offenses and the sequential pattern they take:

> I could tell as soon as he told me he had four prior drunk charges that he was just another of these Skid-Row bums. You could look at him and tell.
>
> When you see a whole string of forgery counts in the past you pretty much know what kind of case you're dealing with. You either get those who commit an occasional forgery, or those that do nothing but. ... With a whole bunch of prior checks (prior forgery convictions) you can bet that he cashes little ones. I didn't even have to ask for the amount you know. I seldom come across one over a hundred bucks.
>
> From the looks of him and the way he said "I wasn't doing anything, just playing with her," you know, it's the usual kind of thing, just a little diddling or something. We can try to get it out on a simple assault.

When a P.D. puts questions to the defendant he is less concerned with recording nuances of the instant event (e.g., how many feet from the bar were you when the cops came in, did you break into the back gate or the front door?), than with establishing its similarity with "events of this sort." That similarity is established, not by discovering statutorily relevant events of the present case, but by locating the event in a sociologically constructed class of "such cases." The first questions directed to the defendant are of the character that answers to them either confirm or throw into question the assumed typicality. First questions with ADWs are of the order: "How long had you been drinking before this all started?" with "child molestation" cases: "How long were you hanging around before this began?" with "forgery" cases: "Was this the second or third check you cashed in the same place?"

We shall present three short excerpts from three first interviews. They all begin with the first question asked after preliminary background data is gathered. The first is with a 288 (child molestation), the second with a 459 (burglary) and the last with a 11530 (possession of marijuana). Each interview was conducted by a different Public Defender. In each case the P.D. had no information about the defendant or this particular crime other than that provided by the penal code number:

288

P.D.: O.K., why don't you start out by telling me how this thing got started?

DEF.: Well, I was at the park and all I did was to ask this little girl if she wanted to sit on my lap for awhile and you know, just sit on my lap. Well, about twenty minutes later I'm walkin' down the street about a block away from the park and this cop pulls up and there the same little girl is, you know, sitting in the back seat with some dame. The cop asks me to stick my head in the back seat and he asks the kid if I was the one and she says yes. So he puts me in the car and takes a statement from me and here I am in the joint. All I was doin' was playin' with her a little . . .

P.D.: (*interrupting*) . . . O.K. I get the story, let's see what we can do. If I can get this charge reduced to a misdemeanor then I would advise you to plead guilty, particularly since you have a record and that wouldn't look too well in court with a jury.

(*The interview proceeded for another two or three minutes, and the decision to plead guilty was made.*)

459

P.D.: Why don't you start by telling me where this place was that you broke into?

DEF.: I don't know for sure . . . I think it was on 13th street or something like that.

P.D.: Had you ever been there before?

DEF.: I hang around that neighborhood you know, so I guess I've been in the place before, yeah.

P.D.: What were you going after?

DEF.: I don't know, whatever there was so's I could get a little cash. Man, I was pretty broke that night.

P.D.: Was anyone with you?

DEF.: No, I was by myself.

P.D.: How much did you break up the place?

DEF.: I didn't do nothing. The back window was open a little bit, see, and I just put my hand in there and opened the door. I was just walking in when I heard police comin', so I turn around and start to run. And they saw me down the block and that was that.

P.D.: Were you drunk at the time?

DEF.: I wasn't drunk, no, I maybe had a drink or two that evening but I wasn't drunk or anything like that.

11530

P.D.: Well, Smith, why don't you tell me where they found it [the marijuana]?

DEF.: I was driving home from the drugstore with my friend and this cop car pulls me up to the side. Two guys get out, one of them was wearing a uniform and the other was a plain-clothesman. They told us to get out of the car and then they searched me and then my friend. Then this guy without the uniform he looked over into the car and picked up this thing from the back floor and said something to the other one. Then he asked me if I had any more of the stuff and I said I didn't know what he was talking about. So he wrote something down on a piece of paper and made me sign it. Then he told my friend to go home and they took me down here to the station and booked me on possession of marijuana. I swear I didn't have no marijuana.

P.D.: You told me you were convicted of possession in 1959.

DEF.: Yeah, but I haven't touched any of the stuff since then. I don't know what it was doing in my car, but I haven't touched the stuff since that last time.

P.D.: You ought to know it doesn't make any difference whether or not they catch you using, just so as they find it on your possession or in a car, or in your house, or something.

DEF.: Man, I swear I don't know how it got there. Somebody must have planted it there.

P.D.: Look, you know as well as I do that with your prior conviction and this charge now that you could go away from here for five years or so. So just calm down a minute and let's look at this thing reasonably. If you go to trial and lose the trial, you're stuck. You'll be in the joint until you're 28 years old. If you plead to this one charge without the priors then we can get you into jail maybe, or a year or two at the most in the joint. If you wait until the preliminary hearing and then they charge the priors, boy you've had it, it's too late.

DEF.: Well how about a trial?

(*After ten minutes, the defendant decided to plead guilty to one charge of possession, before the date of the preliminary hearing.*)

Let us consider, in light of the previous discussion, some of the features of these interviews.

1. In each case the information sought is not "data" for organizing the particular facts of the case for deciding proper penal code designations (or with a view toward undermining the assignment of a

designation in an anticipated trial). In the 288 instance, the P.D. interrupted when he had enough information to confirm his sense of the case's typicality and construct a typifying portrayal of the present defendant. The character of the information supplied by the defendant was such that it was specifically lacking detail about the particular occurrences, e.g., the time, place, what was said to the girl, what precisely did the defendant do or not do, his "state of mind," etc. The defendant's appearance and prior record (in this case the defendant was a fifty-five-year-old white, unemployed, unskilled laborer, with about ten prior drunk arrests, seven convictions, and two prior sex offense violations) was relied upon to provide the sense of the present occasion. The P.D. straightforwardly approached the D.A. and arranged for a "contributing to the delinquency of a minor" reduction. In the burglary case, the question, "Had you ever been there before?" was intended to elicit what was received, e.g., that the place was a familiar one to the defendant. Knowing that the place was in the defendant's neighborhood establishes its character as a Skid-Row area business; that the First Federal Bank was not entered has been confirmed. "What were you going after?" also irrelevant to the 459 section of the penal code, provides him with information that there was no special motive for entering this establishment. The question, "Was anyone with you?" when answered negatively, placed the event in the typical class of "burglaries" as solitary, non-coordinated activities. The remaining questions were directed as well to confirming the typical character of the event, and the adequacy of the defendant's account is not decided by whether or not the P.D. can now decide whether the statutory definition of the contemplated reduction or the original charge is satisfied. Its adequacy is determined by the ability with which the P.D. can detect its normal character. The accounts provided thus may have the character of anecdotes, sketches, phrases, etc. In the first instance, with the 288, the prior record and the defendant's appearance, demeanor and style of talking about the event was enough to warrant his typical treatment.

2. The most important feature of the P.D.'s questioning is the presupposition of guilt that makes his proposed questions legitimate and answerable at the outset. To pose the question, "Why don't you start by telling me where this place was that you broke into?" as a lead question, the P.D. takes it that the defendant is guilty of a crime and that the crime for which he is charged probably describes what essentially occurred.

The P.D.'s activity is seldom geared to securing acquittals for clients. He and the D.A., as co-workers in the same courts, take it for granted that the persons who come before the courts are guilty of

crimes and are to be treated accordingly: "Most of them have records
as you can see. Almost all of them have been through our courts
before. And the police just don't make mistakes in this town. That's
one thing about———, we've got the best police force in the state."
As we shall argue below, the way defendants are "represented" (the
station manning rather than assignment of counselors to clients), the
way trials are conducted, the way interviews are held and the penal
code employed—all of the P.D.'s work is premised on the supposition
that people charged with crimes have committed crimes.

This presupposition makes such first questions as "Why don't you
start by telling me where this place was . . ." reasonable questions.
When the answer comes: "What place? I don't know what you are
talking about," the defendant is taken to be a phony, making an
"innocent pitch." The conceivable first question: "Did you do it?" is
not asked because it is felt that this gives the defendant the notion
that he can try an "innocent pitch":

> I never ask them, "did you do it?" because on one hand I know
> they did and mainly because then they think that they can play
> games with us. We can always check their records and usually
> they have a string of offenses. You don't have to, though, be-
> cause in a day or two they change their story and plead guilty.
> Except for the stubborn ones.

Of the possible answers to an opening question, bewilderment, the
inability to answer, or silence, is taken to indicate that the defendant
is putting the P.D. on. For defendants who refuse to admit anything,
the P.D. threatens: "Look, if you don't want to talk, that's you business. I can't help you. All I can say is that if you go to trial on this
beef you're going to spend a long time in the joint. When you get
ready to tell me the story straight, then we can see what can be
done."

If the puzzlement comes because the wrong question is asked, e.g.,
"There wasn't any fight—that's not the way it happened," the defendant will start to fill in the story. The P.D. awaits to see if, how far,
and in what ways the instant case is deviant. If the defendant is
charged with burglary and a middle-class establishment was bur-
glarized, windows shattered, a large payroll sought, and a gun used,
then the reduction to petty theft, generally employed for "normal
burglaries," would be more difficult to arrange.

Generally, the P.D. doesn't have to discover the atypical kinds of
cases through questioning. Rather, the D.A., in writing the original
complaint, provides the P.D. with clues that the typical recipe, given
the way the event occurred, will not be allowable. Where the way
it occurs is such that it does not resemble normal burglaries and the
routinely used penalty would reduce it *too far* commensurate with

the way the crime occurred, the D.A. frequently charges various situationally included offenses, indicating to the P.D. that the procedure to employ here is to suggest "dropping" some of the charges, leaving the originally charged greatest offense as it stands.

In the general case he doesn't charge all those offenses that he legally might. He might charge "child molesting" and "loitering around a schoolyard" but typically only the greater charge is made. The D.A. does so, so as to provide for a later reduction that will appear particularly lenient in that it seemingly involves a *change* in the charge. Were he to charge both molesting and loitering, he would be obliged, moreover, should the case come to trial, to introduce evidence for both offenses. The D.A. is thus always constrained not to set overly high charges or not situationally included multiple offenses by the possibility that the defendant will not plead guilty to a lesser offense and the case will go to trial. Of primary importance is that he doesn't charge multiple offenses so that the P.D. will be in the best position vis-à-vis the defendant. He thus charges the first complaint so as to provide for a "setup."

The alteration of charges must be made in open court. The P.D. requests to have a new plea entered:

> P.D.: Your Honor, in the interests of justice, my client would like to change his plea of not guilty to the charge of burglary and enter a plea of guilty to the charge of petty theft.
> JUDGE: Is this new plea acceptable to the prosecution?
> D.A.: Yes, your Honor.

The prosecutor knows beforehand that the request will be made, and has agreed in advance to allow it.

I asked a P.D. how they felt about making such requests in open court, i.e., asking for a reduction from one offense to another when the latter is obviously not necessarily included and often (as is the case in burglary-to-petty theft) not situationally included. He summarized the office's feeling:

> In the old days, ten or so years ago, we didn't like to do it in front of the judge. What we used to do when we made a deal was that the D.A. would dismiss the original charge and write up a new complaint altogether. That took a lot of time. We had to rearraign him all over again back in the muni court and everything. Besides, in the same courtroom, everyone used to know what was going on anyway. Now we just ask for a change of plea to the lesser charge regardless of whether it's included or not. Nobody thinks twice about asking for petty theft on burglary, or drunkenness on car theft, or something like that. It's just the way it's done.

Some restrictions are felt. Assaultive crimes (e.g., ADW, simple assault, attempted murder, etc.) will not be reduced to or from "money offenses" (burglary, robbery, theft) unless the latter involve weapons or some violence. Also, victimless crimes (narcotics, drunkenness) are not reduced to or from assaultive or "money offenses," unless there is some factual relation, e.g., drunkenness with a fight might turn out to be simple assault reduced to drunkenness.

For most cases that come before their courts, the P.D. and D.A. are able to employ reductions that are formulated for handling typical cases. While some burglaries, rapes, narcotics violations, and petty thefts are instigated in strange ways and involve atypical facts, some manipulation in the way the initial charge is made can be used to set up a procedure to replace the simple charge-alteration form of reducing.

Recalcitrant Defendants

Most of the P.D.'s cases that "have to go to trial" are those where the P.D. is not able to sell the defendant on the "bargain." These are cases for which reductions are available, reductions that are constructed on the basis of the typicality of the offense and allowable by the D.A. These are normal crimes committed by "stubborn" defendants.

So-called stubborn defendants will be distinguished from a second class of offenders, those who commit *crimes which are atypical in their character (for this community, at this time, etc.) or who commit crimes which while typical (recurrent for this community, this time, etc.) are committed atypically.* The manner in which the P.D. and D.A. must conduct the representation and prosecution of these defendants is radically different. To characterize the special problems the P.D. has with each class of defendants, it is first necessary to point out a general feature of the P.D.'s orientation to the work of the courts that has hitherto not been made explicit. This orientation will be merely sketched here.

As we noticed, the defendant's guilt is not attended to. That is to say, the presupposition of guilt, as a *presupposition,* does not say "You are guilty" with a pointing accusatory finger, but "You are guilty, you know it, I know it, so let's get down to the business of deciding what to do with you." When a defendant agrees to plead guilty, he is not *admitting* his guilt; when asked to plead guilty, he is not being asked, "Come on, admit it, you know you were *wrong,*" but rather, "Why don't you be sensible about this thing?" What is sought is not a *confession,* but reasonableness.

The presupposition of guilt as a way of attending to the treatment of defendants has its counterpart in the way the P.D. attends to the entire court process, prosecuting machinery, law enforcement techniques, and the community.

For P.D. and D.A. it is a routinely encountered phenomenon that persons in the community regularly commit criminal offenses, are regularly brought before the courts, and are regularly transported to the state and county penal institutions. To confront a "criminal" is, for D.A. and P.D., no special experience, nothing to tell their wives about, nothing to record as outstanding in the happenings of the day. Before "their court" scores of "criminals" pass each day.

The morality of the courts is taken for granted. The P.D. assumes that the D.A., the police, judge, the narcotics agents and others all conduct their business as it must be conducted and in a proper fashion. That the police may hide out to deceive petty violators; that narcotics agents may regularly employ illicit entrapment procedures to find suspects; that investigators may routinely arrest suspects before they have sufficient grounds and only later uncover warrantable evidence for a formal booking; that the police may beat suspects; that judges may be "tough" because they are looking for support for higher office elections; that some laws may be specifically prejudicial against certain classes of persons—whatever may be the actual course of charging and convicting defendants—all of this is taken, as one P.D. put it, "as part of the system and the way it has to be." And the P.D. is part of the team.

While it is common to overhear private attorneys call judges "bastards," policemen "hoodlums," and prosecutors "sadists," the P.D., in the presence of such talk, remains silent. When the P.D. "loses" a case —and we shall see that *losing* is an adequate description only for some circumstances—he is likely to say "I knew *he* couldn't win." Private attorneys, on the other hand, will not hesitate to remark, as one did in a recent case, "You haven't got a fucking chance in front of that son-of-a-bitch dictator." In the P.D. office, there is a total absence of such condemnation.

The P.D. takes it for granted and attends to the courts in accord with the view that "what goes on in this business is what goes on and what goes on is the way it should be." It is rare to hear a public defender voice protest against a particular law, procedure, or official. One of the attorneys mentioned that he felt the new narcotics law (which makes it mandatory that a high minimum sentence be served for "possession or sale of narcotics") wasn't too severe "considering that they wanted to give them the chair." Another indicated that the more rigid statute "will probably cure a lot of them because they'll be in for so long." One P.D. feels that wiretapping would be a useful adjunct to police procedure. It is generally said, by everyone in the office, that "——— is one of the best cities in the state when it comes to police."

In the P.D.'s interviews, the defendant's guilt becomes a topic only when the defendant himself attempts to direct attention to his innocence. Such attempts are never taken seriously by the P.D. but are seen as "innocent pitches," as "being wise," as "not knowing what is good for him." Defendants who make "innocent pitches" often find themselves able to convince the P.D. to have trials. The P.D. is in a professional and organizational bind in that he requires that his "clients" agree with whatever action he takes "on their behalf":

> Can you imagine what might happen if we went straight to the D.A. with a deal to which the client later refused to agree? Can you see him in court screaming how the P.D. sold him out? As it is, we get plenty of letters purporting to show why we don't do our job. Judges are swamped with letters condemning the P.D. Plenty of appeals get started this way.

Some defendants don't buy the offer of less time as constituting sufficient grounds for avoiding a trial. To others, it appears that "copping out" is worse than having a trial regardless of the consequences for the length of sentence. The following remarks, taken from P.D. files, illustrate the terms in which such "stubborn" defendants are conceived:

> Def wants a trial, but he is dead. In lieu of a possible 995, D.A. agreed to put note in his file recommending a deal. This should be explored and encouraged as big break for Def.
> Chance of successful defense negligible. Def realizes this but says he ain't going to cop to no strong-arm. See if we can set him straight.
> Dead case. Too many witnesses and ... used in two of the transactions. However, Def is a very squirmy jailhouse lawyer and refuses to face facts.
> Possibly the D.A. in Sup/Ct could be persuaded into cutting her loose if she took the 211 and one of the narco counts. If not, the Def, who is somewhat recalcitrant and stubborn, will probably demand a JT [jury trial].

The routine trial, generated as it is by the defendant's refusal to make a lesser plea, is the "defendant's fault": "What the hell are we supposed to do with them? If they can't listen to good reason and take a bargain, then it's their tough luck. If they go to prison, well, they're the ones who are losing the trials, not us." When the P.D. enters the courtroom, he takes it that he is going to lose, e.g., the defendant is going to prison. When he "prepares" for trial, he doesn't prepare to "win." There is no attention given to "how am I going to construct a defense in order that I can get this defendant free of the charges against him." In fact, he doesn't "prepare for trial" in any "ordinary" sense. (I use the term *ordinary* with hesitation; what *preparation for trial* might in fact involve with other than P.D. lawyers has not, to my knowledge, been investigated.)

For the P.D., "preparation for trial" involves, essentially, learning what "burglary cases" are like, what "rape cases" are like, what "assaults" are like. The P.D.'s main concern is to conduct his part of the proceedings in accord with complete respect for proper legal procedure. He raises objections to improper testimony; introduces motions whenever they seem called for; demands his "client's rights" to access to the prosecution's evidence before trial (through so-called discovery proceedings); cross-examines all witnesses; does not introduce evidence that he expects will not be allowable; asks all those questions of all those people that he must in order to have addressed himself to the task of insuring that the corpus delicti has been established; carefully summarizes the evidence that has been presented in making a closing argument. Throughout, at every point, he conducts his "defense" in such a manner that no one can say of him, "He has been negligent, there are grounds for appeal here." He systematically provides, in accord with the prescriptions of due process and the fourteenth amendment, a completely proper "adequate legal representation."

At the same time the district attorney and the county, which employs them both, can rely on the P.D. not to attempt to morally degrade police officers in cross-examination; not to impeach the state's witnesses by trickery; not to attempt an exposition of the entrapment methods of narcotics agents; not to condemn the community for the "racial prejudice that produces our criminals" (the phrase of a private attorney during closing argument); not to challenge the prosecution of "these women who are trying to raise a family without a husband" (the statement of another private attorney during closing argument on a welfare fraud case); in sum, not to make an issue of the moral character of the administrative machinery of the local courts, the community, or the police. He will not cause any serious trouble for the routine motion of the court conviction process. Laws will not be challenged, cases will not be tried to test the constitutionality of procedures and statutes, judges will not be personally degraded, police will be free from scrutiny to decide the legitimacy of their operations, and the community will not be condemned for its segregative practices against Negroes. The P.D.'s defense is completely proper, in accord with correct legal procedure, and specifically amoral in its import, manner of delivery, and perceived implications for the propriety of the prosecution enterprise.

In "return" for all this, the district attorney treats the defendant's guilt in a matter-of-fact fashion, doesn't get hostile in the course of the proceedings, doesn't insist that the jury or judge "throw the book," but rather "puts on a trial" (in their way of referring to their daily tasks) in order to, with a minimum of strain, properly place the defendant behind bars. Both prosecutor and public defender thus protect the moral character of the other's charges from exposure. Should the P.D. attend to demonstrating the innocence of his client by attempting to undermine the legitimate character of police operations, the prosecutor might feel obliged in return to employ devices to degrade the moral character of the P.D.'s client. Should the D.A. attack defendants in court, by pointing to the specifically immoral character of their activities, the P.D. might feel obligated, in response, to raise into relief the moral texture of the D.A.'s and police's and community's operations. Wherever possible, each holds the other in check. But the "check" need not be continuously held in place, or even attended to self-consciously, for both P.D. and D.A. trust one another implicitly. The D.A. knows, with certainty, that the P.D. will not make a closing argument that resembles the following by a private attorney, from which I have paraphrased key excerpts:

> If it hadn't been for all the publicity that this case had in our wonderful local newspapers, you wouldn't want to throw the book at these men.
> If you'd clear up the problems with the Negro in ———— maybe you wouldn't have cases like this in your courts.
> [*After sentence was pronounced*]:Your Honor, I just would like to say one thing—that I've never heard or seen such a display of injustice as I've seen here in this court today. It's a sad commentary on the state of our community if people like yourself pay more attention to the local political machines than to the lives of our defendants. I think you are guilty of that, your Honor.

(At this last statement, one of the P.D.s who was in the courtroom turned to me and said, "He sure is looking for a contempt charge.")

The P.D. knows how to conduct his trials because he knows how to conduct "assault with deadly weapons" trials, "burglary" trials, "rape" trials, and the rest. The corpus delicti here provides him with a basis for asking "proper questions," making the "proper" cross-examinations, and pointing out the "proper" things to jurors about "reasonable doubt." He need not extensively gather information about the specific facts of the instant case. Whatever is needed in the way of "facts of the case" arise in the course of the D.A.'s presentation. He employs the "strategy" of directing the same questions to the witness as were put by the D.A. with added emphasis on the question mark, or an inserted "Did you really see————?" His "defense" consists of attempting to "bring out" slightly variant aspects of the D.A.'s story by questioning his own witnesses (whom he seldom interviews before beginning trial but who are interviewed by the office's two "investigators") and the defendant.

With little variation the same questions are put to all defendants charged with the same crimes. The P.D. learns with experience what to expect as the "facts of the case." These facts, in their general structure, portray social circumstances that he can anticipate by virtue of his knowledge of the normal features of offense categories and types of offenders. The "details" of the instant case are "discovered" over the course of hearing them in court. In this regard, the "information" that "comes out" is often as new to him as to the jury.

Employing a common sense conception of what criminal lawyers behave like in cross-examination and argument, and the popular portrayal of their demeanor and style of addressing adversary witnesses, the onlooker comes away with the sense of having witnessed not a trial at all, but a set of motions, a perfunctorily carried off event. A sociological analysis of this sense would require a systematic attempt to describe the features of adversary trial conduct.

A Note on Special Cases

To conduct trials with "stubborn" defendants, so-called, is no special trouble. Here trials are viewed as a "waste of time." Murders, embezzlements, multiple rape cases (several defendants with one victim), large-scale robberies, dope ring operations, those cases that arouse public attention and receive special notice in the papers—these are cases whose normal features are not constructed and for which, even were a guilty plea available, both parties feel uncomfortably obliged to bring issues of moral character into the courtroom. The privacy of the P.D.-D.A. conviction machinery through the use of the guilty plea can no longer be preserved. Only "normal defendants" are accorded this privacy. The pressure for a public hearing, in the sense of "bringing the public in to see and monitor the character of the proceedings," must be allowed to culminate in a full-blown jury trial. There is a general preference in the P.D. office to handle routine cases without a jury, if it must go to trial at all. In the special case the jury must be employed and with them a large audience of onlookers, newspapermen, and daily paper coverage must be tolerated.

To put on a fight is a discomforting task for persons who regularly work together as a team. Every effort is made to bind off the event of a special case by heightened interaction outside the courtroom. In the routine case, with no jury or at least no press coverage, the whole trial can be handled as a backstage operation. With special cases there can be no byplay conversation in the courtroom between D.A.

and P.D., and no leaving court together, arm in arm. Metaphorically, two persons who regularly dance together must now appear, with the lights turned on, to be fighting.

The P.D. office reserves several of its attorneys to handle such cases. By keeping the regular personnel away from particular court-rooms, their routine interactions with the D.A. can be properly maintained. An older, more experienced attorney, from each side, comes to court to put on the show. The device of so handling the assignment of attorneys to cases serves to mark off the event as a special occasion, to set it outside the regular ordering of relationships that must resume when the special, and dreaded, case becomes a statistic in the penal institution records.

With the special cases, the client-attorney assignment procedure is instituted. The head of the P.D. office, along with a coterie of older attorneys, goes to the first interview in the jail, and these same attorneys, or some of them, take over the case and stay with it, handling its development with kid gloves. The concern to provide "adequate legal representation" may be relegated to a back seat. Both P.D. and D.A. must temporarily step outside their typical modes of mutual conduct and yet, at the same time, not permanently jeopard-ize the stability of their usual teamlike relationship.

Some Conclusions

An examination of the use of the penal code by actually practicing attorneys has revealed that categories of crime, rather than being "unsuited" to sociological analysis, are so employed as to make their analysis crucial to empirical understanding. What categories of crime are, i.e., who is assembled under this one or that, what consti-tute the behaviors inspected for deciding such matters, what "etio-logically significant" matters are incorporated within their scope, is not, the present findings indicate, to be decided on the basis of an *a priori* inspection of their formally available definitions. The sociol-ogist who regards the category "theft" with penal code in hand and proposes necessary, "theoretically relevant" revisions, is construct-ing an imagined use of the penal code as the basis for his criticism. For in their actual use, categories of crime, as we have reiterated continuously above, are, at least for this legal establishment, the shorthand reference terms for that knowledge of the social structure and its criminal events upon which the task of practically organiz-ing the work of "representation" is premised. That knowledge in-cludes, embodied within what burglary, petty theft, narcotics violations, child molestation and the rest *actually stand for,* knowl-edge of modes of criminal activity, ecological characteristics of the community, patterns of daily slum life, psychological and social biographies of offenders, criminal histories and futures; in sum, practically tested criminological wisdom. The operations of the Public Defender system, and it is clear that upon comparative analysis with other legal "firms" it would be somewhat distinctive in character, are routinely maintained via the proper use of categories of crime for everyday decision-making. The proprieties of that use are not described in the state criminal code, nor are the operations of reduction, detailed above.

A cautionary word is required. It will appear as obvious that the system of providing "defense" to indigent persons described above is not representative of criminal defense work generally. How the penal code is employed, i.e., how behaviors are scrutinized under its jurisdiction and dispensations made via operations performed on its categories, in other kinds of legal establishments, has not been investigated here. The present case, albeit apparently specialized, was chosen as an example only. It may well be that, in certain forms of legal work, the penal code as a statutory document is accorded a much different and more "rigorous" scrutiny. The legalistic character of some criminal prosecutions leads one to suspect that the "letter of the law" might constitute a key reference point in preparing for a criminal defense, aiming for acquittal, or changing a statutory regulation.

The Practice of Law as Confidence Game
Organizational Cooptation of a Profession

Abraham S. Blumberg

A recurring theme in the growing dialogue between sociology and law has been the great need for a joint effort of the two disciplines to illuminate urgent social and legal issues. Having uttered fervent public pronouncements in this vein, however, the respective practitioners often go their separate ways. Academic spokesmen for the legal profession are somewhat critical of sociologists of law because of what they perceive as the sociologist's preoccupation with the application of theory and methodology to the examination of legal phenomena, without regard to the solution of legal problems. Further, it is felt that "contemporary writing in the sociology of law . . . betrays the existence of painfully unsophisticated notions about the day-to-day operations of courts, legislatures and law offices."[1] Regardless of the merit of such criticism, scant attention—apart from explorations of the legal profession itself—has been given to the sociological examination of legal institutions, or their supporting ideological assumptions. Thus, for example, very little sociological effort is expended to ascertain the validity and viability of important court decisions, which may rest on wholly erroneous assumptions about contextual realities of social structure. A particular decision may rest upon a legally impeccable rationale; at the same time it may be rendered nugatory or self-defeating by contingencies imposed by aspects of social reality of which the lawmakers are themselves unaware.

Within this context, I wish to question the impact of three recent landmark decisions of the United States Supreme Court; each hailed as destined to effect profound changes in the future of criminal law administration and enforcement in America. The first of these,

SOURCE: *Law and Society Review* 1 (June 1967): 15–39. Copyright © 1967 by the Law and Society Association and reprinted by its permission.

[1]H. W. Jones, "A View from the Bridge," *Law and Society,* Supplement to summer 1965 issue of *Social Problems* 42 (1965). See G. Geis, "Sociology, Criminology, and Criminal Law," *Social Problems* 7, (1959), 40–47. N. S. Timasheff, "Growth and Scope of Sociology of Law," in *Modern Sociological Theory in Community and Change,* H. Becker and A. Boskoff, eds., 1957, pp. 424–49, for further evaluation of the strained relations between sociology and law.

Gideon v. *Wainwright,* 372 U.S. 335 (1963) required states and locali-
ties henceforth to furnish counsel in the case of indigent persons
charged with a felony.[2] The *Gideon* ruling left several major issues
unsettled, among them the vital question: What is the precise point
in time at which a suspect is entitled to counsel?[3] The answer came
relatively quickly in *Escobedo* v. *Illinois,* 378 U.S. 478 (1964), which
has aroused a storm of controversy. Danny Escobedo confessed to the
murder of his brother-in-law after the police had refused to permit
retained counsel to see him, although his lawyer was present in the
station house and asked to confer with his client. In a 5–4 decision,
the court asserted that counsel must be permitted when the process
of police investigative effort shifts from merely investigatory to that
of accusatory, "when its focus is on the accused and its purpose is to
elicit a confession—our adversary system begins to operate, and,
under the circumstances here, the accused must be permitted to
consult with his lawyer."

As a consequence, Escobedo's confession was rendered inadmissible. The decision triggered a national debate among police, district
attorneys, judges, lawyers, and other law enforcement officials,
which continues unabated, as to the value and propriety of confes-

[2]This decision represented the climax of a line of cases which had begun to chip
away at the notion that the Sixth Amendment of the Constitution (right to assistance
of counsel) applied only to the federal government, and could not be held to run
against the states through the Fourteenth Amendment. An exhaustive historical
analysis of the Fourteenth Amendment and the Bill of Rights will be found in C.
Fairman, "Does the Fourteenth Amendment Incorporate the Bill of Rights? The Original Understanding," *Stan. L. Rev.* 2: (1949), 5–139. Since the *Gideon* decision, there is
already evidence that its effect will ultimately extend to indigent persons charged
with misdemeanors—and perhaps ultimately even traffic cases and other minor
offenses. For a popular account of this important development in connection with the
right to assistance of counsel, see A. Lewis, *Gideon's Trumpet* (1964). For a sholarly
historical analysis of the right to counsel see W. M. Beaney, *The Right to Counsel in
American Courts* (1955). For a more recent comprehensive review and discussion of
the right to counsel and its development, see Note, "Counsel at Interrogation," *Yale
L. J.* 73 (1964), 1000–57.

With the passage of the Criminal Justice Act of 1964, indigent accused persons in
the federal courts will be defended by federally paid legal counsel. For a general
discussion of the nature and extent of public and private legal aid in the United States
prior to the *Gideon* case, see E. A. Brownell, *Legal Aid in the United States* (1961);
also R. B. von Mehren et al., *Equal Justice for the Accused* (1959).

[3]In the case of federal defendants the issue is clear. In *Mallory* v. *United States,* 354
U.S. 449 (1957), the Supreme Court unequivocally indicated that a person under federal
arrest must be taken "without any unnecessary delay" before a U.S. Commissioner
where he will receive information as to his rights to remain silent and to assistance
of counsel which will be furnished, in the event he is indigent, under the Criminal
Justice Act of 1964. For a most interesting and righly documented work in connection
with the general area of the Bill of Rights, see C. R. Sowle, *Police Power and Individual Freedom* (1962).

sions in criminal cases.[4] On June 13, 1966, the Supreme Court in a 5–4 decision underscored the principle enunciated in *Escobedo* in the case of *Miranda* v. *Arizona*.[5] Police interrogation of any suspect in custody, without his consent, unless a defense attorney is present, is prohibited by the self-incrimination provision of the Fifth Amendment. Regardless of the relative merit of the various shades of opinion about the role of counsel in criminal cases, the issues generated thereby will be in part resolved as additional cases move toward decision in the Supreme Court in the near future. They are of peripheral interest and not of immediate concern in this paper. However, the *Gideon, Escobedo,* and *Miranda* cases pose interesting general questions. In all three decisions, the Supreme Court reiterates the traditional legal conception of a defense lawyer based on the ideological perception of a criminal case as an *adversary, combative* proceeding, in which counsel for the defense assiduously musters all the admittedly limited resources at his command to *defend* the accused.[6] The fundamental question remains to be answered: Does the Supreme Court's conception of the role of counsel in a criminal case square with social reality?

The task of this paper is to furnish some preliminary evidence toward the illumination of that question. Little empirical understanding of the function of defense counsel exists; only some ideologically oriented generalizations and commitments. This paper is based upon observations made by the writer during many years of legal practice in the criminal courts of a large metropolitan area. No claim is made as to its methodological rigor, although it does reflect a conscious and sustained effort for participant observation.

[4]See *N.Y. Times,* Nov. 20, 1965, p. 1, for Justice Nathan R. Sobel's statement to the effect that based on his study of 1,000 indictments in Brooklyn, N.Y., from February–April, 1965, fewer than 10 percent involved confessions. Sobel's detailed analysis will be found in six articles which appeared in the *New York Law Journal,* beginning November 15, 1965, through November 21, 1965, titled "The Exclusionary Rules in the Law of Confessions: A Legal Perspective—A Practical Perspective." Most law enforcement officials believe that the majority of convictions in criminal cases are based upon confessions obtained by police. For example, the District Attorney of New York County (a jurisdiction which has the largest volume of cases in the United States), Frank S. Hogan, reports that confessions are crucial and indicates "if a suspect is entitled to have a lawyer during preliminary questioning . . . any lawyer worth his fee will tell him to keep his mouth shut," *N.Y. Times,* Dec. 2, 1965, p. 1. Concise discussions of the issue are to be found in D. Robinson, Jr., "Massiah, Escobedo and Rationales for the Exclusion of Confession," *J. Crim. L. C. & P.S.* 56 (1965), 412–31; D. C. Dowling, "Escobedo and Beyond: The Need for a Fourteenth Amendment Code of Criminal Procedure," *J. Crim. L. C. & P.S.* 56 (1965), 143–57.

[5]*Miranda* v. *Arizona,* 384 U.S. 436 (1966).

[6]Even under optimal circumstances a criminal case is a very much one-sided affair, the parties to the "contest" being decidedly unequal in strength and resources. See A. S. Goldstein, "The State and the Accused: Balance of Advantage in Criminal Procedure," *Yale L. J.* 69 (1960), 1149–99.

Court Structure Defines Role of Defense Lawyer

The overwhelming majority of convictions in criminal cases (usually over 90 percent) are not the product of a combative trial-by-jury process at all, but instead merely involve the sentencing of the individual after a negotiated, bargained-for plea of guilty has been entered.[7] Although more recently the overzealous role of police and prosecutors in producing pretrial confessions and admissions has achieved a good deal of notoriety, scant attention has been paid to the organizational structure and personnel of the criminal court itself. Indeed, the extremely high conviction rate produced without the features of an adversary trial in our courts would tend to suggest that the "trial" becomes a perfunctory reiteration and validation of the pretrial interrogation and investigation.[8]

The institutional setting of the court defines a role for the defense counsel in a criminal case radically different from the one traditionally depicted.[9] Sociologists and others have focused their attention on the deprivations and social disabilities of such variables as race, ethnicity, and social class as being the source of an accused person's defeat in a criminal court. Largely overlooked is the variable of the court organization itself, which possesses a thrust, purpose, and direction of its own. It is grounded in pragmatic values, bureaucratic priorities, and administrative instruments. These exalt maximum production and the particularistic career designs of organizational incumbents, whose occupational and career commitments tend to

[7]F. J. Davis et al., *Society and the Law: New Meanings for an Old Profession* (1962), 301; L. Orfield *Criminal Procedure from Arrest to Appeal (1947)*, 297.

D. J. Newman, "Pleading Guilty for Considerations: A Study of Bargain Justice," *J. Crim. L. C. & P.S.* 46 (1954), 780–90. Newman's data covered only one year, 1954, in a midwestern community, however, it is in general confirmed by my own data drawn from a far more populous area, and from what is one of the major criminal courts in the country, for a period of fifteen years from 1950 to 1964 inclusive. The English experience tends also to confirm American data, see N. Walker, *Crime and Punishment in Britain: An Analysis of the Penal System* (1965). See also D. J. Newman, *Conviction: The Determination of Guilt or Innocence without Trial* (1966), for a comprehensive legalistic study of the guilty plea sponsored by the American Bar Foundation. The criminal court as a social system, an analysis of "bargaining" and its functions in the criminal court's organizational structure, are examined in my forthcoming book, *The Criminal Court: A Sociological Perspective*, to be published by Quadrangle Books, Chicago.

[8]G. Feifer, *Justice in Moscow* (1965). The Soviet trial has been termed "an appeal from the pretrial investigation" and Feifer notes that the Soviet "trial" is simply a recapitulation of the data collected by the pretrial investigator. The notions of a trial being a "tabula rasa" and presumptions of innocence are wholly alien to Soviet notions of justice. "The closer the investigation resembles the finished script, the better" (at 86).

[9]For a concise statement of the constitutional and economic aspects of the right to legal assistance, see M. G. Paulsen, *Equal Justice for the Poor Man* (1964); for a brief traditional description of the legal profession, see P. A. Freund, "The Legal Profession." *Daedalus* (1963), 689–700.

generate a set of priorities. These priorities exert a higher claim than the stated ideological goals of "due process of law" and are often inconsistent with them.

Organizational goals and discipline impose a set of demands and conditions of practice on the respective professions in the criminal court, to which they respond by abandoning their ideological and professional commitments to the accused client, in the service of these higher claims of the court organization. All court personnel, including the accused's own lawyer, tend to be coopted to become agent-mediators[10] who help the accused redefine his situation and restructure his perceptions concomitant with a plea of guilty.

Of all the occupational roles in the court the only private individual who is officially recognized as having a special status and concomitant obligations is the lawyer. His legal status is that of "an officer of the court" and he is held to a standard of ethical performance and duty to his client as well as to the court. This obligation is thought to be far higher than that expected of ordinary individuals occupying the various occupational statuses in the court community. However, lawyers, whether privately retained or of the legal-aid, public defender variety, have close and continuing relations with the prosecuting office and the court itself through discreet relations with the judges via their law secretaries or "confidential" assistants. Indeed, lines of communication, influence and contact with those offices, as well as with the Office of the Clerk of the court, Probation Division, and with the press, are essential to present and prospective requirements of criminal law practice. Similarly, the subtle involvement of the press and other mass media in the court's organizational network is not readily discernible to the casual observer. Accused persons come and go in the court system schema, but the structure and its occupational incumbents remain to carry on their respective career, occupational, and organizational enterprises. The individual stridencies, tensions, and conflicts a given accused person's case may present to all the participants are overcome, because the formal and informal relations of all the groups in the court setting require it. The probability of continued future relations and interaction must be preserved at all costs.

This is particularly true of the "lawyer regulars" i.e., those defense lawyers, who by virtue of their continuous appearances in behalf of defendants, tend to represent the bulk of a criminal court's nonindigent case workload, and those lawyers who are not "regulars," who appear almost casually in behalf of an occasional client. Some of the "lawyer regulars" are highly visible as one moves about the major

---

[10]I use the concept in the general sense that Erving Goffman employed it in his *Asylums: Essays on the Social Situation of Mental Patients and Other Inmates (1961).*

urban centers of the nation, their offices line the back streets of the courthouses, at times sharing space with bondsmen. Their political "visibility" in terms of local clubhouse ties, reaching into the judge's chambers and prosecutor's office, are also deemed essential to successful practitioners. Previous research has indicated that the "lawyer regulars" make no effort to conceal their dependence upon police, bondsmen, jail personnel. Nor do they conceal the necessity for maintaining intimate relations with all levels of personnel in the court setting as a means of obtaining, maintaining, and building their practice. These informal relations are the *sine qua non* not only of retaining a practice, but also in the negotiation of pleas and sentences.[11]

The client, then, is a secondary figure in the court system as in certain other bureaucratic settings.[12] He becomes a means to other ends of the organization's incumbents. He may present doubts, contingencies, and pressures which challenge existing informal arrangements or disrupt them; but these tend to be resolved in favor of the continuance of the organization and its relations as before. There is a greater community of interest among all the principal organizational structures and their incumbents than exists elsewhere in other settings. The accused's lawyer has far greater professional, economic, intellectual and other ties to the various elements of the court system than he does to his own client. In short, the court is a closed community.

This is more than just the case of the usual "secrets" of bureaucracy which are fanatically defended from an outside view. Even all elements of the press are zealously determined to report on that which will not offend the board of judges, the prosecutor, probation, legal-aid, or other officials, in return for privileges and courtesies granted in the past and to be granted in the future. Rather than any view of the matter in terms of some variation of a "conspiracy" hypothesis, the simple explanation is one of an ongoing system handling delicate tensions, managing the trauma produced by law enforcement and administration, and requiring almost pathological distrust of "outsiders" bordering on group paranoia.

[11]A. L. Wood, "Informal Relations in the Practice of Criminal Law." *Am. J. Soc.* 62, (1956); 48–55; J. E. Carlin, *Lawyers on Their Own* (1962), 105–109; R. Goldfarb, *Ransom —A Critique of the American Bail System* (1965), 114–15. Relatively recent data as to recruitment to the legal profession, and variables involved in the type of practice engaged in, will be found in J. Ladinsky, "Careers of Lawyers, Law Practice, and Legal Institutions," *Am. Soc. Rev.* 28 (1963); 47–54. See also S. Warkov and J. Zelan, *Lawyers in the Making (1965).*

[12]There is a real question to be raised as to whether in certain organizational settings, a complete reversal of the bureaucratic ideal has not occurred. That is, it would seem, in some instances the organization appears to exist to serve the needs of its various occupational incumbents, rather than its clients. A. Etzioni, *Modern Organizations (1964), 94–104.*

The hostile attitude toward "outsiders" is in large measure engendered by a defensiveness itself produced by the inherent deficiencies of assembly line justice, so characteristic of our major criminal courts. Intolerably large caseloads of defendants, which must be disposed of in an organizational context of limited resources and personnel, potentially subject the participants in the court community to harsh scrutiny from appellate courts, and other public and private sources of condemnation. As a consequence, an almost irreconcilable conflict is posed in terms of intense pressures to process large numbers of cases on the one hand, and the stringent ideological and legal requirements of "due process of law," on the other hand. A rather tenuous resolution of the dilemma has emerged in the shape of a large variety of bureaucratically ordained and controlled "work crimes," short cuts, deviations, and outright rule violations adopted as court practice in order to meet production norms. Fearfully anticipating criticism on ethical as well as legal grounds, all the significant participants in the court's social structure are bound into an organized system of complicity. This consists of a work arrangement in which the patterned, covert, informal breaches, and evasions of "due process" are institutionalized, but are, nevertheless, denied to exist.

These institutionalized evasions will be found to occur to some degree in all criminal courts. Their nature, scope, and complexity are largely determined by the size of the court and the character of the community in which it is located, e.g., whether it is a large, urban institution or a relatively small rural county court. In addition, idiosyncratic local conditions may contribute to a unique flavor in the character and quality of the criminal law's administration in a particular community. However, in most instances a variety of stratagems are employed—some subtle, some crude—in effectively disposing of what are often too large caseloads. A wide variety of coercive devices are employed against an accused client, couched in a depersonalized, instrumental, bureaucratic version of due process of law, and which are in reality a perfunctory obeisance to the ideology of due process. These include some very explicit pressures which are exerted in some measure by all court personnel, including judges, to plead guilty and avoid trial. In many instances the sanction of a potentially harsh sentence is utilized as the visible alternative to pleading guilty, in the case of recalcitrants. Probation and psychiatric reports are "tailored" to organizational needs, or are at least responsive to the court organization's requirements for the refurbishment of a defendant's social biography, consonant with his new status. A resourceful judge can, through his subtle domination of the proceedings, impose his will on the final outcome of a trial. Stenographers and clerks, in their function as record keepers, are on occasion pressed into service in support of a judicial need to "rewrite" the record of a courtroom event. Bail practices are usually employed for purposes other than simply assuring a defendant's presence on the date of a hearing in connection with his case. Too often, the discretionary power as to bail is part of the arsenal of weapons available to collapse the resistance of an accused person. The foregoing is a most cursory examination of some of the more prominent "short cuts" available to any court organization. There are numerous other procedural strategies constituting due process deviations, which tend to become the work style artifacts of a court's personnel. Thus, only court "regulars" who are "bound in" are really accepted; others are treated routinely and in almost a coldly correct manner.

The defense attorneys, therefore, whether of the legal-aid, public defender variety or privately retained, although operating in terms of pressures specific to their respective role and organizational obligations, ultimately are concerned with strategies which tend to lead to a plea. It is the rational, impersonal elements involving economies of time, labor, expense and a superior commitment of the defense counsel to these rationalistic values of maximum production[13] of court organization that prevail, in his relationship with a client. The lawyer "regulars" are frequently former staff members of the prosecutor's office and utilize the prestige, know-how and contacts of their former affiliation as part of their stock in trade. Close and continuing relations between the lawyer "regular" and his former colleagues in the prosecutor's office generally overshadow the relationship between the regular and his client. The continuing colleagueship of supposedly adversary counsel rests on real professional and organizational needs of a *quid pro quo*, which goes beyond the limits of an accommodation or *modus vivendi* one might ordinarily expect under the circumstances of an otherwise seemingly adversary relationship. Indeed, the adversary features which are manifest are for the most part muted and exist even in their attenuated form largely for external consumption. The principals, lawyer and assistant district attorney, rely upon one another's cooperation for their contin-

[13]Three relatively recent items reported in the *N.Y. Times* tend to underscore this point as it has manifested itself in one of the major criminal courts. In one instance the Bronx County Bar Association condemned "mass assembly-line justice," which "was rushing defendants into pleas of guilty and into convictions, in violation of their legal rights." *N.Y. Times*, March 10, 1965, p. 51. Another item, appearing somewhat later that year reports a judge criticizing his own court system (the New York Criminal Court), that "pressure to set statistical records in disposing of cases had hurt the administration of justice." *N.Y. Times*, Nov. 4, 1965, p. 49. A third, and most unusual recent public discussion in the press was a statement by a leading New York appellate judge decrying "instant justice" which is employed to reduce court calendar congestion "converting our courthouses into counting houses . . ., as in most big cities where the volume of business tends to overpower court facilities." *N.Y. Times*, Feb. 5, 1966. p. 58.

ued professional existence, and so the bargaining between them
tends usually to be "reasonable" rather than fierce.

Fee Collection and Fixing

The real key to understanding the role of defense counsel in a criminal case is to be found in the area of the fixing of the fee to be charged
and its collection. The problem of fixing and collecting the fee tends
to influence to a significant degree the criminal court process itself,
and not just the relationship of the lawyer and his client. In essence,
a lawyer-client "confidence game" is played. A true confidence game
is unlike the case of the emperor's new clothes wherein that mo-
narch's nakedness was a result of inordinate gullibility and
credulity. In a genuine confidence game, the perpetrator manipulates the basic dishonesty of his partner, the victim or mark, toward
his own (the confidence operator's) ends. Thus, "the victim of a con
scheme must have some larceny in his heart."[14]

Legal service lends itself particularly well to confidence games.
Usually a plumber will be able to demonstrate empirically that he
has performed a service by clearing up the stuffed drain, repairing
the leaky faucet or pipe—and therefore merits his fee. He has rendered, when summoned, a visible, tangible boon for his client in
return for the requested fee. A physician who has not performed
some visible surgery or otherwise engaged in some readily discernible procedure in connection with a patient may be deemed by the
patient to have "done nothing" for him. As a consequence, medical
practitioners may simply prescribe or administer by injection a
placebo to overcome a patient's potential reluctance or dissatisfaction in paying a requested fee "for nothing."

In the practice of law there is a special problem in this regard, no
matter what the level of the practitioner or his place in the hierarchy
of prestige. Much legal work is intangible either because it is simply
a few words of advice, some preventive action, a telephone call,
negotiation of some kind, a form filled out and filed, a hurried conference with another attorney or an official of a government agency, a
letter or opinion written, or a countless variety of seemingly innocuous and even prosaic procedures and actions. These are the basic
activities, apart from any possible court appearance, of almost all
lawyers, at all levels of practice. Much of the activity is not in the
nature of the exercise of the traditional, precise professional skills of
the attorney such as library research and oral argument in connection with appellate briefs, court motions, trial work, drafting of
opinions, memoranda, contracts, and other complex documents and
agreements. Instead, much legal activity, whether it is at the lowest
or highest "white shoe" law firm levels, is of the brokerage, agent,

---

[14]R. L. Glasser, "The Confidence Game," *Fed. Prob.* 27 (1963), 47.

sales representative, lobbyist type of activity, in which the lawyer acts for someone else in pursuing the latter's interests and designs. The service is intangible.[15]

The large-scale law firm may not speak as openly of their "contacts," their "fixing" abilities, as does the lower level lawyer. They trade instead upon a façade of thick carpeting, walnut paneling, genteel low pressure, and superficialities of traditional legal professionalism. There are occasions when even the large firm is on the defensive in connection with the fees they charge because the services rendered or results obtained do not appear to merit the fee asked.[16] Therefore, there is a recurrent problem in the legal profession in fixing the amount of fee and in justifying the basis for the requested fee.

Although the fee at times amounts to what the traffic and the conscience of the lawyer will bear, one further observation must be made with regard to the size of the fee and its collection. The defendant in a criminal case and the material gain he may have acquired during the course of his illicit activities are soon parted. Not infrequently the ill-gotten fruits of the various modes of larceny are sequestered by a defense lawyer in payment of his fee. Inexorably, the amount of the fee is a function of the dollar value of the crime committed, and is frequently set with meticulous precision at a sum which bears an uncanny relationship to that of the net proceeds of the particular offense involved. On occasion, defendants have been known to commit additional offenses while at liberty on bail, in order to secure the requisite funds with which to meet their obligations for payment of legal fees. Defense lawyers condition even the most obtuse clients to recognize that there is a firm interconnection between fee payment and the zealous exercise of professional expertise, secret knowledge, and organizational "connections" in their behalf. Lawyers, therefore, seek to keep their clients in a proper state of tension, and to arouse in them the precise edge of anxiety which is calculated to encourage prompt fee payment. Consequently, the client attitude in the relationship between defense counsel and an accused is in many instances a precarious admixture of hostility, mistrust, dependence, and sycophancy. By keeping his client's anxieties aroused to the proper pitch and establishing a seeming causal relationship between a requested fee and the accused's ultimate extrication from his onerous difficulties, the lawyer will have established the necessary preliminary groundwork to assure a minimum of haggling over the fee and its eventual payment.

In varying degrees, as a consequence, all law practice involves a manipulation of the client and a stage management of the lawyer-

[15]C. W. Mills, *White Collar* (1951), 121–29; J. E. Carlin, *supra*, note 11.

[16]E. O. Smigel, *The Wall Street Lawyer*, New York: The Free Press of Glencoe, 1964, p. 309.

client relationship so that at least an *appearance* of help and service
will be forthcoming. This is accomplished in a variety of ways, often
exercised in combination with each other. At the outset, the lawyer-
professional employs with suitable variation a measure of sales-puff
which may range from an air of unbounding self-confidence, adequacy, and dominion over events to that of complete arrogance. This
will be supplemented by the affectation of a studied, faultless mode
of personal attire. In the larger firms, the furnishings and office
trappings will serve as the backdrop to help in impression management and client intimidation. In all firms, solo or large-scale, an
access to secret knowledge, and to the seats of power and influence,
is inferred or presumed to a varying degree as the basic vendible
commodity of the practitioners.

The lack of visible end product offers a special complication in the
course of the professional life of the criminal court lawyer with
respect to his fee and in his relations with his client. The plain fact
is that an accused in a criminal case always "loses" even when he has
been exonerated by an acquittal, discharge, or dismissal of his case.
The hostility of an accused which follows as a consequence of his
arrest, incarceration, possible loss of job, expense and other traumas
connected with his case is directed, by means of displacement, toward his lawyer. It is in this sense that it may be said that a criminal
lawyer never really "wins" a case. The really satisfied client is rare,
since in the very nature of the situation even an accused's vindica-
tion leaves him with some degree of dissatisfaction and hostility. It
is this state of affairs that makes for a lawyer-client relationship in
the criminal court which tends to be a somewhat exaggerated version of the usual lawyer-client confidence game.

At the outset, because there are great risks of nonpayment of the
fee, due to the impecuniousness of his clients, and the fact that a man
who is sentenced to jail may be a singularly unappreciative client,
the criminal lawyer collects his fee *in advance.* Often, because the
lawyer and the accused both have questionable designs of their own
upon each other, the confidence game can be played. The criminal
lawyer must serve three major functions or, stated another way, he
must solve three problems. First, he must arrange for his fee; second,
he must prepare and then, if necessary, "cool out" his client in case
of defeat[17] (a highly likely contingency); third, he must satisfy the

---

[17]Talcott Parsons indicates that the social role and function of the lawyer can be
therapeutic, helping his client psychologically in giving him necessary emotional
support at critical times. The lawyer is also said to be acting as an agent of social
control in the counseling of his client and in the influencing of his course of conduct.
See T. Parsons, *Essays in Sociological Theory* (1954), 382 et seq.; E. Goffman, "On
Cooling the Mark Out: Some Aspects of Adaptation to Failure," in *Human Behavior
and Social Processes,* A. Rose ed. (1962), 482–505. Goffman's "cooling out" analysis is
especially relevant in the lawyer-accused client relationship.

court organization that he has performed adequately in the process of negotiating the plea, so as to preclude the possibility of any sort of embarrassing incident which may serve to invite "outside" scrutiny.

In assuring the attainment of one of his primary objectives, his fee, the criminal lawyer will very often enter into negotiations with the accused's kin, including collateral relatives. In many instances, the accused himself is unable to pay any sort of fee or anything more than a token fee. It then becomes important to involve as many of the accused's kin as possible in the situation. This is especially so if the attorney hopes to collect a significant part of a proposed substantial fee. It is not uncommon for several relatives to contribute toward the fee. The larger the group, the greater the possibility that the lawyer will collect a sizable fee by getting contributions from each.

A fee for a felony case which ultimately results in a plea, rather than a trial, may ordinarily range anywhere from $500 to $1,500. Should the case go to trial, the fee will be proportionately larger, depending upon the length of the trial. But the larger the fee the lawyer wishes to exact, the more impressive his performance must be, in terms of his stage-managed image as a personage of great influence and power in the court organization. Court personnel are keenly aware of the extent to which a lawyer's stock in trade involves the precarious stage management of an image which goes beyond the usual professional flamboyance, and for this reason alone the lawyer is "bound in" to the authority system of the court's organizational discipline. Therefore, to some extent, court personnel will aid the lawyer in the creation and maintenance of that impression. There is a tacit commitment to the lawyer by the court organization, apart from formal etiquette, to aid him in this. Such augmentation of the lawyer's stage-managed image as this affords is the partial basis for the *quid pro quo* which exists between the lawyer and the court organization. It tends to serve as the continuing basis for the higher loyalty of the lawyer to the organization; his relationship with his client, in contrast, is transient, ephemeral and often superficial.

Defense Lawyer as Double Agent

The lawyer has often been accused of stirring up unnecessary litigation, especially in the field of negligence. He is said to acquire a vested interest in a cause of action or claim which was initially his client's. The strong incentive of possible fee motivates the lawyer to promote litigation which would otherwise never have developed.

However, the criminal lawyer develops a vested interest of an entirely different nature in his client's case: to limit its scope and duration rather than do battle. Only in this way can a case be "profitable." Thus, he enlists the aid of relatives not only to assure payment of his fee, but he will also rely on these persons to help him in his agent-mediator role of convincing the accused to plead guilty, and ultimately to help in "cooling out" the accused if necessary.

It is at this point that an accused-defendant may experience his first sense of "betrayal." While he had perhaps perceived the police and prosecutor to be adversaries, or possibly even the judge, the accused is wholly unprepared for his counsel's role performance as an agent-mediator. In the same vein, it is even less likely to occur to an accused that members of his own family or other kin may become agents, albeit at the behest and urging of other agents or mediators, acting on the principle that they are in reality helping an accused negotiate the best possible plea arrangement under the circumstances. Usually, it will be the lawyer who will activate next of kin in this role, his ostensible motive being to arrange for his fee. But soon latent and unstated motives will assert themselves, with entreaties by counsel to the accused's next of kin, to appeal to the accused to "help himself" by pleading. *Gemeinshaft* sentiments are to this extent exploited by a defense lawyer (or even at times by a district attorney) to achieve specific secular ends, that is, of concluding a particular matter with all possible dispatch.

The fee is often collected in stages, each installment usually payable prior to a necessary court appearance required during the course of an accused's career journey. At each stage, in his interviews and communications with the accused, or in addition, with members of his family, if they are helping with the fee payment, the lawyer employs an air of professional confidence and "inside-dopesterism" in order to assuage anxieties on all sides. He makes the necessary bland assurances, and in effect manipulates his client, who is usually willing to do and say the things, true or not, which will help his attorney extricate him. Since the dimensions of what he is essentially selling, organizational influence and expertise, are not technically and precisely measurable, the lawyer can make extravagant claims of influence and secret knowledge with impunity. Thus, lawyers frequently claim to have inside knowledge in connection with information in the hands of the D.A., police, probation officials or to have access to these functionaries. Factually, they often do, and need only to exaggerate the nature of their relationships with them to obtain the desired effective impression upon the client. But, as in the genuine confidence game, the victim who has participated is loath to do anything which will upset the lesser plea which his lawyer has "conned" him into accepting.[18]

In effect, in his role as double agent, the criminal lawyer performs an extremely vital and delicate mission for the court organization and the accused. Both principals are anxious to terminate the litigation with a minimum of expense and damage to each other. There is no other personage or role incumbent in the total court structure more strategically located, who by training and in terms of his own requirements is more ideally suited to do so than the lawyer. In recognition of this, judges will cooperate with attorneys in many important ways. For example, they will adjourn the case of an accused in jail awaiting plea or sentence if the attorney requests such action. While explicitly this may be done for some innocuous and seemingly valid reason, the tacit purpose is that pressure is being applied by the attorney for the collection of his fee, which he knows will probably not be forthcoming if the case is concluded. Judges are aware of this tactic on the part of lawyers, who, by requesting an adjournment, keep an accused incarcerated awhile longer as a not too subtle method of dunning a client for payment. However, the judges will go along with this, on the ground that important ends are being served. Often, the only end served is to protect a lawyer's fee.

The judge will help an accused's lawyer in still another way. He will lend the official aura of his office and courtroom so that a lawyer can stage-manage an impression of an "all-out" performance for the accused in justification of his fee. The judge and other court personnel will serve as a backdrop for a scene charged with dramatic fire, in which the accused's lawyer makes a stirring appeal in his behalf. With a show of restrained passion, the lawyer will intone the virtues of the accused and recite the social deprivations which have reduced him to his present state. The speech varies somewhat, depending on whether the accused has been convicted after trial or has pleaded guilty. In the main, however, the incongruity, superficiality, and ritualistic character of the total performance is underscored by a

---

[18]The question has never been raised as to whether "bargain justice," "copping a plea," or justice by negotiation is a constitutional process. Although it has become the most central aspect of the process of criminal law administration, it has received virtually no close scrutiny by the appellate courts. As a consequence it is relatively free of legal control and supervision. But, apart from any questions of the legality of bargaining, in terms of the pressures and devices that are employed which tend to violate due process of law, there remain ethical and practical questions. The system of bargain-counter justice is like the proverbial iceberg, much of its danger is concealed in secret negotiations and its least alarming feature, the final pleas, being the one presented to public view. See A. S. Trebach, *The Rationing of Justice* (1964), 74–94; Note, "Guilty Plea Bargaining: Compromises by Prosecutors to Secure Guilty Pleas," *U. Pa. L. Rev.* 112 (1964), 865–95.

visibly impassive, almost bored reaction on the part of the judge and other members of the court retinue.

Afterward, there is a hearty exchange of pleasantries between the lawyer and district attorney, wholly out of context in terms of the supposed adversary nature of the preceding events. The fiery passion in defense of his client is gone, and the lawyers for both sides resume their offstage relations, chatting amiably and perhaps including the judge in their restrained banter. No other aspect of their visible conduct so effectively serves to put even a casual observer on notice, that these individuals have claims upon each other. These seemingly innocuous actions are indicative of continuing organizational and informal relations, which, in their intricacy and depth, range far beyond any priorities or claims a particular defendant may have.[19]

Criminal law practice is a unique form of private law practice since it really only appears to be private practice.[20] Actually it is bureaucratic practice, because of the legal practitioner's enmeshment in the authority, discipline, and perspectives of the court organization. Private practice, supposedly, in a professional sense, involves the maintenance of an organized, disciplined body of knowledge and learning; the individual practitioners are imbued with a spirit of autonomy and service, the earning of a livelihood being incidental. In the sense that the lawyer in the criminal court serves as a double agent, serving higher organizational rather than professional ends, he may be deemed to be engaged in bureaucratic rather than private practice. To some extent the lawyer-client "confidence game," in addition to its other functions, serves to conceal this fact.

---

[19]For a conventional summary statement of some of the inevitable conflicting loyalties encountered in the practice of law, see E. E. Cheatham, *Cases and Materials on the Legal Profession* (2d ed., 1955), 70–79.

[20]Some lawyers at either end of the continuum of law practice appear to have grave doubts as to whether it is indeed a profession at all. J. E. Carlin, *supra,* note 11, at 192; E. O. Smigel, *supra,* note 16, at 304–5. Increasingly, it is perceived as a business with widespread evasion of the Cannons of Ethics, duplicity and chicanery being practiced in an effort to get and keep business. The poet, Carl Sandburg, epitomized this notion in the following vignette: "Have you a criminal lawyer in this burg?" "We think so but we haven't been able to prove it on him." C. Sandburg, *The People, Yes* (1936), 154.

Thus, while there is a considerable amount of dishonesty present in law practice involving fee splitting, thefts from clients, influence peddling, fixing, questionable use of favors and gifts to obtain business or influence others, this sort of activity is most often attributed to the "solo" private practice lawyer. See A. L. Wood, "Professional Ethics among Criminal Lawyers," *Social Problems* (1959), 70–73. However, to some degree, large-scale "downtown" elite firms also engage in these dubious activities. The difference is that the latter firms enjoy a good deal of immunity from these harsh charges because of their institutional and organizational advantages, in terms of near monopoly over more desirable types of practice, as well as exerting great influence in the political, economics, and professional realms of power.

The Client's Perception

The "cop-out" ceremony, in which the court process culminates, is not only invaluable for redefining the accused's perspectives of himself, but also in reiterating publicly in a formal structured ritual the accused person's guilt for the benefit of significant "others" who are observing. The accused not only is made to assert publicly his guilt of a specific crime, but also a complete recital of its details. He is further made to indicate that he is entering his plea of guilt freely, willingly, and voluntarily, and that he is not doing so because of any promises or in consideration of any commitments that may have been made to him by anyone. This last is intended as a blanket statement to shield the participants from any possible charges of "coercion" or undue influence that may have been exerted in violation of due process requirements. Its function is to preclude any later review by an appellate court on these grounds, and also to obviate any second thoughts an accused may develop in connection with his plea.

However, for the accused, the conception of self as a guilty person is in large measure a temporary role adaptation. His career socialization as an accused, if it is successful, eventuates in his acceptance and redefinition of himself as a guilty person.[21] However, the transformation is ephemeral in that he will, in private, quickly reassert his innocence. Of importance is that he accept his defeat, publicly proclaim it, and find some measure of pacification in it.[22] Almost immediately after his plea, a defendant will generally be interviewed by

[21]This does not mean that most of those who plead guilty are innocent of any crime. Indeed, in many instances those who have been able to negotiate a lesser plea have done so willingly and even eagerly. The system of justice-by-negotiation, without trial, probably tends to better serve the interests and requirements of guilty persons, who are thereby presented with formal alternatives of "half a loaf," in terms of, at worst, possibilities of a lesser plea and a concomitant shorter sentence as compensation for their acquiescence and participation. Having observed the prescriptive etiquette in compliance with the defendant role expectancies in this setting, he is rewarded. An innocent person, on the other hand, is confronted with the same set of rule prescriptions, structures, and legal alternatives, and in any event, for him this mode of justice is often an ineluctable bind.

[22]"Any communicative network between persons whereby the public identity of an actor is transformed into something looked on as lower in the local scheme of social types will be called a 'status degradation ceremony.'" H. Garfinkel, "Conditions of Successful Degradation Ceremonies," *Am. J. Soc.* 61 (1956), 420–24. But contrary to the conception of the "cop out" as a "status degradation ceremony" is the fact that it is in reality a charade, during the course of which an accused must project an appropriate and acceptable amount of guilt, penitence, and remorse. Having adequately feigned the role of the "guilty person," his hearers will engage in the fantasy that he is contrite, and thereby merits a lesser plea. It is one of the essential functions of the criminal lawyer that he coach and direct his accused-client in that role performance. Thus, what is actually involved is not a "degradation" process at all, but is instead, a highly structured system of exchange cloaked in the rituals of legalism and public professions of guilt and repentance.

a representative of the probation division in connection with a presentence report which is to be prepared. The very first question to
be asked of him by the probation officer is: "Are you guilty of the
crime to which you pleaded?" This is by way of double affirmation
of the defendant's guilt. Should the defendant now begin to make
bold assertions of his innocence, despite his plea of guilty, he will
be asked to withdraw his plea and stand trial on the original charges.
Such a threatened possibility is, in most instances, sufficient to cause
an accused to let the plea stand and to request the probation officer
to overlook his exclamations of innocence. The table that follows is
a breakdown of the categorized responses of a random sample of
male defendants in Metropolitan Court[23] during 1962, 1963, and 1964
in connection with their statements during presentence probation
interviews following their plea of guilty.

It would be well to observe at the outset that, of the 724 defendants
who pleaded guilty before trial, only 43 (5.94 percent) of the total
group had confessed prior to their indictment. Thus, the ultimate
judicial process was predicated upon evidence independent of any
confession of the accused.[24]

As the data indicate, only a relatively small number (95) out of the
total number of defendants actually will even admit their guilt,
following the "cop-out" ceremony. However, even though they have
affirmed their guilt, many of these defendants felt that they should
have been able to negotiate a more favorable plea. The largest aggregate of defendants (373) were those who reasserted their "innocence"
following their public profession of guilt during the "cop-out" ceremony. These defendants employed differential degrees of fervor,
solemnity, and credibility, ranging from really mild, wavering assertions of innocence which were embroidered with a variety of stock
explanations and rationalizations, to those of an adamant, "framed"
nature. Thus, the "Innocent" group, for the most part, were largely
concerned with underscoring for their probation interviewer their

---

[23]The name is of course fictitious. However, the actual court which served as the
universe from which the data were drawn is one of the largest criminal courts in the
United States, dealing with felonies only. Female defendants in the years 1950
through 1964 constituted from 7–10 percent of the totals for each year.

[24]My own data in this connection would appear to support Sobel's conclusion (see
note 4 *supra*), and appears to be at variance with the prevalent view, which stresses
the importance of confessions in law enforcement and prosecution. All the persons
in my sample were originally charged with felonies ranging from homicide to forgery; in most instances the original felony charges were reduced to misdemeanors by
way of a negotiated lesser plea. The vast range of crime categories which are available
facilitates the patterned court process of plea reduction to a lesser offense, which is
also usually a socially less opprobrious crime. For an illustration of this feature of the
bargaining process in a court utilizing a public defender office, see D. Sudnow. "Normal Crimes: Sociological Features of the Penal Code in a Public Defender Office," *Social
Problems* 12 (1964), 255–76.

Table 1. Defendant Responses as to Guilt or Innocence after Pleading Guilty
(N = 724; Years, 1962, 1963, 1964)

Nature of Response		N of Defendants
Innocent (Manipulated)	"The lawyer or judge, police or D.A. 'conned me'"	86
Innocent (Pragmatic)	"Wanted to get it over with" "You can't beat the system" "They have you over a barrel when you have a record"	147
Innocent (Advice of counsel)	"Followed my lawyer's advice"	92
Innocent (Defiant)	"Framed" "Betrayed by Complainant," "Police," "Squealers," "Lawyer," "Friends," "Wife," "Girlfriend"	33
Innocent (Adverse social data)	Blames probation officer or psychiatrist for "bad report," in cases where there was prepleading investigation	15
Guilty	"But I should have gotten a better deal" Blames Lawyer, D.A., Police, Judge	74
Guilty	Won't say anything further	21
Fatalistic (Doesn't press his "Innocence," won't admit "Guilt")	"I did it for convenience" "My lawyer told me it was only thing I could do" "I did it because it was the best way out"	248
No Response		8
Total		724

essential "goodness" and "worthiness," despite their formal plea of guilty. Assertion of his innocence at the post-plea stage, resurrects a more respectable and acceptable self-concept for the accused defendant who has pleaded guilty. A recital of the structural exigencies which precipitated his plea of guilt serves to embellish a newly proffered claim of innocence, which many defendants mistakenly feel will stand them in good stead at the time of sentence, or ultimately with probation or parole authorites.

Relatively few (33) maintained their innocence in terms of having been "framed" by some person or agent-mediator, although a larger number (86) indicated that they had been manipulated or "conned" by an agent-mediator to plead guilty, but as indicated, their assertions of innocence were relatively mild.

A rather substantial group (147) preferred to stress the pragmatic aspects of their plea of guilty. They would only perfunctorily assert their innocence and would in general refer to some adverse aspect of their situation which they believed tended to negatively affect their bargaining leverage, including in some instances a prior criminal record.

One group of defendants (92), while maintaining their innocence, simply employed some variation of a theme of following "the advice of counsel" as a covering response, to explain their guilty plea in the light of their new affirmation of innocence.

The largest single group of defendants (248) were basically fatalistic. They often verbalized weak suggestions of their innocence in rather halting terms, wholly without conviction. By the same token, they would not admit guilt readily and were generally evasive as to guilt or innocence, preferring to stress aspects of their stoic submission in their decision to plead. This sizable group of defendants appeared to perceive the total court process as being caught up in a monstrous organizational apparatus, in which the defendant role expectancies were not clearly defined. Reluctant to offend anyone in authority, fearful that clear-cut statements on their part as to their guilt or innocence would be negatively construed, they adopted a stance of passivity, resignation, and acceptance. Interestingly, they would in most instances invoke their lawyer as being the one who crystallized the available alternatives for them, and who was therefore the critical element in their decision-making process.

In order to determine which agent-mediator was most influential in altering the accused's perspectives as to his decision to plead or go to trial (regardless of the proposed basis of the plea), the same sample of defendants were asked to indicate the person who first suggested to them that they plead guilty. They were also asked to indicate which of the persons or officials who made such suggestion was most influential in affecting their final decision to plead.

Table 2 indicates the breakdown of the responses to the two questions.

It is popularly assumed that the police, through forced confessions, and the district attorney, employing still other pressures, are most instrumental in the inducement of an accused to plead guilty.[25] As Table 2 indicates, it is actually the defendant's own

[25]Failures, shortcomings and oppressive features of our system of criminal justice have been attributed to a variety of sources including "lawless" police, overzealous district attorneys, "hanging" juries, corruption and political connivance, incompetent judges, inadequacy or lack of counsel, and poverty or other social disabilities of the defendant. See A. Barth, *Law Enforcement versus the Law* (1963), for a journalist's account embodying this point of view; J. H. Skolnick, *Justice without Trial: Law Enforcement in Democratic Society* (1966), for a sociologist's study of the role of the police in criminal law administration. For a somewhat more detailed, albeit legalistic and somewhat technical, discussion of American police procedures, see W. R. LaFave, *Arrest: The Decision to Take a Suspect into Custody* (1965).

Table 2. Role of Agent-Mediators in Defendant's Guilty Plea

Person or Official	First Suggested Plea of Guilty	Influenced the Accused Most in His Final Decision to Plead
Judge	4	26
District attorney	67	116
Defense counsel	407	411
Probation officer	14	3
Psychiatrist	8	1
Wife	34	120
Friends and kin	21	14
Police	14	4
Fellow inmates	119	14
Others	28	5
No response	8	10
Total	724	724

counsel who is most effective in this role. Further, this phenomenon tends to reinforce the extremely rational nature of criminal law administration, for an organization could not rely upon the sort of idiosyncratic measures employed by the police to induce confessions and maintain its efficiency, high production, and over-all rational legal character. The defense counsel becomes the ideal agent-mediator since, as "officer of the court" and confidant of the accused and his kin, he lives astride both worlds and can serve the ends of the two as well as his own.[26]

While an accused's wife, for example, may be influential in making him more amenable to a plea, her agent-mediator role has, nevertheless, usually been sparked and initiated by defense counsel. Further, although a number of first suggestions of a plea came from an accused's fellow jail inmates, he tended to rely largely on his counsel as an ultimate source of influence in his final decision. The defense counsel, being a crucial figure in the total organizational scheme in constituting a new set of perspectives for the accused, the same sample of defendants were asked to indicate at which stage of their contact with counsel was the suggestion of a plea made. There are three basic kinds of defense counsel available in Metropolitan Court: legal-aid, privately retained counsel, and counsel assigned by the court (but may eventually be privately retained by the accused).

The overwhelming majority of accused persons, regardless of type of counsel, related a specific incident which indicated an urging or

[26]Aspects of the lawyer's ambivalences with regard to the expectancies of the various groups who have claims upon him, are discussed in H. J. O'Gorman, "The Ambivalence of Lawyers," paper presented at the Eastern Sociological Association meetings, April 10, 1965.

suggestion, either during the course of the first or second contact, that they plead guilty to a lesser charge if this could be arranged. Of all the agent-mediators, it is the lawyer who is most effective in manipulating an accused's perspectives, notwithstanding pressures that may have been previously applied by police, district attorney, judge, or any of the agent-mediators that may have been activated by them. Legal-aid and assigned counsel would apparently be more likely to suggest a possible plea at the point of initial interview as response to pressures of time. In the case of the assigned counsel, the strong possibility that there is no fee involved, may be an added impetus to such a suggestion at the first contact.

Table 3.   Stage at Which Counsel Suggested Accused to Plead
(N = 724)

| Contact | Counsel Type | | | | | | | |
| | Privately Retained | | Legal-aid | | Assigned | | Total | |
	N	%	N	%	N	%	N	%
First	66	35	237	49	28	60	331	46
Second	83	44	142	29	8	17	233	32
Third	29	15	63	13	4	9	96	13
Fourth or more	12	6	31	7	5	11	48	7
No response	0	0	14	3	2	4	16	2
Total	190	100	487	100*	47	101*	724	100

*Rounded percentage.

In addition, there is some further evidence in Table 3 of the perfunctory, ministerial character of the system in Metropolitan Court and similar criminal courts. There is little real effort to individualize, and the lawyer's role as agent-mediator may be seen as unique in that he is in effect a double agent. Although, as "officer of the court" he mediates between the court organization and the defendant, his roles with respect to each are rent by conflicts of interest. Too often these must be resolved in favor of the organization which provides him with the means for his professional existence. Consequently, in order to reduce the strains and conflicts imposed in what is ultimately an overdemanding role obligation for him, the lawyer engages in the lawyer-client "confidence game" so as to structure more favorably an otherwise onerous role system.[27]

[27]W. J. Goode, "A Theory of Role Strain." Am. Soc. Rev. 14 (1960), 483–96; J. D. Snoek, "Role Strain in Diversified Role Sets, Am. J. Soc. 71 (1966), 363–72.

Conclusion

Recent decisions of the Supreme Court, in the area of criminal law administration and defendant's rights, fail to take into account three crucial aspects of social structure which may tend to render the more libertarian rules as nugatory. The decisions overlook (1) the nature of courts as formal organizations; (2) the relationship that the lawyer-regular *actually* has with the court organization; and (3) the character of the lawyer-client relationship in the criminal court (the routine relationships, not those unusual ones that are described in "heroic" terms in novels, movies, and TV).

Courts, like many other modern large-scale organizations possess a monstrous appetite for the cooptation of entire professional groups as well as individuals.[28] Almost all those who come within the ambit of organizational authority, find that their definitions, perceptions, and values have been refurbished, largely in terms favorable to the particular organization and its goals. As a result, recent Supreme Court decisions may have a long-range effect which is radically different from that intended or anticipated. The more libertarian rules will tend to produce the rather ironic end result of augmenting the *existing* organizational arrangements, enriching court organizations with more personnel and elaborate structure, which in turn will maximize organizational goals of "efficiency" and production. Thus, many defendants will find that courts will possess an even more sophisticated apparatus for processing them toward a guilty plea!

---

[28]Some of the resources which have become an integral part of our courts, e.g., psychiatry, social work and probation, were originally intended as part of an ameliorative, therapeutic effort to individualize offenders. However, there is some evidence that a quite different result obtains, than the one originally intended. The ameliorative instruments have been coopted by the court in order to more "efficiently" deal with a court's caseload, often to the legal disadvantage of an accused person. See F. A. Allen, *The Borderland of Criminal Justice* (1964); T. S. Szasz, *Law, Liberty and Psychiatry* (1963) and also Szasz's most recent, *Psychiatric Justice* (1965); L. Diana, "The Rights of Juvenile Delinquents: An Appraisal of Juvenile Court Procedures," *Journal of Criminal Law, Criminology and Police Science* 47 (1957), 561–69.

"Hogan's Office"
A Kind of Ministry of Justice

Martin Mayer

Nobody in the history of New York City has held a single elective office so long as Frank Smithwick Hogan, the tall, deliberate, pipe-smoking organizer and administrator who is now in his 26th year as District Attorney of New York County. Though he likes to say that everything he has done as D.A. has been merely an attempt to carry forward the policies of his predecessor Thomas E. Dewey—and though men first appointed during the Dewey regime still make up the majority of his bureau chiefs—lawyers who live in and off the criminal courts and who speak of "the Bronx D.A." and "the Queens D.A." will, when they speak of Manhattan, say simply "Hogan's office." It is a unique institution, thoroughly professional, truly non-political, and very nearly noncontroversial. The people who burn about the infrequent mistakes the office does make are usually law school professors and professional libertarians, whose contact with the criminal courts is remote. Defense lawyers, who can daily compare performance in Manhattan with performance in the other boroughs and the suburban counties, are uniformly enthusiastic about the great majority of Hogan's assistants and their schooling in his office. Other boroughs have contests for D.A., but Hogan has been unopposed since Dewey and Judge John A. Mullen (or maybe Tammany leader Christy Sullivan) jointly arranged his nomination by all parties in 1941.

In theory, the function of the District Attorney is to prosecute in the courts people charged with committing felonies and misdemeanors. In fact, so far as serious crimes are concerned, Hogan's office determines whether accused people are guilty or not. Once the New York D.A. decides you are guilty of a felony, you are. As of June 23, the office had prosecuted to a conclusion this year, 2,182 people accused of a felony. Seven of them—one-third of 1 percent—had been acquitted. Seventy-two had been convicted by juries, and 2,103 had entered a plea of guilty to something (not necessarily the full original indictment). "Our record of convictions," Hogan says, "does not show greater proficiency in the courtroom, but a better screening process. I ask a question whenever there's an acquittal, because it means the jury thinks we brought an innocent man to trial, and I think a jury is usually right."

Defendants plead guilty in New York County because their law-yers can demonstrate to them that they have no earthly hope of winning in court. Though Hogan has no firm policy on disclosing the prosecution's case, and an Assistant District Attorney who feels the defense lawyer is a crook is empowered to give him no more than the law demands, standard operating procedure is to lay out the people's evidence in a conference with the defendant's lawyer and then begin to negotiate about the severity of the charge to which the defendant should plead.

"Other jurisdictions have a lot of problems we don't have in New York," says Anthony F. Marra, chief of the criminal division of the New York Legal Aid Society, which represents about 70 percent of all the defendants in Manhattan. "Elsewhere everything is done on motion—if you want information about the people's case you have to demand a bill of particulars. Here you just ask the D.A.—they'll make full disclosure. That saves us a lot of paper work. Then you can go to your client and say, 'Here's what the People have on you.' And that saves defendants a lot of time they'd serve if they went to trial and got convicted on the top count."

Even more remarkable, the defense lawyers in these conferences will usually reveal whatever evidence they may have. Except per-haps in the rackets and organized crime area, where the office retains a crusading zeal which also stems from the Dewey days, a defendant with a case stands a much better chance of persuading Hogan's assistant to dismiss than of persuading a jury to acquit. As against seven acquittals prior to June 23, there were 85 felony cases where, after indictment and assignment of the case to a court for trial, the Hogan office either dismissed the matter or discharged the defen-dant.

In other jurisdictions an indication that a witness is not trustwor-thy may provoke from an Assistant D.A. a comment such as, "Well, that's for the jury to say"—and then the prosecution prepares to counter the defendant's arguments at trial. In New York, because Hogan does not like acquittals, an assistant is more likely to get in trouble by proceeding with a shaky case than he is by recommend-ing that a case be dropped. "You can disclose," says Gil Rosenthal, one of the city's more belligerent defense lawyers, "without worry-ing that they'll take unfair advantage." At a defendant's request, the D.A. may give him a lie-detector test on a risk-free basis. If the polygraph says the fellow is lying, everybody forgets about it; if the machine says he is telling the truth, says Marra, "ninety-nine times out of a hundred Hogan will drop the case."

Our legal theory and textbooks, our Supreme Court, our newspa-pers and magazines all discuss an "adversary system" of criminal justice, in which witnesses are examined and cross-examined in open court and a jury votes that it has or has not heard proof beyond a reasonable doubt. But in New York County—and to only somewhat lesser degree in other jurisdictions—what we really have is an administrative system of criminal justice, where the evidence is weighed and the important decisions are taken in the prosecutor's office. In Manhattan the primacy of administrative process is so thoroughly recognized that cases are assigned for trial not to a judge but to an Assistant D.A., and do not go onto a judge's calendar until the D.A. puts them there.

The classic (or Jim Garrison) image of the fighting D.A. is today an intolerable anachronism. If our system of criminal law is to be even minimally fair, the D.A.'s office must become, county by county, a ministry of justice. Hogan likes to say that his office is "ever-mindful of its quasi-judicial function."

The offices of the New York District Attorney occupy most of the sixth through ninth floors of the block-long, seventeen-story, Rockefeller-Center-style Criminal Courts Building on Centre Street in lower Manhattan. Like most New York public offices built in this century, they are stark and uncomfortable, inadequately lighted, with dirty plaster walls, bare wood chairs and old wood desks. The decorations on the walls are framed diplomas and certificates of appointment and photographs of ceremonial occasions. Only the bureau chiefs enjoy the luxury of air-conditioning, and not even all of them have carpets on the floor.

The legal work of the office is broken into eight bureaus—complaint, indictment, criminal courts (for trying misdemeanors), Supreme Court (for trying felonies), homicide, rackets, frauds, and appeals. As the names indicate, the complaint bureau processes the problems of aggrieved citizens who want the People to take up their cause, and the appeals bureau defends the D.A.'s convictions against challenge in the higher courts. (To the great annoyance of the office, however, the appeals bureau does not defend postconviction habeas corpus challenges in the Federal courts: such proceedings are brought against the warden of the prison, who is a state official, and Attorney General Louis Lefkowitz insists that only his men may defend state officials.) The rackets and frauds bureaus, introduced by Dewey, run investigations and "make cases," often with the help of grand juries, at least four of which are in session in the building every day. The other bureaus are involved in disposing of the business which the police department supplies in great quantities—about 60,000 cases a year, roughly one-third of the entire criminal caseload in New York State.

Mayor Lindsay's 1967–68 budget allocates $2.3-million and 260 positions to the District Attorney of New York County, 102 of the positions to be filled by lawyers, at salaries ranging from $6,750 for newcomers to $37,000 for Hogan. A separate "D.A.'s Squad" of 75 detectives, permanently assigned to the office, though paid by the Police Department, does most of the investigative legwork, but the office also maintains its own staff of about ten to look into situations out of town where there is some reason to distrust the local police (who would necessarily—*noblesse oblige*—be the main source of contacts and information for a visiting New York detective) or situations close to home where the subject of the inquiry is one or more of New York's Finest. Another D.A.'s squad of six or seven accountants checks out cases for the frauds bureau and for the rackets bureau. "Many crimes," says Jerome Kidder, the tall, rather sorrowful chief of the frauds bureau, "are concealed in the books." The office also has its own photographer, pathologist, and engineer.

Every lawyer enters the Hogan office at the bottom, whether he comes fresh out of law school or from several years in practice. Despite the low salaries, there are 250 to 300 applicants a year, of whom about 100 pass through interviews with at least two bureau chiefs to the office of David S. Worgan, Hogan's executive assistant. About 50 reach Hogan himself. Ten to fifteen are chosen. The ideal candidate is a boy with a pleasing manner who grew up on the streets of New York and worked his way through Harvard, Yale, Columbia, Cornell, or Pennsylvania Law School and made the law review. Any one of these requirements can be waived, but probably not two of them.

Everybody starts in the complaint bureau, where Melvin D. Glass, the youngest of the bureau chiefs (nine years out of Pennsylvania Law School) offers "a seminar in advanced criminal procedure." In the first week the neophyte learns how to fill out a complaint card, "what to say on the phone and what not to say on the phone," how to tell people that even if what they say is true they have a civil lawsuit rather than a criminal charge against the storekeeper or the landlord or the neighbor or the bigamous husband (bigamy is a crime in New York only if the *second* marriage was performed in the state). Then there are two weeks of following in great detail a hypothetical robbery case, from the policeman at the scene to the decision on appeal. "We introduce them," Glass says, "to police forms, court forms, our forms. They hear lectures from experts on gypsies and con games, burglary, homicide, larceny; visit the prison; observe the summons procedure; watch a full trial; do a moot court on a gambling case."

The new men now begin to meet the public. About 2,000 complainants a year visit the D.A.'s office, and Hogan insists that everybody must be treated courteously. ("It is not our function," the manual for the complaint bureau explains, "to advise any person that he needs psychiatric treatment.") Generally, if the matter is one that should be handled by a private lawyer, the visitor will be referred to the bar association or Legal Aid. (There are exceptions: as a courtesy to the tourist industry, for example, the D.A. will call a local store accused, by letter, of failure to deliver the merchandise.)

Only about 35 complaints a year lead to arrest (an assistant must check with Glass before authorizing an arrest), but during the course of processing the bulk of noncriminal or self-serving complaints the new Assistant D.A. learns a great deal that law school never taught him about interviewing members of the general public to get their stories out of them. The lawyers of the complaint bureau also take calls from policemen who want advice about how to handle a situation, and toward the end of their six months or so in the bureau they get to try a few cases, if that is the right phrase for it, in the gamblers' court, where a ritualized ballet is played out by the police and the old men who have become the city's policy runners since the Legislature made prison sentences mandatory for gambling.

Next in the training program comes half a year in the indictment bureau, where the assistant learns to check out felony cases prepared by the police, and to present witnesses before the sympathetic audience of the grand jury. Older members of the 11-man indictment bureau run Part 1-A, the courtroom where prisoners are brought by the police for a judge to determine whether or not there is enough evidence that they committed a crime to justify holding them. Since January, under a new dispensation, Part 1-A operates around the clock, and over the course of the year half the whole office will take a turn presenting to a judge a policeman's reasons for wanting the person he has just arrested to be placed in the pipeline of criminal process. Until recently, that was the full extent of the assistant's duties in 1-A; now there is a complaint room where the assistant can talk over the arrest with the officer and the complainant and throw out before it ever reaches the court a case where no actual crime occurred or the evidence is already tainted or the policeman seems to have made a mistake.

The D.A.'s first tight sieve, however, is operated between arraignment in 1-A and indictment. "We want to see if these are proper cases," says Karl Grebow, chief of the bureau, who next January will celebrate his 30th anniversary with the New York District Attorney's office. "If they're not proper cases we want to get rid of them."

For each case which is to be presented to the 23-man grand jury (a majority indicts), an assistant makes up a fact sheet consisting of the crime and its circumstances and the evidence available for prosecution. Witnesses are called in rapid-fire order to give the bones of their story to the grand jury (in a proceeding from which defense lawyers are barred); the defendant may testify if he wishes, but of course waives his immunity to self-incrimination if he does so. About 6,000 indictments a year are sought by the New York D.A.'s office, and disposition of the average request takes a grand jury about 15 minutes.

The assistant in the indictment bureau has some authority to dismiss or reduce a charge on his own—"in an obvious situation," Grebow explains, "a rape without corroboration, when a man knows there's no case." Normally, however, it is simpler to let the grand jury make this decision itself, and over the course of the year, usually but not always following a hint from the assistant, the grand jury will dismiss about 13 percent of the indictments and reduce 12 percent to charges of misdemeanor. The work of the assistants is tightly supervised: either Grebow or his deputy Sal Pino reads every fact sheet and every indictment.

The final phase of the training program is a term, usually a year, in the criminal courts bureau, trying the misdemeanor cases that flood in from the police—shoplifting, unarmed assault, purse-snatching, simple theft, "resisting arrest," complicated disorderly conduct. (Traffic offenses, prostitution, and drunk cases are processed directly by the police and not through the D.A.'s office.) Trials are considerably more common in this area. Of 8,202 cases pressed to a conclusion in the first four months of the year, 6,327 produced guilty pleas, 971 resulted in convictions after trial, and 904 yielded acquittals. This huge volume was handled by a staff of only 18 men, headed by bureau chief Joseph Stone. The courts in which this activity occurs are monkey-houses, complete to official proceedings in corridors and cloakrooms; and everyone professionally involved—judges, prosecutors, defense lawyers, police—is under the most intense imaginable pressure to keep the business moving.

After a man has been two years in the office, one of them in the criminal courts bureau, he is eligible for more or less permanent assignment to the less frenetic trial work of more serious crimes in Supreme Court, the more profound responsibilities of the homicide bureau (which supervises investigations as well as trying cases), the mostly investigative labors of the rackets or frauds bureaus (which also, however, try their own cases when there are cases to be tried), or the intellectual labors of the appeals bureau.

Promotions within the bureaus are by seniority, to guarantee against any return to the pre-Dewey days when jobs in the D.A.'s office at all levels are the property of district leaders, who could give them as rewards to deserving followers or their children. Everybody hired into the Hogan office promises to stay at least four years; but when the four years are up a man is likely to look around, note that he is still making less than the $9,200 the Wall Street law firms pay their new recruits, and begin counting how many years must pass

before death or retirement will give him a crack at the better jobs
in the office.

The resulting turnover of 12 to 15 men a year has meant that
apprentices have to be hustled through Hogan's training program
faster than the book says they should move—some have even
skipped the criminal courts year entirely. Not everybody feels,
though, that the turnover is bad: "You hate to lose a man who's good
and useful and grown up," says a lawyer now in private practice
who ran a prosecutor's office, "but that's just when you ought to lose
him. A long-range career at the D.A.'s office tends to warp a mind;
a man doesn't have a full professional life just on that side of the bar."
Hogan of course disagrees with that judgment. He has a remarkably
developed sense of loyalty and about the best thing he can say about
a man is that "he's been here a *long* time."

The turnover has put what is probably a wholesome pressure on
the policy of promotion by seniority. Though six of the eight bureau
chiefs are men who have been with the office more than 20 years,
and their deputies have almost equivalent service records, rapid
advance has become a possibility for a really extraordinary man.
H. Richard Uviller, a patiently ironic Yale Law graduate (and ama-
teur painter whose abstractions are about the only art in the office),
became chief of the appeals bureau after only seven years; and the
eager and earnest Melvin Glass was appointed chief of the complaint
bureau after only eight years, partly as a reward for his work in
demonstrating that the police had not solved the Janice Wylie murders when they drew a confession out of George Whitmore Jr.

Hogan runs this establishment from a very high eminence. He has
not himself tried a case since 1945: "To be away from administrative
work for four or five weeks is not a wise thing to do," he says, "even
though it may be more satisfying personally." He speaks every day
with his bureau chiefs, usually on the telephone—only executive
assistant Worgan is a frequent visitor to his large office—and he
receives a daily written report on work done before the grand jury
and in the Supreme Court bureau.

Apart from the men in the rackets bureau, where Hogan maintains continuing personal interest, assistants below the senior level
are likely to see him only at occasional office social functions—
especially at the softball games. Until a few years ago, Hogan played
third base for the office team, who wear shirts identifying them as
Hogan's Hooligans; and he threatens to return to action next year.

Hogan has his own way of keeping up with his office. He reads the
mail—"Everything," he says, "that comes into the office. Every
morning the mail room brings me two big folders. The smaller one
is my own mail; the larger one is the mail for everybody else in the
office. It doesn't take me that much time to read it all, because I've

been doing it so long." Letters that indicate possible trouble get passed on to the man to whom they were originally sent with a copy of Form 38-2M-800230 (61), on which Hogan can check one of ten boxes—"See me about this," or "Let me see proposed reply," or "Telephone me," etc.

Part of the purpose of reading the mail is simply to enforce Hogan's rules of courtesy. A ceramic plaque with gold Gothic lettering stands on the table beside his desk: "Courtesy is the Golden Key that unlocks all the doors." Joseph Stone says, "We all know one thing Hogan won't stand for is being late with appointments or not answering letters. Around here you've got to handle people with plenty of Tender Loving Care." But the letters also keep Hogan informed about what defense lawyers are asking from his assistants, and tip him off to any situations which seem to be developing badly. New bureau chiefs quickly learn that when they call Hogan to talk over a problem he usually knows about it already.

Hogan reads the mail rather than discussing things with juniors because he is at bottom rather shy. He puffs his pipe and looks away when he talks with you. Dewey at the time of Hogan's nomination called him "the most sweetly honorable man I've ever known," which is an interesting description. (Hogan doesn't think much of it.) "He's formal with people," says appeals chief Uviller. "Gallant with ladies. He believes assistants should wear coats when ladies are in the room. He dislikes profanity, and believes in old-fashioned virtues, loyalty and courtesy. But he's a remarkably astute judge of the capabilities of the staff. He knows strengths, weaknesses and proclivities quite far down the line—knows who gets hot-headed, who takes trivia too seriously, who's a fighter, who's a scholar and how to use them. He has a remarkable ability to judge and respond to people." He can also be quietly funny, with the faintly acrid wit of a man who is successfully controlling a considerable temper.

The one major outside interest in Hogan's life is Columbia University, which he serves as a life trustee and, currently, as co-chairman of the giant new fund-raising drive. He and his wife, Mary, whom he married in 1936, live as they always have near Columbia at 404 Riverside Drive. They entertain modestly: Hogan is no part of a politician, as his dull race for the Senate in 1958 conclusively demonstrated. When Dewey listed Hogan as one of the four men on his staff whom he would be prepared to support as his successor, nobody had ever heard of him. Though he had helped Dewey on a couple of cases and had tried some cases himself, his job had been essentially that of his title, "administrative assistant." A few days after Tammany had announced that it would accept Hogan (the only Democrat on Dewey's list), and Dewey had, over La Guardia's protests, forced the Republicans to go along, the new D.A. made ritual visits to the headquarters of all the parties to meet the leaders, none of whom he had ever met before.

Frank S. Hogan was born 65 years ago in Waterbury, Conn., where "my people had a grocery store." He got his first job in the plating room of the New England Watch Company while he was a freshman in high school (the high school was on double-session, which gave him pretty much a full day's work), and he has held one job or another ever since. Some of them were pretty exotic. One summer he was an installment plan collector for a clothing store which sold suits for $1 a week; his salary was $20 a week plus 3 percent commission. Another year he sold the People's Home Library—"Not a book, Mrs. Jones, but a complete library: medical book, cookbook, stock book." While he was a student at Columbia, he waited on table and played on the football team. ("In those youthful days," he told an alumni meeting in 1954, "I regret to say that a varsity 'C' was just a little more important to me than a degree. More deplorable, it still is.") In the summers he worked as a Pullman conductor all over the Northeast and once as a steward on the *Leviathan*.

On graduation from college, Hogan took a job as "organizing secretary" for a Russian baron who had discovered "the science of being," and who gave free large lectures to ladies' groups, followed by courses of small-group lectures at $50 a head for ten meetings. "After four or five months," he recalls, "we didn't get along. I was beginning to feel like a con man." Leaving the baron, Hogan went to Guatemala as tutor to the sons of the superintendent of a gold mine, "moonlighting as an accountant for the company." Then he returned to Columbia for law school. One summer he worked as a steamfitter's helper on the construction of the Columbia-Presbyterian Medical Center; and then he got a steady year-round job, five in the afternoon to midnight, in the showroom of the New York Edison Company on 42nd Street between Fifth and Sixth Avenues. This paid $25 a week, and gave him a feeling of affluence.

On graduation from law school, Hogan worked two years as a junior associate in a downtown firm, then became half of one of the many struggling two-man partnerships in New York in the depression. He was still trying to put together a practice in 1935 when he read in the newspapers that Governor Herbert H. Lehman had appointed Thomas E. Dewey, from the U.S. Attorney's office, to run a special investigation of rackets in the city, and he wrote a letter of application. Hogan believes he was accepted strictly on the basis of the letter, but he was a classmate and fraternity brother of Paul E. Lockwood, who was to be Dewey's deputy, and Lockwood put in the necessary good word. In any event, Hogan was one of the original group of seven sworn in with Dewey on July 29, 1935, and he moved over to the D.A.'s office with the rest of Dewey's staff of special assistants when the future Governor won his first election in 1937.

The most publicized feature of both Dewey's and Hogan's administration of the office has been the separate rackets bureau, now headed by Alfred J. Scotti (another bureau chief who started with the original Dewey team), and staffed by a dozen to 15 lawyers, plus most of the D.A.'s squad. A highly persistent little man with extra supplies of bouncing energy, Scotti enjoys thinking of theories by which wrongdoing not explicitly covered by the penal code can be brought into the crime category, and his bureau does not qualify for the general encomium given to the Hogan office by defense lawyers. "He sees everything in black and white," one of them says, "and the world is full of grays."

Of all that happens in his office, Hogan is proudest of the self-starting pressure the rackets bureau applies impartially to government, business, and labor, and of the "hundreds of convictions" for corruption, extortion, and fraud which the D.A.'s own investigators have uncovered. The cases have included the basketball fixes; the TV quiz scandal; bribery in the State Liquor Authority (for which former Republican State Chairman L. Judson Morhouse went to jail); hanky-panky with labor welfare funds (resulting in the incarceration of George Scalise); the conviction of gamblers Frank Costello and Frank Ericson (and the accompanying disclosure of Costello's influence on judicial nominations); the revelation of waterfront racketeering, black market baby rings, and a series of extortions by the city Fire and Building Departments which, among other results, led to a permanent residence in Mexico of former Mayor William O'Dwyer.

It is in defense of the work of this bureau that Hogan has spoken up for wiretapping and eavesdropping. Thus the other day, in an appeal to a Senate subcommittee to authorize new legislation on the subject, he called wiretapping "the single most valuable and effective weapon" in law enforcement.

"Without wiretapping," Scotti says, "we'd be in the dark—who's going to come in and tell us about these things?" Among the tasks Hogan accepted for himself as D.A. was the personal processing of applications for court-approved taps, bugs, and extensions. "There weren't so many of them," he says. "About 125 a year."

Like most prosecutors, Hogan is less than enchanted with several recent Supreme Court decisions. "In the old days we had more leeway," he says. "You didn't have motions to suppress evidence, confessions were more ... simplistic, you could use wiretaps without any court order. Now the delay is unconscionable, it's extremely difficult to move cases."

To Hogan's office the most troublesome of the decisions is the limitation on the use of confessions. In his recent appeal to the subcommittee, he declared that such decisions had "significantly increased the chances that a criminal will escape judgment." The homicide bureau has been particularly disturbed, partly because the

absence of confessions makes convictions slightly more difficult to
obtain (although two out of three accused killers still waive their
right to counsel and make statements), partly because the assistant
in charge of the case, who comes in at the beginning (the New York
police make arrests for homicide only on the advice of the D.A.'s
office), finds it more difficult to convince himself.

"If you have a case with four independent eyewitnesses and the
guy confesses," says bureau chief Vincent J. Dermody, "you can sleep
easy. But a case where you have one witness—he was passing by, he
heard a shot, a man came running out with a revolver, he never saw
him before . . . and a month later he picks him out of the lineup—
then you've got a hot potato.

"You go into the whole background of the witness, what sort of job
does he have, what sort of person is he, how good is his eyesight,
what was the wattage of the bulb, when was the globe cleaned last,
are we dealing with a nut or a guy who wants to be in the limelight
or, worst of all, a guy who is honestly mistaken?"

Evidence other than the testimony of witnesses, or a confession,
is unusual. (Fingerprints, Dermody says, are " a real rarity—maybe
once in a thousand times.") Deprived of the chance to question and
size up the prospective defendant, the Assistant District Attorney
worries that ("God forbid") he may be prosecuting an innocent man.
The worry is compounded by his knowledge that he will very probably get his conviction from the jury whether the man is innocent
or not.

"A lot of people in the office believe," Uviller says, "that the courts
are working against us." Still, nobody is crying, and Hogan has not
noted any crime wave. "There hasn't been much change in ten
years," he says, "in the number of cases in the felony parts." One
observer feels that Hogan, who reads appellate decisions (and *The
Congressional Record*) with considerable care, has come out of the
experiences of the last few years a better and wiser lawyer: "He
never used to think much about criminal law, just about doing his
own job. Now he sits on a lot of committees that wouldn't have
interested him at all in the beginning."

Richard A. Green, director of the American Bar Association study
on Minimum Standards of Effective Criminal Justice, believes that
the uncertainties attendant on the Supreme Court decisions may
have improved the performance of the office. "There's always a danger," Green says, "that you consider yourself so objective you're *sure*
you can't possibly be prosecuting an innocent man. And you can be."
Dissenting judges on the Court of Appeals and a Federal district
judge have recently criticized Hogan's office for failure to make
available to the defense derogatory information about prosecution
witnesses. Behind this failure, obviously, was the attitude that the

office had investigated these people and decided they were telling the truth, so why waste time going over it again. But even a ministry of justice must not have the right to suppress.

Hogan worries about the trial court judges—especially those who since court consolidation have been sitting on criminal cases for the first time in their lives. "They're not conversant with the criminal law," he says. "They don't like the work and have no hesitancy about saying it." He wishes the Mayor would look more often in the direction of his bureau chiefs when choosing judges, and likes to point out that Mayor Hylan appointed to the bench 30 assistants of Joab Banton, who held the office from 1921 to 1929 and is one of the few D.A.s before Dewey whom Hogan respects. "It would be wonderful for morale," he says rather wistfully. "But La Guardia never did it, and Lindsay's taken only one. It's the penalty we pay for being a nonpolitical office."

Hogan's greatest concern is about the office's future pulling power on the new law school graduates. The alumni roster is distinguished —it includes, for example, Chief Judge Stanley H. Fuld and Associate Judge Charles D. Breitel of the Court of Appeals, former Attorney General William Rogers and Charles Tillinghast, president of T.W.A. Nobody is confident that men of this potential are coming to the D.A.'s office today.

Others at the office are concerned about what may happen, both to the office and to themselves, when Hogan leaves. Most of his bureau chiefs are his age or near it; and none of them seems a likely candidate to capture the nomination of all parties. Return to the political maelstrom would be a tragedy for the office and for the city, but civic tragedy is commonplace in New York.

Hogan's criminal courts bureau doubtless passes by some stones it should turn, not every assistant is the model of fairness Hogan thinks his men should be, and the operation of the seniority system has moved into high positions some men whose capacity does not greatly impress students of the office. But lawyers who work in other counties of the city—and in other cities around the country— envy Manhattan its D.A. and his office. "There are no hacks," says a defense lawyer. "Some bureau chiefs may be mediocre, but they're professionals. They're concerned about their cases." Practicing before a bench where many judges are disgracefully weak, pinched by a budget which allots less than $40 per case for the volume of work that passes through the building, Hogan has indeed made his office a functioning ministry of justice. He has had few imitators anywhere, but among the rather wistful hopes of the President's National Crime Commission is that more D.A.s will try to be like Hogan. If Washington's current interest in the problems of criminal justice should persist, Hogan's accomplishment may have national significance.

The Defendant's Perspective

Jonathan D. Casper

The bargaining that occurs—and it occurs frequently—can center around either charge or sentence. A defendant charged with robbery with violence may eventually plead guilty to simple robbery; a charge of assault with intent to kill may be reduced to aggravated assault; burglary may be broken down to breaking and entering. The charge is of importance, for it determines, to some extent, the maximum sentence that a defendant can receive. If he is sent to prison, the minimum term (e.g., on a two-to-five-year sentence, the two-year minimum) determines the date of his eligibility for parole. The maximum is important too, though less so, for it affects his eligibility for discharge from parole after he is released.

Even more frequent is bargaining over the sentence to be imposed. For most crimes the judge has discretion to impose any sentence up to the maximum permitted by statute. Thus, breaking and entering can be penalized by five years in prison or by a lesser sentence (e.g., two to five years). In addition to bargaining over the sentence for a particular offense, many defendants have been charged with several crimes; for example, eight counts of B and E [breaking and entering], nine counts of forgery. In theory a plea of guilty to each count could result in a series of terms in prison for each count. In the plea-bargaining process a defendant may be offered an agreement about a series of concurrent sentences: the eight counts of B and E will produce eight concurrent sentences of two to five years in prison.

[Here] we will discuss the process in more detail: the choices that the defendant feels he has available to him, his view of his relationship with his attorney, and the ways in which he interprets the behavior of the prosecutor and the judge. This brief account suggests the structure of the proceeding: the formal appearances in court and the informal bargaining that underlies and in many ways determines the results that these formal appearances produce.

To begin to flesh out the reality of the process—as seen by the defendant—let us listen at length to two defendants. They represent somewhat different experiences: in one the defendant was relatively passive, and events simply occurred; in the other the defendant engaged in an extensive variety of tactics and bargained actively.

Source: Jonathen D. Casper, *American Criminal Justice: The Defendant's Perspective* (Englewood Cliffs, N.J.: Prentice-Hall, 1972), pp. 54–65. Copyright © 1972. Reprinted by permission of Prentice-Hall, Inc.

The first man was arrested and charged, on complaint of his girl-friend, with assault with intent to rape. He refused to make a statement to the police. In discussing his case, he indicated that he was probably guilty of assault, but not assault with intent to rape. The report of a "double-cross" by the public defender was not typical, but neither was it uncommon.

"I got arraigned before the judge and got ten thousand dollars bail, and then I stayed in jail ever since then."

"Now, did you intend to plead not guilty to this charge?"

"Yes, I was gonna plead not guilty."

"So you were arraigned: they gave you a bond you can't make; so you're back in jail."

"Right."

"What happened then?"

"I just stayed there and kept going back and forth to court."

"What did you go to court for?"

"For the same charge."

"What was happening?"

"The lawyer didn't seem to be doing nothin. Every time I'd go there he would—he wouldn't, he wasn't sayin nothin."

"He was a public defender?"

"Yes."

"Did you appear in circuit court? Did you have the probable-cause hearing?"

"Naw, he said it's better not to have it."

"So you were bound over?"

"Yes. To high court."

"So you had a different public defender in superior court?"

"Yes, I had a different one there."

"Now, when was the first time you met him?"

"It was about three months."

"You were taken over to superior court, and you met the public defender?"

"Yes. See, I had started off with Moore; then they switched me to some other guy. And no one was takin interest in—"

"Did any of them ever come visit you in jail?"

"Naw."

"The only time you saw them was in the bullpen or around court?"

"Yes."

"Did you eventually plead guilty?"

"Yes, he told me, 'With your record and stuff, you'd better plead guilty.' "

"Who told you that?"

"The lawyer."

"And this is one day in court?"

"Yes. He told me I would probably get a year; that's why I pleaded guilty."

"Did he first ask you what you wanted to plead?"

"Yes. I said, 'I want to plead not guilty; I'm not guilty of it.' And then—see I'd been in prison before; so he says, 'Well, you take this to a jury trial, you might get a lot of time.' He had me pretty scared. So he said, 'You better—I think I can get you a year.' So I said OK, and then I got up there, and I got five years."

"You got the feeling he wanted you to plead guilty?"

"Yes."

"And when he said, 'I think I can get you a year,' did he say he'd talked to the prosecutor about it, or—?"

"Yes, he said the prosecutor wasn't gonna recommend nothin. In other words, he wasn't gonna recommend I got time or nothin. But when I got up there in court, the prosecutor recommended I go to prison and aw, everything changed, you know."

"Do you think the lawyer thought you were innocent or guilty?"

"I think he thought I was innocent, but he just didn't want to go into too much trouble. He asked me, 'You got any money?' I told him no."

"The implication was if you had some money, he'd do a better job for you?"

"Yeah, he says, 'Have you got any money you can give me?' I said, 'No, I haven't got no money.' "

"Did you go first to plead in the superior court, and then there was a presentence, and then you got sentenced? or did they do it all at once?"

"No, I went down there about three or four different times. Pled not guilty, and then I went down there once, and nothin happened—didn't even get to see the judge—and then back again."

"To plead guilty?"

"Yeah, they just kept runnin me back and forth, hopin you get sick of waitin there and then plead guilty."

"If you had to pick out a sort of crucial factor that changed your mind from the time you were going to plead not guilty to the time you decided to cop out, what was it?"

"I started thinking—you know, I did have a prison record, and I really didn't want to plead guilty to that attempted rape, because with the statement he had and everything, I should have got off. And it was really mixed up. I didn't try to run. I could have left the house. I waited there; I thought I was just gonna get threw out [by the police officers]."

"You were charged with attempted rape or assault with intent to rape?"

"Assault with intent to rape."

"Yeah. At one point you thought you could beat that."

"Yeah."

"But then you changed your mind."

"Yeah, well, when I see he didn't try to do nothin—the law-yer he just got up there and say, 'Yes sir, yes sir,' He didn't even try to argue with the judge. I figured I'd better plead guilty here, or else I'm gonna get a lot of time."

"Now, you got two to five?"

"Two to five."

"If the lawyer had come to you and said, 'I'll get you two to five,' would you have pled guilty?"

"I don't think I would have, no."

"So it was the fact that he said he could get you a year?"

"He said he could get me a year there."

"And you thought that was a pretty good deal?"

"Yeah, I figured better than going to prison [i.e., a year in jail is better than a longer term in prison]."

"Now, thinking about this from the time you were arrested till the time you got sentenced, if you had it to do over again, would you do it different?"

"Yes."

"What would you do?"

"The first thing I'd do is probably get in contact with my family, get my own lawyer. I'd never believe that lawyer again, never. They'd never give me no public defender; I wouldn't take him."

The next young man was charged with two counts of burglary (carrying a potential maximum sentence of twenty years on each count), one count of resisting arrest, and one count of larceny. He was apprehended and shot by police officers in the course of one of the breaks and placed under a bail of ten thousand dollars by police officers. He asserted that he could have made the bond, but a parole-violation warrant had been lodged against him, making him ineligible for release.

"So you went to court the next day?"

"Yeah, I went to court, and they presented the charges. Then they continued it."

"Did you have a lawyer when you went to court the next day?"

"No, I had a public defender."

"Did you talk to him at all?"

"Yeah, he ran the facts and all that stuff. You know, how much time they carry and stuff like that."

"How did you intend to plead at that point?"

"He said that if I pleaded guilty, they drop resistance and larceny and bound the two burglaries over to superior court."

"He said they would do that?"

"Yeah."

"He said you ought to do that?"

"Yeah."

"So did you do it?"

"Yeah."

"Were you guilty of both of them?"

"No, just one."

"The other one you were innocent of?"

"Yeah."

"Did you tell them that?"

"No."

"How come?"

"I mean yeah, I told them, yeah."

"You told them. What did he say?"

"He say nothin. He just said, 'It's up to you.' I guess he thought I was lying."

"So why did you plead guilty to the second one that you didn't do?"

"Cause I knew if I'd a went to high court that they would eventually break it down to a breaking and entering without permission. Cause I was planning on getting my own lawyer, but then I was gonna see what my public defender was gonna do first."

"So the deal he offered was, Plead guilty to two burglaries. They'll drop the resisting and the larceny."

"Yeah."

"And then what happens? Did he say they'd knock it down to B and E in superior court?"

"No, he just said they bound it over."

"So you waived the probable-cause hearing?"

"Yeah, I waived it."

"And you pled guilty to the one you didn't do because you figured they'd drop it eventually anyway?"

"No, they'd break it down for a misdemeanor, breaking into without permission. If the public defender wasn't going to do it—if he didn't want to hear it, I figured eventually he'd make a deal because, you see, I waited four months to go to court. I was in the state jail, and from state jail I went to 'Northport'— the hospital."

"Drugs?"

"No, suicidal. And I laid up there for a while, and then I came back and went back. I was doing this just to_____"

"You were purposely delaying the superior court case?"

"Yeah."

"Figuring that they'd break it down?"

"No, well, see at that time the superior court in Eastport was real crowded. You come in there with a case, and they wanted to dispose of it as quick as possible, see. So I figured if I kept on delaying and delaying and delaying, they'd eventually break it down, you know what I mean. He'd come up with some kind of a deal. I sorta like pressed him to come up with a deal, and he came up with a deal."

"Who's he?"

" 'Franklin.' "

"The public defender?"

"Yeah."

"This is the public defender in superior court?"

"Superior court, yeah."

"Well, when did you first run into him?"

"The day I went to superior court."

"And this was shortly after you were bound over? How long between the time you were bound over and you first went to superior court?"

"Well, I was bound over at superior court. I didn't know I— I didn't know when I was going to superior court; so what I did —you know, I cut up [attempted suicide]."

"Yeah."

"And they sent me to [the hospital], see. So then from [the hospital] I came back, and I went to court."

"And at this point how were you intending to plead? You hadn't pled in superior court."

"No, I hadn't pleaded at all. I was just rapping, like I went to superior court once or twice. Three times. You know, the first two times I didn't plead at all; I just rapped."

"About what?"

"About the finish, you know."

"What kind of stuff did you talk about?"

"Well, the first time I went to court, [the judge] just told me, Did I got a lawyer. I said no. I said, at that time, I wanted my own lawyer, see. I didn't really want one, but again I was still delaying. So he said, You gonna get your own lawyer? I said yeah. You know, in front of the judge I said I'd like to get my own lawyer. So he said, We'll continue the case until tomorrow. So I went back again the next day, and I think I told him the same story; I'm not sure. Well, anyway, then I met Franklin. I was rapping to him, and he said, It looks like you're not going to have a public defender. I said I'm still working on getting [a private attorney], you know. I said he's busy. You see, at first I was going to have a lawyer by the name of—'DeAngelo.' Now DeAngelo was in the courtroom, but my mother hadn't notified him. You see, I told him—my mother—I'm still delaying it."

"Wait, I'm not clear. Did you really want a private lawyer, or are you just saying that so you could delay it?"

"No, you see, I was pressing em for a deal, hoping that they would say, Well, look, we gotta get this case; this case has been continued so long let's get it over with. And then they come up with a deal. So I went back to court the next day. [The judge] says, We're going to appoint you public defender. So all right.

I didn't get to see him at all that day. I went back to jail. Then
I didn't hear any more when my court case gonna come up."

"So the guy came to visit you in jail?"

"No."

"The public defender?"

"No. So then I cut up again and went back to [the hospital]
and stayed about a month and a half; so altogether it was 112
days before I went to court. Finally, the last day I went, and my
mother was there and everything; and my social worker, he
was talking; he came to see me. He said, If you plead guilty,
we're going to see if we can get it dropped down to a misdemeanor. This means you get a year. You know, those two burglaries were carrying a maximum of forty years; so I said it
sounds all right. Just what I wanted. So I went to court the next
day—a couple of days after I saw my social worker—and we
rapped about it. He says, All right? and I says yeah."

"You're getting all this not directly from the public defender
but through your social worker?"

"No, but what I'm saying now is that I went to court after I
talked to my public defender, and I talked to him, I mean after
I talked to my social worker. Then I talked to my public defender, Franklin. He said, 'Yeah, well, I was talking to the
district attorney, and he said he was going to see if he could get
you your charges dropped down to misdemeanor.' You know,
if you cop out guilty. And so 90 percent of the time you cop out;
he usually gets you what you want or what he offers you; so
I says, Well, that sounds right."

"You're going to cop out to both of them?"

"Right."

"One of them you were innocent of?"

"Right. So then my mother was there and everything, and I
went before the judge, and the judge, he asked me, Did I make
any deals, you know. I said nah, no deals. He says, How you
plead? I says guilty. So Franklin, he starts running off his
mouth. He says, 'Yeah, well ah, I file that we have the charges
lessened to misdemeanor carrying a maximum of one year,' so
public defender, I mean prosecutor, 'Broussard,' he went along
with it; so the judge went along with it, and they sentenced me
to a year in the state jail, and then they transferred me from the
state jail up here."

"Let me ask you a few questions. Where did you learn all
these things about delay, they'll break it down, and this kind
of stuff? Past experience?"

"No, well, I talk to a lot of people in jail, but they didn't delay
it or anything like that. But, see, I knew Franklin, he didn't
want to make this deal. You know, he wanted to hang me."

"The public defender wanted to hang you?"

"Yeah, I think he wanted to hang me. So what I was doing,
you know, I knew it was all over; the courts were flooded with

all kinds of cases; so I guess they were disposing of them like mad; so they'd do anything just to get the case over with. So I delay them about three and a half months."

"Are you telling me that you pled guilty to two, one which you did and one which you didn't?"

"Right."

"How did you feel about pleading guilty to something that you didn't do?"

"Well, if I would've—he told me that if I would of went ahead with a jury trial, now they would of definitely hung me on one of them. Now, if I woulda went to the court and pleaded not guilty to one of them, asked for a jury trial on both the cases, they couldn't pay; they'd probably dismiss one of them, you see, but they'd hang me on the other one."

"Did he tell you that?"

"Naw, but this is the way it works, you know what I mean. Like, let's say you have a whole lot of charges—aggravated assault, breach of peace. I had big charges. They'll drop all the big charges and leave you with the one little one and hang you on the little one. They'll give you the maximum time on the little one. You know what I mean? I figured this way: if I copped the both of them, I would of got a year; but if they would of hung me on the last one—in which they would have done cause I was caught dead in the act—I probably would have had an indefinite or a three-to-seven or a one-to-three—two-to-five, you know. Understand what I mean?"

"Yeah."

"This is why I copped out."

"Do you feel bitter about having to plead guilty to something you didn't do, or is it just the way it is?"

"That's the way; that's the name of the game. That's the game, you know, the game."

"The prosecutor obviously let you off relatively easy and gave you a deal that was much less than you could have gotten."

"Well, sure."

"Why do you think they agreed to it?"

"Now you know a jury trial costs the state money, costs them quite a bit of money, and I was going to ask for jury of twelve, and I was going to go through a whole lot of hassle and cost the state a whole lot of money. So he figured we could avoid the state, like paying the jury—that, $150, $250—I don't know how much they're paying them—we gotta pay each jury, each guy on the jury, a sum of money, and it's costing the state, you see? This is why a guy, guys make this kind of deals, because the state don't want to pay all that money. They got like a little racket, the court racket. The public defender knows the prosecutor, you know; they drink together and play cards and _____."

"Now, if you had it to do all over again, from the time you were arrested to the time you got sentenced, would you do anything different, or do you think you came out all right?"

"I would've done the same thing."

"You think you did about as good as you could?"

"I think I made out like a bandit. I mean I had forty years hanging, the maximum. They could've gave me a ten-to-twenty on just one of them, cause twenty years is the maximum on burglary. They coulda gave me ten-to-twenty; they coulda gave me anything. They gave me twenty, nineteen, on the way down. Or they coulda gave me a one-to-two or two-to-five, but whatever he offers you, you better take it, cause if you don't, you're going to get more than he offered; so take what you get."

"You came out pretty well?"

"Yeah, I mean from forty down to one year, you know—good."

Both of these men pleaded guilty. Both expressed some reservations (though somewhat muted and perhaps ritualistic) about their actual guilt. One was quite dissatisfied with the outcome of his case; the other felt he "made out like a bandit." Both accepted bargains. Both distrusted their attorneys. Both in some ways felt that their adversary in the proceeding was not only the state and its representative, the prosecutor, but also their own attorney.

Plea Bargains without Bargaining
Routinization of Misdemeanor Procedures
Richard G. Mendes and John T. Wold

The negotiated plea of guilty is a highly significant vehicle for case disposition in American trial courts. More than 85 percent of all nonfederal prosecutors reportedly engage in "bargain justice" in order to obtain guilty pleas from defendants.[1] Roughly 90 percent of all convictions are the products of pleas of guilty rather than criminal trials,[2] and a large percentage of these pleas are the result of negotiations between prosecutors and defense attorneys.

Here we shall analyze the negotiated-plea process in one of the busiest urban courtrooms in the nation—Division 81 of the Los Angeles Municipal Court. Our study differs from earlier studies of plea bargaining[3] in two important respects. First, it focuses exclusively on misdemeanor, rather than felony, plea bargaining in an urban court. Second, it focuses on a highly formalized system of plea bargaining inaugurated after the decision of the U.S. Supreme Court in *Brady* v. *U.S.*[4] and the subsequent similar ruling of the California Supreme Court in *People* v. *West.*[5] These decisions definitively upheld the constitutionality of the guilty-plea process and allowed judges openly to accept the results of plea negotiations in court.

Our task is threefold: to describe the recent history of Division 81 and its setting in the court system, to examine the significant fea-

Source: Previously unpublished, this article is a revised version of a paper presented at the meeting of the Western Political Science Association, 4–6 April 1974, Denver, Colorado. Printed by permission of the authors.

[1]"Note, Guilty Plea Bargaining: Compromises by Prosecutors to Obtain Guilty Pleas," *University of Pennsylvania Law Review* 112 (1964), 865, at 901.

[2]See, e.g., Donald J. Newman, *Conviction: The Determination of Guilt or Innocence without Trial* (Boston: Little, Brown, 1966), p. 3; Arthur Rosett, "The Negotiated Guilty Plea," *The Annals of the American Academy of Political and Social Science* 70 (November 1967), at 71.

[3]In addition to the works cited in notes 1 and 2, cf. Albert W. Alschuler, "The Prosecutor's Role in Plea Bargaining," *University of Chicago Law Review* 36(1968), 50; Abraham S. Blumberg, *Criminal Justice* (Chicago: Quadrangle Books); "Comment, Official Inducement to Plead Guilty: Suggested Morals for a Marketplace," *University of Chicago Law Review* 32 (1964), 167; H. Jay Folberg, "The 'Bargained For' Guilty Plea —An Evaluation," *Criminal Law Bulletin* 4, 201; Donald J. Newman, "Pleading Guilty for Considerations: A Study of Bargain Justice," in George F. Cole, *Criminal Justice: Law and Politics* (Belmont, Calif.: Duxbury Press, 1972), pp. 183–96; and "The Unconstitutionality of Plea Bargaining," *Harvard Law Review* 83 (1970), 1387.

[4]397 U.S. 742 (1970).

[5]91 Cal. Rptr. 385, 477 P.2d 409 (1970).

tures of misdemeanor plea bargaining in this court, and to assess the
roles of the various participants.

Methodology

The two major techniques employed in this investigation were in-
depth, elite interviews and direct observation. Quantitative data
were almost impossible to obtain because of the archaic record-
keeping system of the Los Angeles Municipal Court, the failure of
Division 81 to maintain adequate records in many important areas
(e.g., the number of persons on summary probation to the court), and
the lack of interface among the various component districts of the
Los Angeles municipal bench. We were able to obtain a limited
amount of aggregate data, and these were generally supportive of
our other materials. These data came from the internal records of
Division 81 and also from the reports of the presiding judge of the
Municipal Court of Los Angeles (1968–74).

The personal interviews we conducted during 1973–74 are the
basis for our role analyses. Each of the major items in our instrument
was designed to tap a broad attitudinal dimension (e.g., fairness of
system, political ideology, opinions concerning other actors in the
system, and role expectations) while allowing the respondents to
structure their own answers. Most interviews were conducted in
single sessions of one to two hours, but a few interviews were completed in two or three parts because of the press of court business.
All interviews were conducted by the authors themselves, singly or
together. No attempt was made to divide up the interviewing on any
systematic basis (e.g., job category of respondent) or in a mathemati-
cally random fashion; nevertheless, we could discern no systematic
differences among the interviews based upon the method of interviewing.

Our sample for this study, 43 persons, included almost all the
prosecutors and judges who had worked in Division 81 since 1971.
We also included a nonsystematic sample of pre-1971 and branch-
court judges and prosecutors, mainly as a control device. We used a
quota-control sample of public and private defense counsel stratified
on the basis of "favorability toward the present plea-bargaining system."

In addition to interviewing, we spent a great deal of time directly
observing the operation of the court, visiting the court nearly every
day for almost two months. Our presence was quickly accepted, and
within a few days we were able to wander about virtually unnoticed. We were given the same degree of access to court areas as were
the prosecutors and public defenders. We were allowed to observe
plea-bargaining sessions in both the prosecutor's office and cham-

bers. And we spent many hours in the prosecutor's office watching the passing parade of bargain seekers.

In sum, our insights into the basic features of Division 81 stem primarily from our observation of court sessions, plea bargaining, and day-to-day interactions among and within the various groups of actors.

Setting

Division 81 is the arraignment court for nontraffic misdemeanors for most of Los Angeles. Its jurisdiction is the Central District, which contains ten of the city's seventeen police divisions, including the Southwest and 77th Street divisions (predominantly black areas, which were the center of the 1965 disturbances), the Ramparts division (basically a lower-class Chicano area), and the Hollywood division (center of the Los Angeles drug, streetwalking, and various sexual subcultures). Division 81 is faced with a massive flow of cases common to urban areas: petty theft, prostitution, public lewdness, obscenity, drug-related offenses, gambling, battery, and the like.

The importance of this court lies not only in the nature of its clientele but also in its position vis-à-vis the rest of the municipal

Division 81 Caseload and Dispositions, 1972-74

		1972	1973	1974
I.	Caseload:			
	Plea of guilty or			
	nolo contendere	19,651	14,746	12,496
	Plea of not guilty	4,923	5,412	6,006
	Miscellaneous[a]	6,529	10,062	10,294
	Probation hearing	[b]	3,112	4,344
	Total dispositions[c]	31,103	33,332	33,140
II.	Dispositions:			
	Guilty or nolo contendere percentage of cases receiving terminal dispositions in Division 81	84.2%	74.4%	68.8%
	Guilty or nolo contendere as percentage of all pleas (Guilty, Nolo, or Not Guilty)	80.0%	73.2%	67.5%

[a] Includes dismissal, expungement, issuance of bench warrant, motions, probation and sentencing, referral to juvenile authorities, determination of mental incompetence.

[b] Data are not available.

[c] Total number of appearances minus continuances. This number represents the number of cases processed by Division 81.

bench. Division 81 is the initial filter for the entire system. Its policies have consequences throughout the Central District in that each
case that is not disposed of at arraignment requires additional time
from at least one and often two other courts.

Before 1970, little plea bargaining occurred in Division 81; most
bargains were struck at the master-calendar of pretrial conference
stage. One judge who presided over the court during this period
estimates that only 20 percent of the cases were disposed of at the
arraignment stage while the remaining 80 percent went on to the
master-calendar court. As the table below illustrates, this proportion
has now been reversed. Furthermore, changes in the operation of
Division 81 have been associated with a reduction in the caseload of
the criminal and civil courts of the Central District.[6]

In 1970 and early 1971, several developments provided impetus for
change, particularly the *Brady* and *West* decisions as well as a
considerable increase in the workload of Division 81 and a policy
determination by the municipal bench to expedite its civil calendar.
But perhaps most important was the coalescence in Division 81 of a
group of judges and prosecutors who were dissatisfied with the high
rate of recidivism and with what they perceived as the "uselessness"
of the arraignment stage in criminal proceedings.[7]

Our interviews indicated that these officials tended to view the
misdemeanor defendants in Division 81 as basically weak-willed
persons who lacked the self-restraint necessary to end their lives of
petty crime. This view was in sharp contrast to their attitude toward
felons, whom they tended to regard as genuinely evil and dangerous.
In speaking with us, prosecutors and judges frequently stressed the
need for systematically increased punishments, not for the sake of
vengeance but to convince misdemeanants that the court was aware
of their activities and would punish misbehavior.

It is our observation that these officials acted upon their perceptions in attempting to create new uses for plea bargaining by adapt-
ing the practice to the needs of an arraignment court.

New Uses

Summary Probation

The most striking characteristic of plea bargaining in Division 81
is the court's extensive and atypical use of summary, or bench,

[6]For a more extensive discussion of this point, see John T. Wold and Richard
Mendes, "Innovation in an Inner City Arraignment Court," *Judicature* 52 (1974), 289,
at 293–95.

[7]Of course, one may question whether an arraignment court which does not produce a large number of dispositions is "useless," since arraignments are fundamental
safeguards against the illegal detention of the accused.

probation. Summary probation is simply probation to the court itself and does not involve formal supervision of an individual's behavior by probation officers. The interviewees indicated that a basic reason for the frequent use of summary probation in misdemeanor cases is the belief among judges and prosecutors that brief jail terms have little rehabilitative effect upon lawbreakers. As one municipal court judge claimed: "County jail is just a warehouse. No one is going to be rehabilitated by going to jail for three or six months. . . . I see the use of summary probation as a way of countering mere jailing for a brief time. . . . for idle purposes."

However, respondents alleged that courts typically grant summary probation without including any specific behavioral guidelines for the probationer. The usual requirement is that he simply "obey the laws." The distinctiveness of the Los Angeles experiment is that specific conditions are attached to the grant of probation for selected categories of offenders.

Since probation is a discretionary act of leniency, the court may attach conditions that are reasonably related to the original charge. Although formally the defendant must accept these conditions freely and voluntarily, as a practical matter the court may simply refuse to grant him probation if he does not agree to them.

One goal of the conditions of probation used in Division 81 is to deprive certain types of offenders of the temptation and opportunity to commit their particular offense. Conditions are designed, for example, to keep prostitutes off the streets and homosexual offenders out of the public parks. Prosecutors and judges contended that their use of increasingly severe penalties and attempts to convince defendants of judicial omniscience are deterrents to future wrongdoing. As one deputy city attorney asserted: "Our conditions give some defendants who are not yet hardened criminals the motivation to avoid further wrongdoing. The threat, the mere idea, that the government is watching them deters some probationers from further crime."

The second primary goal is to keep probationers "on the string"— that is, to make it possible for the police to arrest them for behavior which, though not illegal as such, violates their conditions of probation. In other words, one intended effect is to expand substantially the scope of police and prosecutorial control over the lives of certain probationers.

To date, officials have devised sets of conditions for six separate categories of offenders, including persons arrested on obscenity charges, for homosexual behavior in public parks, for streetwalking, for narcotics and marijuana use, for battery and gun violations, and for bookmaking.

Officials estimate that 95 percent of all defendants pleading guilty in Division 81 are placed on summary probation, and that for half of them probation is subject to special conditions.[8] The other half are subject only to the traditional requirement that they obey all laws. For some, such as gamblers and petty thieves, officials have been unable to devise any workable sets of conditions. For others, such as those committing offenses for which arrests are made only infrequently, officials have not yet considered it necessary to devise any conditions.

In numerical terms alone, the results of the court's experiment with summary probation have been remarkable. By mid-1974, an estimated 60,000–100,000 persons were on probation to Division 81.[9]

Standard Deals

Another striking feature about the operation of Division 81 is the virtual routinization of the dispositional process, from the filing of charges through formal arraignment. In charging defendants, for example, the deputy city attorneys almost always follow the initial accusation contained in the police report. In fact, one deputy estimated that the prosecutors changed the original charge in only about 2 percent of all cases filed.

The practice of "overcharging" defendants, alleged to exist in many other parts of the nation, is thus virtually nonexistent in Division 81.[10] We observed that defendants typically have only a single count of a single charge filed against them—probably because there is only one charge that *can* be leveled against them. For instance, almost all streetwalkers are arrested for having accosted a plainclothes police officer. There is normally no other charge that can reasonably be filed. Arrests for lewd conduct in a park restroom or "porno" theater are likewise typically uncomplicated, and there is logically or practically only a particular misdemeanor violation that can be alleged against the defendant.

While prosecutors could conceivably charge some defendants— such as those accused of narcotics violations or bookmaking—with multiple offenses, as a matter of course this is not done. Prosecutors typically file additional charges only when the defendant appears to have committed offenses that are wholly separate and distinct from the original charge, such as resisting arrest or obstructing a police officer in the exercise of his duty.

[8]In observing the court, we kept track of such parameters as caseload and nature of dispositions, observations we used as an independent check on the estimates of officials. Our own data indicated that the estimate of 95 percent was, if anything, conservative.

[9]No official tally is kept; this figure is the composite estimate of officials most closely associated with the system.

[10]For a discussion of the alleged practice of "overcharging" by prosecutors to improve their subsequent bargaining position, see Alschuler, *op. cit.*, pp. 85–105.

Plea bargaining in Division 81 is also virtually routinized. The participants in bargaining make deals not on an individualized basis but according to the current policies of the court. Deputies have only limited discretion when "dealing" with defense attorneys. Thus, "plea bargaining" in Division 81 is typically devoid of any real bargaining. As one deputy city attorney observed: "Ninety-eight percent of the stuff here is routine. There is a policy covering almost every charge." And one judge asserted that "bargains are almost always predetermined. I can look at the defendant's arrest report and prior record and know in advance what the bargain will be. The actual bargaining is over the number of days of jail time to be credited or other relatively minor questions."

Policies governing bargaining are proposed by the "dealing" prosecutors to the judge(s) presiding in Division 81. Ultimate authority over dispositions remains in the hands of the judiciary, since all judges who have served in the arraignment court have insisted that any proposed policy may not be implemented without their prior approval. The impetus for revisions in bargaining policy may be either "internal"—because of changes in judicial or prosecutorial personnel or dissatisfaction with the results of existing policy—or "external"—e.g., because of an influx of a "new set" of defendants. When, in the summer of 1973, Los Angeles police began for the first time to make numerous arrests of male customers of streetwalkers, the deputies in Division 81 had to devise a policy for negotiating with the attorneys of these defendants.

Bargaining policies are predicated upon the notion of systematically increased punishments for defendants who continue to commit the same offense. Virtually all persons who are arrested in the Central District for the first time on any given charge—regardless of the number of convictions they have on other charges—are offered a standard deal in exchange for a guilty plea. That is, they are permitted to plead guilty to charges that do not bear the stigma of the original charge. They are also given suspended sentences and 24 months of summary probation, one of the conditions of which is that they pay a $100 fine or serve five days in the county jail.[11]

As an example, a prostitute arrested for the first time in the Central District for soliciting may plead guilty to a charge of trespass and be placed on summary probation for two years. She must consent to the "100-or-5" requirement and agree to comply with six specific conditions of probation. These include the requirements that she "not solicit or accept a ride from motorists or be parked in a motor

[11]The "100-or-5" requirement is often the result of pro forma "bargaining." Deputies offer just five days in jail at first, then add the $100 option automatically when the public defender asks for the change.

vehicle with lone male motorists," "not approach male pedestrians or motorists or engage them in conversation upon a public street or in a public place," and "not occupy a hotel or motel room or any other residence unless registered in [her] true name."

Persons apprehended for the first time on charges of being under the influence of narcotics may plead guilty to a violation of Section 4143 of the Business and Professions Code, that is, unlawful possession of a hypodermic needle and hypodermic syringe. They likewise must comply with the "100-or-5" requirement and submit to six specific conditions of probation. These include the stipulations that the probationer not use or possess any marijuana, narcotics, or dangerous drugs, or associate with anyone else who does so.

Defendants arrested for lewd conduct in a public park (a common homosexual offense) may plead guilty to trespass and agree to the standard probation period and jail term or fine. They normally must consent to two specific conditions of probation: that they "stay out of public parks, streets, and sidewalks immediately adjacent to public parks," and "submit to and cooperate in field interrogation by any peace officer at any time of day or night."

First-time defendants on petty theft charges, where the property in question is valued at less than $20, receive a standard offer: trespass charges, summary probation for two years, and the "100-or-5" requirement. But if the property is valued at more than $20, the defendant usually must plead "straight up" to the theft charge. In either case, there are no specific conditions with which the probationer must comply; he or she simply must agree to "obey all laws."

Despite the virtual standardization of deals for first-time offenders, deputies sometimes do have limited discretion as to actual dispositions of cases. In theft cases, for instance, they may allow a plea to trespass if the property involved, though valued at more than $20, consists of only one item. Likewise, they may "bend" if they believe the defendant has stolen food for only his or her own consumption.[12] And deputies sometimes dismiss first-time shoplifting charges altogether—for example, if it appears that the only reason for the theft was the defendant's senility.

Deputies also have some discretion concerning the number of days credited toward completion of the "100-or-5" requirement. For example, if a defendant has served two and one-half days in jail at the time of arraignment, the deputy may choose whether to offer three or only two days' credit for time already served. For defendants with jobs and families the decision on this issue is often an important one, since many of the defendants hold marginal jobs, and a prolonged absence could cause dismissal.

---

[12]Deputies show no leniency, however, if the defendant stole steaks, since these are presumed to have been taken for sale and not merely for personal consumption.

Dispositions for defendants arrested more than once on the same charge are also predetermined, although not to the same extent as for first-time offenders. The most significant factor influencing the ultimate deal for multiple offenders is the recentness of prior arrests on the same charge. Defendants with no recent "priors" (that is, no arrests for at least one year) may again be treated as first-time offenders. However, they may be required to serve more jail time than they served after the first conviction. But if defendants are on probation and have recent "priors," deputies typically insist that they plead "straight up" to the original charge, that their probation be revoked and reinstated for another 24 months, and that they serve longer jail terms as a condition of their new probation.

The actual sequence of jail terms varies from one type of offense to another. For most violations the sequence is 30 days for a second offense, 60 for a third, and 90 for a fourth offense. For some violations, such as prostitution, the sequence of jail terms is simply 45 days for a second offense and 90 days for each subsequent conviction. Probationers arrested for the second time on narcotics charges, if required to plead "straight up," must serve the statutory minimum of 90 days in the county jail.[13]

It is the certainty of increased punishment which prosecutors and judges in Division 81 consider the primary deterrent to future wrongdoing by defendants. As one judge insisted: "You have to give them the right impression. If you promise them something, you must be a man of your word. Otherwise you're a paper tiger. You must let the criminal type know what will happen to him if he keeps doing the same thing."

We should note that the jail terms for multiple offenders are not actual sentences for the crime charged but conditions tied to the reinstatement of probation. Sentences themselves are suspended after each plea of guilty and therefore accumulate. Many jurists and prosecutors agree that most probationers who have been given three-month jail terms do not again commit their particular crimes (not in Los Angeles, at least). Judges base their belief upon casual empiricism rather than objective data, but in any event their sentencing policy reflects a belief in the efficacy of the 90-day sentence.

One aspect of keeping probationers "on a string" is that they may be treated as possible probation violators if they do not plead guilty to any new charges filed against them.[14] In a probation revocation

[13]Deputy city attorneys view the mandatory jail term for narcotics convictions as particularly beneficial to heroin addicts, in that it enables them to overcome their actual physical need for heroin and leads to a temporary reduction in the amount of the drug needed to support their habit.

[14]The arrest of a probationer is usually for another commission of the same crime with which he was originally charged, not for violation of the terms of probation per se.

hearing the prosecutor need only show that a preponderance of evidence exists against the probationer; he need not prove his case beyond a reasonable doubt. Also, there is no trial, the hearing being conducted in the judge's chambers rather than in open court. The customary rule against hearsay evidence is likewise relaxed.[15] If a violation of probation is found, the judge may impose any and all suspended sentences that have accumulated against the defendant. Probationers may thus, in the words of one deputy, be punished merely for "being where they shouldn't be and doing what they shouldn't do."

In sum, plea bargaining in Division 81 involves an extensive use of packaged deals: standardized punishments and summary probation, which is often tied to specific behavioral guidelines. Plea bargaining of this nature differs in many respects from the types of plea bargaining discussed in much of the earlier literature.

Roles

Because of its heavy caseload and extensive use of summary probation, Division 81 is heavily staffed. A large number of bailiffs and clerical personnel are needed to process the enormous amount of paperwork generated by the policies of the court.

Currently the entire caseload is handled by a single judge, although, in the past, the court often used the services of two judges, or one judge and one commissioner. One judge would preside in the courtroom, overseeing the endless paper-shuffling, official stamping, and queueing of defendants. At the same time the second judge would be in chambers helping to work out difficult deals or holding probation-violation hearings. During the day, the judges would periodically exchange positions.

The City Attorney's Office provides six to eight deputies for Division 81. Usually two of these prosecutors are novices who are spending a short time in the court to learn about the plea-bargaining system. These deputies do no dealing but are "disposition readers." That is, they represent the prosecution in the courtroom itself and literally read the agreed-upon plea bargains from forms given to them by the other deputies. As one of these trainees commented, "All I do is read the disposition slip. If the disposition slip says 'I am a monkey,' I say 'I am a monkey.'" Deputies other than the deputy-in-charge sit in their office or roam the corridors conducting case discussions with the defense attorneys, who likewise roam the corridors looking for someone to bargain with.

[15]However, the right to counsel and the exclusionary rule with respect to searches and seizures are about the same as those pertaining to trials.

The deputy-in-charge does a very limited amount of routine dealing but is called upon to handle cases which are unusual and hence fall outside the guidelines of the standard deals. He is also responsible administratively to the City Attorney's Office.

The Public Defender's Office provides a staff of about 25 deputies. One is the administrative head of the group and the remainder are divided into two "teams" of about 12 each. The teams alternate every three weeks between bargaining and trial work. A team spends three weeks in Division 81 handling arraignments and attempting to negotiate pleas. At the end of this period they move to the trial courts to represent clients for whom they could not strike satisfactory bargains. Generally, each public defender remains with the same clients in both stages.

It is possible that this rotational system has an impact upon the decision not to accept proffered bargains in some cases. Several respondents suggested that many public defenders "hold off" on "bargaining out" a number of cases so that they will have enough cases to fill their three weeks of trial work.

The groups in Division 81 differ not only in their roles but also in their perception of the fairness of the dispositional process. The prosecutors are the pivotal group since they are the ones who do the actual bargaining in each case. They serve as a bridge between the broad policy guidelines of the judges and the specifics of each case presented by the defense attorneys. In this sense they act more as administrators than as advocates. Indeed, one former prosecutor stated that his very reason for leaving his position was the administrative nature of his duties; he felt he was moving "further and further away from the law."

When present and former bargaining prosecutors were asked to verbalize the normative objectives of their role, they tended to emphasize three major goals: to protect the public, "see that justice is done," and guarantee equality of punishment to defendants. The first two goals are applicable to all facets of prosecutorial work, not just plea bargaining. The third goal, however, was portrayed as primarily an administrative norm rather than a purely legalistic one.

Almost all the prosecutors acknowledged that they had a responsibility to represent the "people" vis-à-vis the defendants in particular and the criminal element in general. Most prosecutors viewed themselves as a shield for the community. Some saw themselves as weights holding the lid on a bubbling cauldron of criminal activity which would overflow, were the prosecutor not diligent, and swamp the city with crime. For instance, one prosecutor stated that the role of the plea bargainer was to "use criminal law as a deterrent ... to remove from society someone who seems to have trouble adjusting to it. Not rehabilitation, but taking this type of person out of society."

Most of the prosecutors felt that the "crime prevention" they were practicing was neither understood nor appreciated by the community at large. One former deputy stated that "city attorneys [in the criminal division] are like garbagemen and morticians; the public wants them to do the dirty work and not to bother the public with it."

A second goal mentioned by the prosecutors was to see that "justice is done." To most prosecutors this meant giving the childlike defendant direction rather than exacting the last ounce of vengeance. As one prosecutor stated: If the defendant is a first-time offender, with education and all, you can deal with him through discussion and counseling. . . . The average person, though, has to have a club put over his head so he won't come back. Many are just weak-willed people who lack self-discipline or will power."

It is the relationship implicit in the goal of "seeing that justice is done" that supplies the prosecutor with a sense of power and authority in the plea-bargaining system. Both defense attorneys and defendants appearing in their own behalf must seek out the prosecutor to ask for a favorable disposition. Also, although the system of standardized deals limits the prosecutor's actual discretion, it apparently does not significantly diminish his sense of efficacy. One prosecutor stated: "We sometimes say we should put on our black robes in the morning, because we really do act as judges. I love the feeling of *power.* You just hope it doesn't go to your head." In short, the norm of "seeing that justice is done" was the justification for substituting benevolent despotism for vengeance and in the process enhancing the self-esteem of the prosecutor.

The third goal prosecutors discussed was the need to ensure equal punishment to offenders who plead guilty. The system of standardized deals described earlier probably engenders and reinforces this attitude on the individual level. Deputies assigned to Division 81 quickly become aware of the norm of equal punishment and tend to internalize it. As one deputy asserted, the major goal is "to get equality in the sentence for every charge. For example, I try to see that every defendant charged with petty theft [for the first time] in this court will receive the same sentence. That makes me blind as to who or what the person is."

The role of the judge in the current plea-bargaining system is somewhat paradoxical in that he is at the same time more and less powerful than his predecessors. He is certainly less powerful in his courtroom presence in that he infrequently refuses a deal agreed upon by the prosecutor and the defense. A judge's courtroom activities often seem confined literally to rubber-stamping negotiated deals and attempting to explain these agreements to generally bewildered defendants. At times the courtroom assumes the atmosphere of a bazaar. One jurist commented that "the disadvantage [of massive plea bargaining] is that the procedure gives the appearance of marketplace justice. I deplore this. But the advantages, I think, outweigh the disadvantages."

Because of the sheer volume of the caseload a judge has little or no opportunity to investigate the merits of each case. Almost every jurist with whom we spoke indicated that a more thorough judicial screening of cases would vastly improve the quality of the system. Since time will not permit this screening, however, the judge relies heavily upon the prosecutor to present a reasonable disposition. One judge observed: "The city attorney helps take the burden off the court. He can work out dispositions and take such work away from the judge. This gives the judge time to work on [more general] problems." This reliance upon the prosecution may be what prompted some respondents to refer to plea-bargaining judges as "emasculated" or "ciphers."

Such characterizations are simplistic for two reasons. First, the judge does reserve to himself the right to take an active role in the disposition of a case. One judge remarked that an arraignment court judge "has no role as a fact-finder, but should take an active role in the plea bargaining itself." Another jurist asserted that "in trials the judge should be passive, but in plea bargaining the judge should participate."

A more important reason is that although the judge has abdicated much of his courtroom decision-making power, he has apparently acquired considerable policy-making power. It is the judge who ultimately determines the limits of plea bargaining. One jurist stated that during his tenure he "talked with the city attorneys once a week, to tell them what I considered to be reasonable plea bargains. The last word on plea bargains comes from the judge." In addition, although a judge rarely rejects a bargain, when he does so he is usually setting a new standard. The ability to make broad-range policy obviously enhances the power of judges in Division 81.

This ability is also of enormous consequence for the municipal trial courts. As mentioned earlier, Division 81 is a filter for the rest of the system, and the judges in this court have been keenly aware of the behavioral demands of their unique position. One judge stated that his major goal was to "try to cut down the calendar—that doesn't mean anything goes, but we must move the courts along. A lot of the court cases are a waste of time, and [this system] saves time for everyone." Another jurist estimated that "if even 10 percent more [defendants] pleaded not guilty than do now, the courts couldn't handle the caseload. It sounds terrible, but we have to move the cases along."

In sum, the role of the judge in Division 81 is that of a policy-maker and an administrator rather than an impartial mediator or finder-of-fact. Not all jurists wish to fulfill the demands of the plea-bargaining role. Many municipal judges assigned to Division 81 have found the system of massive plea bargaining either incomprehensible or distasteful. Some have attempted to change the system, only to be quickly "rotated out" by the presiding municipal judge when the disposition rate of the court dropped.

The perceptions of the judges and prosecutors were remarkably similar. They saw the system as both extremely efficient and generally fair (perhaps even overly lenient) to the defendant. Since the judges and prosecutors possess unusually high status in this type of operation, it is not unreasonable for them to view it in a positive fashion.

On the other hand, many public defenders expressed serious reservations about, and often outright hostility toward, the same system. Unlike prosecutors, who stated that their duty to represent "the people" was tempered by the need to see that "justice is done," the public defenders believed that their sole loyalty was to their clients. As one remarked: "I should be protecting, on an individual basis, the legal positions of individuals charged . . . to see that they have every legal right. My responsibility is almost exclusively to the defendant." Only the ethical boundaries of the legal profession were perceived as the limits of the defender's obligation to his clients. As one respondent said: "The public defender has no function in making up defenses or aiding perjury, but he should take advantage of every technical and legal defense which is ethical. The law is the law. If a loophole exists, then the system [the legislature] should take care of it."

Although the public defenders viewed their role as that of the complete advocate, counterpressures forced them to compromise this ideal. Most agreed that there was great pressure to "help keep the system moving." "You can't treat the clients as human beings," one defender claimed, "because of the caseload. People become mere cases. . . . You're dropping bodies into a meatgrinder, and if one balks it is a problem for the system."

Another counterpressure on the public defenders stemmed from their own clientele. Unlike the prosecutors, the defenders must actually discuss each case with the defendant, and many become very cynical about the basic character of their clients. It is very disillusioning for individuals who became public defenders in order to "help the poor and oppressed" to find that their clients often see them as merely an extension of an oppressive criminal justice system. Many defenders in fact claimed that their clients heaped more abuse and mistrust upon them than upon any other actor in the system, including the prosecutor. This should not be surprising. After all, it is often the defender who advises his client to stay in jail and wait for trial while the prosecutor is offering the same defendant a tempting deal.

Buffeted among the demands of a heavy caseload, a powerful judge-prosecutor alliance, and an abusive and distrustful clientele, it is small wonder that many public defenders felt extremely ambivalent about their roles. In the words of one: "At the most cynical, I'm part of the railroad with respect to my client. At the most idealistic, the idea is to screw the police and the prosecutors."

It is our contention that the type of plea bargaining used in this court is significantly related to the atypical roles of its actors. Its judges, for example, devote most of their efforts to making policy concerning standard deals and conditions of probation. Prosecutors act as administrators of court policies, processing defendants in accordance with the bureaucratic norms of efficiency and uniformity. Public defenders appear cross-pressured by the system of the court. They are pressed to conform to the administrative norms mentioned above but still feel a strong commitment to their clients. For them, the contrast between the goals of an administrator and the ideals of a traditional advocate creates a serious emotional and intellectual dilemma.

Conclusion

Most actors in Division 81 possess either a predominantly favorable or unfavorable attitude toward the court's method of operation, depending upon their particular role within the system. In the course of our research, however, we developed distinctly ambivalent attitudes toward the court's policies.

On the one hand, the system does constitute an attempt to respond to the apparent constraints which the public and/or legislature place upon the courts. Many respondents perceived three major constraints. First, most legislatures appear unwilling to finance sufficient courtrooms and personnel to provide every defendant with a trial. At the same time, lawmakers seem unwilling to decriminalize much behavior now defined as criminal. (The longstanding controversy over so-called victimless crimes is of course relevant here.) Furthermore, police agencies that fail to enforce existing statutes run the risk of public censure.

In addition, the plea-bargaining system used in Division 81 may indeed deter or reform many misdemeanants and in doing so provide a service to both society and offenders.

On the other hand, some features of Division 81 are especially vulnerable to negative criticism. It may well be, for example, that the liberality of the "deals" offered induces defendants to give up their right to trial and hence sometimes makes criminals out of innocent individuals. Likewise, the apparent use of threats of probation revocation to induce guilty pleas casts doubt upon the voluntariness of such pleas. If voluntariness be lacking, a basic guideline laid down in *Brady* v. *U.S.* would be violated.

Similarly, according to many respondents, the court's emphasis on expediency makes prosecutors, judges, and defenders *all* susceptible to the desire merely to "process" defendants rather than to try them. Judges were especially vulnerable to criticism in that they were viewed as having exchanged the traditional juridical role of impartial arbiter for that of expediter.

Finally, some of the conditions of probation used are of questionable constitutionality. Those applied to streetwalkers and many homosexual offenders are most suspect.

In sum, we are unable to make a definitive value judgment about the new uses of plea bargaining employed in Division 81. We do note, however, that its operation reflects the demands that it process a heavy caseload and still protect the rights of defendants—a dilemma that has plagued not only Division 81 but most other urban criminal courts in the United States.

4
Interaction in the Court

We have seen that before the accused offender appears before a judge many things must happen. An observer or a victim must contact the police and complain about criminal activity, a policeman must investigate the matter and decide that it is "serious" enough to warrant further action, and a prosecutor must feel that the accused should be prosecuted.* If courtroom proceedings begin, certain decisions made by persons who play various roles in the court will determine the final outcome of the case.

In order to understand how the criminal justice system operates, therefore, it is necessary to study how these decisions are made. All of the studies in this final part attempt to answer these general questions: What decisions are likely to be made about accused offenders when they are processed through the criminal courts? How are decisions made in the courthouse? And what are the consequences of these decisions for those who are accused of violating the law?

Our ideal of the criminal justice system rests on the assumption that the courtroom is a stage on which adversaries who strictly follow the law compete against each other. The prosecutor tries to win the case for "the people" while the defense attorney argues for the best interests of the client. In many ways the ceremony of the court and its physical structure, including the bench, the jury box, the special tables for prosecution and defense, the area between the attorneys and the judge's bench, encourage this image. The courtroom is like a stage, and those who staff it are like actors in a drama. But, unlike the ideal image, the actual drama of the criminal courts is not written down beforehand, and the crucial interaction that comprises the drama does not have an adversary quality, nor does it literally follow the law. The "administration of justice" cannot be understood merely by reading the law and paying attention to the action on the courthouse stage. In order to comprehend it fully, one must probe behind the scenes and contemplate how the law "as it is written" (Pound, 1930) has been adopted by the actors who have had parts in the play for many years. One can discover what is really going on only by stripping away the façade of legal ceremony to expose the consequential interaction of the players.

*It should be said that grand-jury action can lead to court trial without all these steps.

203

Some scholars have done this and have produced sound professional studies. For instance, Donald Newman (1966) discusses how the formal proceedings of the court give the trial process "an apparent simplicity which does not accord with reality." Even though all the actors realize that the defendant has been induced to enter a plea of guilty rather than request a trial, a ritual is often enacted that the uncritical audience is led to believe represents reality. Newman (1966:7–8) presents the following typical exchange:

COURT: You are charged in the information filed against you in this court with the crime of breaking and entering in the daytime, two counts. Do you understand what this means?
DEFENDANT: Yes.
COURT: And how do you plead to this charge?
DEFENDANT: Guilty.
COURT: Are you pleading guilty because you actually are guilty?
DEFENDANT: Yes.
COURT: Has the prosecuting attorney, any officer of this court, or any other person threatened you or made you any promises or inducements to influence you to plead guilty?
DEFENDANT: No.
COURT: You are pleading guilty freely and voluntarily?
DEFENDANT: Yes.
COURT: Prior to your plea did you understand that you had a constitutional right to a trial by jury and that if you were financially unable to employ counsel the court would appoint a lawyer for you?
DEFENDANT: Yes.
COURT: You do not want a trial or a lawyer?
DEFENDANT: No sir.
COURT: You understand that upon accepting your plea of guilty it is my duty to impose sentence on you?
DEFENDANT: I understand.
COURT: And that the penalty provided for daytime breaking and entering might involve a prison term up to five years?
DEFENDANT: Yes.
COURT: Very well, I will accept your plea of guilty and set the date for sentencing three weeks from today, that is, on December 10.

All the authors represented in this part recognize that the interaction of various actors in the courthouse community does not conform to the ideal written in the law; therefore, they have examined the decision-making processes with skepticism. In their exploration of what goes on in the courtroom, they have searched for standards, informal rules, and formulas that have been developed and are used by courthouse personnel to guide their behavior.

The specific policies and rules that organize interaction are always being refined by the actors in the court. Consequently, some extralegal rule systems may become institutionalized. As the following articles indicate, empirical study had led many scholars to conclude that the informal criteria used by agents of the court have become so routinized that they should not be regarded as extralegal. The law-in-action is for all practical purposes the law. What is written down in the statutes and criminal codes is of little consequence if it remains only an ideal. If the law-in-action is based on informal criteria, these criteria become an essential part of it.

The institutionalized quality of these informal rules developed by the courthouse bureaucracy is attested by the fact that there is little disagreement among agents of the system about what policies to follow. The guidelines used are not written down or codified, but they are well known to the interactors in the courtroom, including lawyers, judges, and to a lesser extent other administrative personnel. This differentially shared knowledge is usually unavailable to outsiders, including those who are charged with crimes. Thus, Frederic Suffet characterizes the typical defendant as a "passive bystander" who contributes little to the proceedings, which are completely bewildering to him. Even those who become regular defendants and thus learn the informal rules are not allowed to contribute significantly to the trial. Jacqueline Wiseman's study shows that the informal policies of the drunk court may become so institutionalized that Skid-Row men are able to predict the sentences drunks will receive in different jurisdictions. Socialization into the court, however, does not change the role the defendant plays in the proceedings. Knowledgeable or not, the defendant has to enact the part of passive client and accept the will of the court.

Because few persons find themselves repeatedly before a judge, most people are not accorded the knowledge that many Skid-Row alcoholics share and are therefore caught in a system they cannot understand. This is true of complainants as well as defendants in many instances. A woman who has been raped, for example, may receive perplexing treatment in a trial. She will soon discover that she is involved in a trial not only as a victim but also as one who is suspected of immoral conduct. Carol Bohmer concludes that the criteria that are used to assess whether a woman has in fact been raped are extremely important to the judge and strongly influence his decision, yet are not established by law as relevant evidence in the determination of culpability. In general the legitimate and illegitimate evidence used by judges in rape cases has an effect similar to that of the character evaluations used in drunk court, bail hearings, and juvenile court in that it largely determines what will happen to the accused. In rape cases, both the victim and the suspect are evaluated, but the determination made about the victim seems to be more important than the one made about the suspect. If a woman is negatively evaluated by a judge, it is unlikely that he will interpret the alleged attack as a rape.

Suffet studied court sessions in which it is decided whether defendants are to be granted release on bail or on their own recognizance or held in jail during the trial. According to Suffet, the court has a community atmosphere. Although each of the various members of the community has his own interests, which he attempts to satisfy, there seems to be a fairly well systematized set of procedures and policies that maintain order and keep open conflict to a minimum.

The fact that there are relatively clear understandings of the informal standards that will be applied to those seeking bail does not mean that all the attorneys in the court will feel that these standards are right or that they will have equal influence on the outcome of a hearing. For example, when conflict occurs between attorneys during a bail hearing, the disagreement is usually resolved in favor of the prosecution. Suffet found that the defense attorney's initial suggestion about the amount of bail that should be set was accepted about 58 percent of the time. Usually bail is set at a higher figure than initially proposed by the defense. The institutionalization of informal policies to guide the decisions of the court does not, therefore, ensure that these policies will be fair. Inequities promoted by informal court policies are particularly evident in rape cases. For instance, Carol Bohmer found that, because judges generally follow an informal policy of being critical of a rape victim's allegations, they tend to treat women in a way that is distinctly different from the treatment given to other victims who appear in court.

Carter and Wilkins suggest that the reason the courts hand down various sentences cannot be understood adequately without appreciating the court as a community. Attorneys, probation officers, and judges are all part of a community, and each is partially responsible for the decisions made regarding sentences. Carter and Wilkins found, for example, that probation officers and judges frequently agree about what should be done with convicted offenders, probably because they share the same informal notions as to which offenders are poor probation risks and what criteria should be used to assess a person's suitability for supervised release. The existence of some informally shared normative system in the court is further suggested by the observation that as probation officers gain experience and are socialized into the system they are more likely to agree with one another about how cases should be handled.

In his analysis of the juvenile court, Aaron Cicourel shows how members of that system rely on numerous informal criteria to determine what to do with juveniles who have gotten into trouble with the police or schools. Cicourel indicates, however, that these criteria are vaguely defined and that their meanings and relevance must be created on those occasions when they are used by juvenile officers and others. The determination that a youth is delinquent is an ad hoc decision. When a young person is labeled a delinquent, the officers of the juvenile court must convince others that the label is appropriate. Evidence cited by juvenile authorities as documentation of delinquency is only as adequate as those in the system make it. They do this by linking features of the youth's behavior to some a priori ideas about delinquents. This means that court policies are *ex post facto* accounts of decisions rather than directives about how to make them.

Bail setting, drunk-court dispositions, rape trials, sentencing of adults, and juvenile hearings all entail some analysis of the character of the accused and the victim. All of the articles in this part indicate that cursory examinations of biography and character play an extremely important part in the proceedings. Bohmer and Wiseman, for example, claim that these evaluations are so common that one can identify the categories into which various defendants are typically placed. For instance, a woman involved in a rape trial may be classified as a vindictive female or a genuine victim. Attached to each biographical category may be a set of qualities that all those placed in that category are assumed to share. In bail hearings, prior arrests may become social indicators of character. In his study of bail hearings Suffet found: "The more serious the charge, the more extensive the prior record, and the weaker the defendant's community ties, the greater the chance for high bail or remand and the smaller is the chance for r.o.r. [release on own recognizance]." Those with previous arrests are considered to be bad risks for probation because they have a "criminal character."

Even a person's appearance may be used as evidence of character. According to Wiseman, defendants who appear to be shaky in drunk court will be treated differently from those who are clean-shaven and able to stand up straight.

Carter and Wilkins show that biographical data about an individual affect the sentence determinations made by the court. Their study reveals: "The proportion of recommendations for probation increased with the number of years of education, average monthly income, higher occupational levels, residence, marital and employment stability, participation in church activities, and a good military record."

Finally, although Cicourel is interested primarily in studying how various aspects of a juvenile's biography are made relevant to the label of delinquency by court personnel, the things he found to be relevant to court officials were also found to be important to legal decisions by the other authors in this section.

References

Newman, Donald J. 1966. *Conviction: The Determination of Guilt or Innocence without Trial.* Boston: Little, Brown.

Pound, Roscoe. 1930. *Criminal Justice in America.* New York: Holt.

Bail Setting
A Study of Courtroom Interaction

Frederic Suffet

In the past ten years there has been an upsurge in empirical studies of the bail system in the United States. Some of them helped trigger the bail reform movement now under way across the nation,[1] and some were done in response to this movement. Most of them, based on data collected from court records, have sought to determine the factors that underlie the amount of bail set in various cases.[2] Many features of the bail system *qua* system still remain relatively unexplored by sociological research. Something is known of the standards that guide the judge in setting bail, but no systematic research has been done on the standards employed by bondsmen in accepting or rejecting potential clients.[3] Research has been done into the legal consequences of pretrail detention,[4] but the social consequences to those detained are all but unknown.[5] Nonfinancial reasons for the

SOURCE: *Crime and Delinquency* (October 1966): 318–31. Reprinted by permission of the author and the National Council on Crime and Delinquency.

[1]For a review of this movement, see *Proceedings and Interim Report of the National Conference on Bail and Criminal Justice* (Washington, D.C., 1965), hereinafter cited as *Proceedings*. See also, Bernard Botein, "The Manhattan Bail Project: Its Impact on Criminology and the Criminal Law Processes," *Texas Law Review* (February 1965), p. 319.

[2]See, e.g., C. Foote, J. Markle, and E. Woolley, "Compelling Appearance in Court: Administration of Bail in Philadelphia," *University of Pennsylvania Law Review* (June 1954), p. 1031. See also, "A Study of the Administration of Bail in New York City," *University of Pennsylvania Law Review* (March 1958), p. 693.

[3]Bondsmen have occasionally been interviewed by reform or study groups in an effort to determine such standards. *The Bail System of the District of Columbia: Report of the Committee on the Administration of Bail* (Washington, D.C., 1963) says (p. 12): "Employment, length of residence, presence of relatives or responsible persons who will vouch for him, and family ties were frequently mentioned [by bondsmen] as criteria." However, how universal these criteria are among bondsmen and whether their application varies according to certain characteristics of the defendants, such as race, are not known.

[4]See Anne Rankin, "The Effect of Pretrial Detention," *New York University Law Review* (June 1964), p. 641.

[5]Occasional cases come to light which illustrate the negative social consequences of detention. For example, there is the oft cited case of Daniel Walker, a victim of mistaken identity, who spent fifty-five days in detention and lost his home and job. (For one account, see Senator Robert Kennedy's statement in the *Hearings on S. 2838, S. 2839 and S. 2840 before the Subcommittee on Constitutional Rights and the Subcommittee on Improvements in the Judicial Machinery of the Committee on the Judiciary,* U.S. Senate, 88th Cong., 2d Sess. [1964], p. 13.) It is not known, however, how widespread such consequences are.

failure to post bail have been investigated,[6] but the social mechanisms that release a defendant on bail have not been fully described.[7]

This study will examine a hitherto uncharted process: what happens in the courtroom when bail is being set. The remarks by the
judge when he sets bail have been reported in occasional studies,[8]
but they have been used to illustrate the factors he takes into account
in arriving at a bail figure. Our present concern extends beyond this
to the following questions:

1. What are the typical patterns of interaction between the judge,
the prosecutor, and the defense attorney at bail setting?

2. How much disagreement over bail is there between these parties? What is the effect of disagreement on bail amount, and whose
side will the judge usually take?

3. Who wields the greatest influence at bail setting?

Method

The study is based on 1,473 bail settings observed during October,
November, and December, 1964, in Part 1A of the New York County
Criminal Court.[9] In each case an observer positioned near the judge's
bench recorded verbatim what was said by the judge, the prosecutor,
and the defense attorney when bail was set.[10] He noted the person
initially suggesting a bail amount, the amount suggested, countersuggestions, and the amount finally set. The defendant's prior criminal record and the current charge against him were determined from
the case papers. For purposes of the study, two categories for each
of these variables were created. Criminal record was dichotomized
as *no record* (never arrested) and *prior record* (any record of arrest,
conviction, or imprisonment).[11] Charges were dichotomized as *ma-*

[6]Suffet, "Patterns of Failure to Raise Bail" (unpublished ms., Vera Foundation, 1965).

[7]No studies have been done of the referral processes which lead clients to bondsmen. Kickback arrangements between bondsmen and jailers are noted in the cata-
logue of abuses of the bail system, but little is known of the legitimate modes of
referral.

[8]Foote, Markle, and Woolley, *supra* note 2, p. 1039.

[9]During this period there were an additional 181 arraignments not included in the
study. In 79 cases observers were not present in the court, and in 102 cases essential
items of information were not available from the case papers at the time of the
analysis.

[10]The observation procedure did not noticeably affect the observed interactions.
The observers were Manhattan Bail Project staff members whose presence in court
was a regular occurrence and who normally stood in the spot used for the observations when discharging their Bail Project duties.

[11]Among those defendants having a prior criminal record, the extent of this record
affects bail disposition. However, the major distinction is between (a) having no
record and (b) having a record, no matter how small.

jor (homicide, forcible rape, and robbery) and *minor* (assault, burglary, carrying a concealed weapon, forgery, larceny, receiving
stolen property, and statutory rape).[12]

Whether there was positive recommendation by the Office of Probation for release on recognizance (hereinafter r.o.r.) was also
recorded. The Manhattan Bail Project, a three-year experiment designed to increase the use of r.o.r., was undertaken in Part 1A of the
Court. The Project provided the judge with a positive recommendation for r.o.r.—which the judge could accept or reject—when the
community ties (family, employment, residence) of the defendant
had been verified, he was not accused of a major crime, and he did
not have an extensive prior record.[13] In no case was a recommendation made *against* r.o.r. The Project was adjudged a success by the
city government,[14] and the prearraignment investigation into the
defendant's community ties was made a permanent citywide court
procedure administered by the Office of Probation.

All observations were made at arraignment, the defendant's first
court appearance. If the case was continued—for trial, for sentencing
(if the accused pleaded guilty), or for obtaining private counsel—bail
was set. Three general bail dispositions are possible: (1) the defendant may be r.o.r.'d, (2) bail may be set in some dollar amount, or (3)
under certain conditions the defendant may be remanded to jail.[15]
Overall, 19 percent of the defendants observed were r.o.r.'d, 77 percent had bail set in an average amount of $1,822, and 4 percent were
remanded.

Bail-Setting Standards

The New York statute clearly specifies the conditions under which
a defendant may be admitted to bail, but it carries only the following
note on the amount of bail: "Elements properly considered in fixing
amount of bail are nature of offense, penalty imposed, probability of

[12]These categories were determined from the bail distributions for each charge. The
term "minor" is used as a complement to "major"; the charges here called minor are
not necessarily the least serious in the overall scale of criminal offenses. The minor
category includes both felonies and misdemeanors; less serious charges—the disorderly conduct offenses—are arraigned in another court.

[13]For a description of the operating procedures of the Manhattan Bail Project, see
Proceedings, supra note 1, pp. 43–46. See also "The Manhattan Bail Project: An Interim
Report on the Use of Pretrial Parole," *New York University Law Review* (January
1963), p. 67.

[14]In three years 3,505 defendants were r.o.r.'d on the recommendation of the Manhattan Bail Project, and the rate of r.o.r. rose from 6 percent to 19 percent. On Sept.
1, 1964, the Project's procedures were taken over by the Office of Probation.

[15]The exact conditions under which a defendant is bailable are set down in §550–556
of the New York Code of Criminal Procedure.

defendant's appearance or flight, pecuniary and social condition, and apparent nature and strength of proof as bearing on the probability of his conviction."[16]

As to how these elements are to be related to the amount of bail, another note says: "Amount of bail is a question of sound discretion and judgment, depending upon primary conditions in the particular case."[17] These notes give little clue to a bail standard since no instruction is given on how the various elements are to be weighted vis-à-vis one another and the direction in which bail is to vary according to these elements is not specified (although perhaps it should be regarded as implicit that the worse an element, the higher the bail).

A clear conception of the standards which govern bail setting in this court is of signal importance, for these standards define the boundaries of the interactions to be examined. No institutionalized social interaction takes place without explicit or implicit "rules of the game." The principal actors in the bail-setting process interact with the standards as well as with each other; the standards set the limits to their initial bail suggestions and to the frequency of, and occasions for, their disagreements. Since the statute does not take us very far toward identifying the standards in the court under observation, we must turn to the cases themselves and let the standards emerge from the data at hand.

The bases ("elements properly considered") of the standards must be known to the actors so that inappropriate behavior will be constrained and interaction facilitated; as reflected in particular cases, they must be matters of fact, not opinion. Charge, prior record, and the presence or absence of an r.o.r. recommendation are all facts of variable status known in each case to the judge and the opposing attorneys, and it is expected that bail is related to these variables. Table 1 shows the final bail dispositions for each combination of charge, record, and r.o.r. recommendation. In cases where bail was set in dollars, the average amount is given in brackets.

The table shows that the three selected variables are related to bail disposition in predictable ways. The presence of a major charge, a prior record, and the absence of an r.o.r. recommendation all increase the chances of an unfavorable bail disposition. Of the three variables, charge has the strongest influence. There is less overall variation in bail disposition according to record and r.o.r. recommendation *within* each of the categories of charge than there is *between* the charge categories when record and r.o.r. recommendation are held constant. A defendant in the major charge category stands a greater chance of being remanded than one in the minor charge category;

[16]New York Code of Criminal Procedure, §550, case note 2.

[17]*Ibid.,* case note 3.

Table 1. Bail Disposition According to Charge, Prior Record, and Presence of R.O.R. Recommendation

Major Charge[a]

Disposition	Prior Record[c] No R.o.r. Rec'd. %	No.	Prior Record[c] R.o.r. Rec'd. %	No.	No Prior Record No R.o.r. Rec'd. %	No.	No Prior Record R.o.r. Rec'd. %	No.
Remand	10.0	18	d	1	14.0	8	0.0	
Bail	89.4	161	d	2	82.5	47	87.5	7
[Average amount]	[$3,863]				[$3,085]		[$2,714]	
R.o.r.	0.6	1	—		3.5	2	12.5	1
	100.0	180		3	100.0	57	100.0	8

Minor Charge[b]

Disposition	Prior Record No R.o.r. Rec'd. %	No.	Prior Record R.o.r. Rec'd. %	No.	No Prior Record No R.o.r. Rec'd. %	No.	No Prior Record R.o.r. Rec'd. %	No.
Remand	4.1	29	1.3	1	2.2	6	0.6	1
Bail	92.1	654	49.4	39	68.3	185	21.2	35
[Average amount]	[$1,587]		[$732]		[$961]		[$760]	
R.o.r.	3.8	27	49.4	39	29.5	80	78.2	129
	100.0	710	100.1	79	100.0	271	100.0	165

[a] Major charges include homicide, forcible rape, and robbery.
[b] Minor charges include assault, burglary, carrying a deadly weapon, forgery, larceny, receiving stolen property, and statutory rape.
[c] Prior record includes any record of arrest, conviction, or prison. No prior record means never previously arrested.
[d] Number of cases is too small for percentage to be meaningful.

few defendants accused of a major charge are r.o.r.'d (few are recommended); and bail averages are uniformly high.

A defendant in the minor charge category who has a prior record *and* a positive r.o.r. recommendation is likely to get a more favorable disposition than the defendant who has no prior record but also does not have an r.o.r. recommendation. Furthermore, a positive r.o.r. recommendation which is not accepted by the judge has the effect of keeping the bail amount low, regardless of prior record. In general, then, the demonstration of verified community ties is of considerable benefit to the defendant at his arraignment.

The standards which govern bail setting emerge as relatively clear and unequivocal. The more serious the charge, the more extensive the prior record, and the weaker the defendant's community ties, the greater is the chance for high bail or remand and the smaller is the chance for r.o.r. It is assumed that the prosecutor and the defense attorney develop a clear sense of this formula, since over the course of many cases they can relate the bail that is set to the charge, the record, and the recommendation in each case.

Patterns of Interaction

Social interaction of any kind is a complex phenomenon which may proceed at many levels. It may be physical, nonverbal, verbal, or any combination of the three. The regular spatial arrangement of the various parties at arraignment—direct physical interaction—is not relevant to bail setting. Nonverbal expressions—the nod, the raised eyebrow, the scowl—are all part of courtroom interaction, but are easily missed by an observer and in the end do not lend themselves easily to interpretation or statistical analysis.[18] In this study we have had to limit our observations to the verbal level. Within the limits of the data employed, verbal statements reveal quite well the basic patterns of interaction at bail setting.

The interactions described are those which take place between the judge, the prosecutor, and the defense attorney. The defendant himself is, to a striking degree, a passive bystander. He does not act; he is acted upon. Occasionally a question is put to him by the judge.

The interactions examined are those between role actors, not the often important individual variations between particular judges or attorneys. To focus on the latter would obscure the way in which roles cohere into broader identifiable social patterns. There is a relatively high degree of interchangeability among the persons who play each role. Individual variations (e.g., "Judge X is tough on car thieves") are taken into account by the various actors, but the varia-

---

[18]The author holds no brief for statistical analysis as the only proper mode of analysis. It is, however, the best method for dealing with a large number of cases.

tions are seen as departures from the expected "normal" behavior prescribed by mutually recognized standards.

During the period studied the average number of cases per day on the court calendar, including arraignments, hearings, and sentencings, was 146 (some with multiple defendants). Given this press of business, the possible patterns of interaction are not infinite. The injunction to keep things moving—"Counselor, the calendar is heavy today"—is often voiced by the judge, and accordingly bail-setting interactions tend to be brief. The charge, the defendant's prior record as shown in the case papers, and the r.o.r. recommendation, if any, provide the judge with most of the information on which he bases his decision. The modal pattern of bail setting is for the judge simply to fix bail without discussing the matter with either of the attorneys. This occurs in 49 percent of the cases. Sometimes one of the attorneys, usually the prosecutor, gives verbal assent to the decision, but the central characteristic of this dominant pattern is that the judge makes the first bail suggestion and meets with no objection from either side.

In the second major pattern, either the prosecutor or the defense attorney suggests a bail amount, often with supporting reasons, and then, without an objection from the opposing attorney, the judge fixes the bail. This pattern occurs in 38 percent of the cases. The judge does not always follow the original suggestion in this simple suggestion-decision pattern: he disagreed with 9 percent of the prosecutor's 374 suggestions, usually setting bail lower than the initial suggestion, and he disagreed with 24 percent of the defense attorney's 189 suggestions, invariably setting higher bail.

The third pattern of interaction is more complex. Here the first bail suggestion is followed by an objection to it and a countersuggestion from one of the attorneys, after which the judge sets bail. This pattern, manifesting an overt verbal "conflict," occurs in 9 percent of the cases. The conflict is of two kinds: one attorney or the other may object to (a) a bail suggestion by the judge or (b) a suggestion by the other attorney. Here, too, the prosecutor's countersuggestions are followed more often.

These three interactional patterns—decision, suggestion-decision, and suggestion-objection-decision—account for the great majority of bail settings. In only 3 percent of the observed cases does the sequence of interaction extend further; these cases, too, are examples of conflict and often involve considerable argument. Though in many ways the most dramatic they are the least typical.

Conflict

The corollary of short bail-setting interactions is the low incidence of disagreement between the judge and the two attorneys. In only

18 percent of the cases is there disagreement of any kind, either when the judge changes the bail amount first suggested by one of the attorneys, or when an attorney objects to an amount suggested by the judge or the opposing counsel. The general lack of disagreement probably reflects the clarity of the bail-setting standards; neither attorney, knowing the relevant facts in the case, suggests an amount greatly different from that usually set, given a particular charge, prior record, and r.o.r. recommendation.

Cases in which a verbal objection is made by one of the attorneys to a bail amount initially suggested by someone else have been labeled "conflict." These cases are instructive, for they provide a measure of the prestige structure in the court. When the attorneys conflict with the judge or with each other, the prosecutor, as expected, asks for higher bail and the defense attorney asks for lower bail. Table 2 shows how often these conflicts occur, in cases manifesting the *suggestion-objection-decision* pattern. (Longer interactions have been omitted so that the eventual effect of the objection in these cases can be ascertained without "contamination" from succeeding objections which mediate between the original objection and the final bail decision.)

Table 2.   Reaction to First Bail Suggestion According to Person Reacting and Person Making Suggestion

| | Prosecutor reacts to: | | | | Defense attorney reacts to: | | | |
| | Judge | | Defense Attorney | | Judge | | Prosecutor | |
Reaction	%	No.	%	No.	%	No.	%	No.
Asks lower bail	0.0		0.0		3.5	25	11.7	45
Does not object	97.5	756	81.5	189	96.5	706	88.3	341
Asks higher bail	2.5	19	18.5	43	0.0		0.0	
	100.0	775	100.0	232	100.0	731	100.0	386

Note: Omitted from the table are 78 cases in which the defendant was not represented by counsel at arraignment.

Table 2 reveals a number of points. First, the prosecutor always asks for higher bail and the defense attorney always asks for lower bail. Since they represent opposing interests, any other configuration of data would be surprising.

Second, the attorneys conflict with each other more often than they do with the judge. To some extent this fact may reflect the normal disinclination of a lower-status person to argue with the decisions of his superior; it is easier to disagree with someone at one's own level. While more prestige is often attributed to the prosecutor than to the defense attorney, in terms of the formal court hierarchy the judge is superior to both. (The difference between the frequency with which the attorneys conflict with each other and the frequency with which either attorney conflicts with the judge may also point to the conflict that more often produces the intended result.)

Third, the prosecutor objects to the first bail suggestion of the defense attorney somewhat more often than the defense attorney objects to the prosecutor's first suggestion. The explanation for this, it turns out, lies in the fact that the objection of the prosecutor is more likely to be heeded by the judge than the defense attorney's objection. Knowing that his objection will often have no effect, the counsel for the defendant will less often argue with his opponent's first suggestion. The conflict cases are presented in Table 3, which shows the effect of the attorneys' objections according to whom each is in conflict with. The term "bail differential," as used in the table, refers to the direction of the difference between the first bail amount suggested and the bail finally set. The differential may be "lower," "higher," or "none" (no difference).

Table 3. Bail Differential According to Person Disagreeing and Person Making First Bail Suggestion

| | Prosecutor asks higher bail | | | | Defense attorney asks lower bail | | | |
| | 1st Suggestion by Judge | | 1st Suggestion by Def. Attorney | | 1st Suggestion by Judge | | 1st Suggestion by Prosecutor | |
Differential	%	No.	%	No.	%	No.	%	No.
Lower	0.0		2.3	1	28.0	7	57.8	26
None	15.8	3	14.0	6	72.0	18	40.0	18
Higher	84.2	16	83.7	36	0.0		2.2	1
	100.0	19	100.0	43	100.0	25	100.0	45

Table 3 reveals that the prosecutor's request for higher bail will achieve the desired results in over four out of five cases no matter to whose original suggestion he is objecting. The defense attorney has no comparable success. In arguing against a first suggestion by the prosecutor, slightly more than half the time he will get the bail amount lowered, and in a direct conflict with the judge his objection will affect the bail decision a little more than a fourth of the time.

The overall difference in their ability to affect a change in bail amount lends credence to the notion that the prosecutor has somewhat more prestige in the courtroom than the defense attorney Of course, to say "more prestige" is simply another way of saying that he stands a better chance of getting his way. In light of the relative inability of the defense attorney to make his objection count, it is not surprising that he does not conflict with the judge very often; he realizes that to raise an objection to a bail amount suggested by the judge is generally useless. He has more success against the prosecutor, but not as much as the prosecutor has against him. This explains why the prosecutor is the more likely of the two to object to a bail suggestion by the opposing counsel. What remains unexplained is why he so infrequently objects to the judge's first bail suggestion, especially since the judge usually follows his countersuggestion. The answer, as Table 4 indicates, is that he and the judge make much the same kinds of initial bail suggestions; in short, they have little to disagree about.

It is revealing of where the judge's sympathies lie to note that he is somewhat stricter in his initial bail suggestions than the prosecutor. This holds true for particular combinations of charge, record and r.o.r. recommendation. When we examine the initial suggestions of the judge and the prosecutor in even the "best" cases—defendants with a minor charge, no prior record, and a recommendation for r.o.r.—we find that the judge suggests r.o.r. 69 percent of the time (total cases, 54) and that the prosecutor suggests r.o.r. 73 percent of the time (total cases, 40). Needless to say, when the defense attorney makes the first suggestion, he recommends r.o.r. for *all* such defendants (total cases, 71).

The totals at the bottom of the columns in Table 4 show that the judge makes the first bail suggestion most of the time (53 percent of all cases), followed by the prosecutor (29 percent), and then by the defense attorney (18 percent). This order of frequency of initial bail suggestions holds in most kinds of cases, except for those described just above, where the defendant shows the most favorable combination of characteristics. Here the defense attorney is more likely than the judge or the prosecutor to make the first suggestion as these defendants offer him the opportunity to make the strongest case for r.o.r.

The defense attorney is expected to make the best suggestion he can on behalf of his client. Four-fifths of his initial suggestions are for r.o.r.; in the remaining cases the suggestion is invariably phrased as a request for "low" bail or "cash" bail. In theory, it may be that the best first suggestion he can make is not that which simply falls at the bottom of the scale of bail amounts, but that which is lower

Table 4. First Bail Suggestion According to Person Suggesting

Suggestion	Judge		Prosecutor		Defense Attorney	
	%	No.	%	No.	%	No.
Remand	6.0	47	3.2	14	0.0	
Bail	84.9	664	76.9	333	17.8	46
R.o.r.	9.1	71	19.9	86	82.2	212
	100.0	782	100.0	433	100.0	258

than the bail amount normally anticipated in a given type of case. For example, the defense attorney might first try to suggest $2,500 in a case which often calls for $5,000. His strategy in limiting himself to relatively infrequent suggestions for r.o.r. and low bail is a forced one: (a) suggesting bail in a specific dollar amount forecloses the possibility that the judge or the prosecutor would have suggested bail in a lower amount and (b) most of the cases do not qualify for r.o.r. under the prevailing standards. Thus, he must let one of the other parties take the lead most of the time and "save" his initial suggestions for situations where, presumably, they would do the most good. The prosecutor can afford to let the judge make most of the initial suggestions, for, as the table shows, the judge makes stronger suggestions on behalf of the people than the prosecutor does himself.

Influence

Do the defense attorney's initial suggestions "do any good"? How often will they be followed, compared to the suggestions of the judge and the prosecutor? Overall, whose first suggestion is the most influential—that is, will result in the amount suggested being set?

Table 5 presents the bail differential according to the person making the first bail suggestion and the content of the suggestions.[19] It shows that the first suggestions of the judge and the prosecutor carry far more weight than the defense attorney's; neither is likely to have his first suggestion changed very often. On the other hand, the de-

Table 5. Bail Differential According to Person
Making First Suggestion and Content of First Suggestion

Differential	Judge Suggests			Prosecutor Suggests			Defense Attorney Suggests		
	Remand %	Bail %	R.o.r. %	Remand %	Bail %	R.o.r. %	Remand %	Bail %	R.o.r. %
Lower	0.0	2.1	0.0	0.0	17.4	0.0	0.0	6.5	0.0
None	100.0	96.1	90.1	100.0	80.2	100.0	0.0	52.2	59.9
Higher	0.0	1.8	9.9	0.0	2.4	0.0	0.0	41.3	40.1
	100.0	100.0	100.0	100.0	100.0	100.0		100.0	100.0
Total no.	47	664	71	14	333	86		46	212

[19]Since the defense attorney rarely specifies an amount in those cases where he suggests bail, we have had to assign a dollar amount to his suggestion in order to calculate the differential. Where "low" bail is asked, the amount of $500 has been taken as the starting point; where "cash" bail is asked, the amount of $100 has been substituted. In this manner the structure of the interaction is preserved for purposes of analysis without, it is hoped, the introduction of a radical bias. Fortunately, cases in which the defense attorney asks for bail are rare.

fense attorney's first suggestion is changed 42 percent of the time, with the change almost always going in an upward direction.

The table shows that no suggestion for remand is ever lowered to a dollar bail amount, no matter who makes it. And a check of these cases revealed that in only one case did the defense attorney object to a remand suggestion. Since the defendants who are remanded are usually charged with a serious offense, and since charge is the primary determinant of bail, it may be assumed that the defense attorney knows he cannot force the issue with any chance of success. It is better, from his point of view, not to take up court time with futile moves.

Where bail differentials do appear, they are often the result of countersuggestions from one or the other of the opposing attorneys. Such countersuggestions accounted for over two-fifths of the cases in which the prosecutor's first suggestion was lowered, and a third of the cases in which the defense attorney's first suggestion was raised. However, the area in which an objection is made to the initial suggestion is limited. When the prosecutor makes an objection it is usually to a suggestion of r.o.r. From his point of view there is no need to object to bail suggestions above r.o.r., since these are either made by himself or by the judge, who tends to make similar suggestions. The counsel for the defendant tends to make his objections in cases where the initial suggestion falls toward the lower end of the scale of bail amounts. Seventy-one percent of the bail suggestions to which he objects are $1,000 or less. Thus, his strategy in making countersuggestions is to take certain cases which are treated relatively leniently to begin with and press for slightly more lenience. The characteristics of these cases—a minor charge, no prior record, or a positive r.o.r. recommendation—give the defense attorney a base from which to make his objection in some hope that it will count.

It is interesting that *all* of the prosecutor's suggestions for r.o.r. are followed, whereas the result of the defense attorney's suggestions for r.o.r. is that two-fifths of the time bail is set in a dollar amount. The suggested r.o.r. cases of the two attorneys bear no substantial difference; both groups have similar charges, prior records, and r.o.r. recommendations.[20] In spite of the similarities, the judge accepts all of the prosecutor's r.o.r. suggestions and rejects a good part of those made by the defense attorney. An examination of the latter's cases showed that when his r.o.r. suggestion is rejected by the judge, the reason usually given is that the defendant has no positive r.o.r. recommendation from the Office of Probation or that he has a prior

[20]Of the prosecutor's cases, 44 percent are backed by a positive probation recommendation for r.o.r., 69 percent have no prior record, and 95 percent are accused of a minor offense. Of the defense attorney's cases, 51 percent have a positive r.o.r. recommendation, 64 percent have no prior record, and 93 percent are accused of a minor offense.

record. These deficiencies are, apparently, offset when the prosecutor makes the r.o.r. suggestion.

In sum, the defense attorney is the least influential member of the court; not only is he the least likely to make the initial bail suggestion, but he has the least chance of making his suggestion stick. The judge and the prosecutor are reciprocally supportive. They subscribe to the same bail-setting standards, they disagree with each other far less often than either disagrees with the defense attorney, and they show the same concern for the people's interest. The role of the prosecutor is prescribed: he represents the public. But the judge is supposed to be, in theory, a neutral "referee" between the two sets of interests. I suggest that the judge's concern for the people's side springs from another source, which I shall now examine.

A Latent Function of Bail

Sociologists make a distinction between those functions of a social practice which are "manifest" and those which are "latent." Manifest functions are intended consequences of the practice; latent functions are consequences which are not originally intended and are often unrecognized. Put another way, manifest functions are "purposes," and latent functions roughly correspond to "side effects" or "by-products."[21]

The major manifest function of setting bail is to guarantee the appearance of the defendant at subsequent court proceedings. Some hold that this is its only legitimate function.[22] Be that as it may, legal officials acknowledge other manifest functions of bail setting, including the following: "To prevent release where flight is likely; to prevent a recurrence of criminal conduct by an accused believed to be dangerous to the community; and to punish the accused by giving him a taste of jail."[23] Whether any of these functions are legitimate under our system of law is a current subject of debate.[24]

A number of critics of the bail system maintain that bail does not truly function to guarantee the appearance of the defendant in court.[25] They point out that, though in theory the defendant's finan-

[21]For a definitive discussion of manifest and latent functions, see Robert K. Merton, *Social Theory and Social Structure* (New York: Free Press, 1957), ch. I.

[22]For example, Daniel J. Freed and Patricia M. Wald, *Bail in the United States: 1964* (Washington, D.C.: National Conference on Bail and Criminal Justice, 1964, p. 8): "Bail in America has developed for a single lawful purpose: to release the accused with assurance he will return for trial."

[23]*Ibid.,* p. 49.

[24]For a statement by a proponent of preventive detention, see the address by Garrett H. Byrne, president of the National District Attorneys Association, *Proceedings, supra* note 1, pp. 160–68.

[25]See, e.g., Botein, *supra* note 1, p. 326.

cial stake in posting bail is supposed to assure his appearance, the bondsman's fee is not returnable and full collateral is not often demanded by New York City bondsmen; thus, the presumed financial stake is virtually nonexistent.[26] Assuming that the criticism is valid, the question arises why bail setting persists as a social practice. The function of preventive detention—setting high bail to prevent release and thus deter flight or recidivism—is not a sufficient explanation since far too many of these defendants raise bail.[27]

Social practices may persist because of their latent functions. One latent function of bail setting is to diffuse the responsibility for the release of the defendant, and we shall argue that this explains, at least in part, why the practice persists and why the judge consistently sides with the prosecutor in fixing bail.

The bail-setting interactions between the judge and the two attorneys cannot be understood if the court is viewed as a closed system. In order to make sense out of what happens in the court, we must take the role of the public into account. Judges are sensitive to public pressure, and some will admit they fear an adverse reaction from the press should they make a mistake. Their position was stated succinctly at the National Conference on Bail and Criminal Justice by Judge Francis Morrissey, who said: "If you let [the defendant] out on personal recognizance, with the understanding that he would reappear again for trial, and then the victim was badly injured, or killed, you have the problem of the newspapers coming in a very critical vein. You have to have some security for the particular judge."[28] In short, judges have a natural reluctance to be responsible for releasing defendants who commit deeds which outrage public opinion.

Fixing high bail to prevent release may explain why $5,000 bail is set in a given case instead of $500, but it does not explain why a judge will set $25 cash bail rather than r.o.r. the defendant. An answer emerges if "responsibility" is seen as coming into play not only when high bail is set, but throughout the range of bail settings, from remand to r.o.r. In this view, the judge who sets $25 cash bail is shifting part of the responsibility for the release of the defendant

[26]This position is taken by Richard H. Kuh, formerly chief of the Criminal Division, New York County District Attorney's Office. Kuh estimates that in 95 percent of the cases, no collateral is asked. (See *Proceedings, supra* note 1, pp. 234–35.) A report in the *New York Times* on a one-week bondsmen's "strike" in New York City agrees that 100 percent collateral is not demanded, although it is at variance with Kuh on exactly how much is asked. The report implies that 20 percent of the face value of the bond is normally demanded in collateral. ("Bondsmen Relax Security Demand," *New York Times,* Jan. 1, 1964.)

[27]The observed cases were not followed to establish the rate of bail raising. The latest available figures for this court show that approximately half the defendants on whom dollar bail is set manage to post it. (Rankin, *supra* note 4, table 2, p. 645.)

[28]*Proceedings, supra* note 1, p. 184.

to the defendant himself. Stated more generally, bail setting serves the latent function of diffusing the responsibility for releasing the defendant, and the three bail dispositions—remand, dollar bail, and r.o.r.—indicate different degrees in the judge's share of this responsibility. (a) When the judge remands the defendant, foreclosing the possibility that the defendant will commit an additional offense, he assumes no responsibility for the release. (b) When the judge sets bail in some dollar amount, he shares the responsibility for releasing the defendant with the bondsman, the defendant's family, or the defendant himself. The higher the amount of the bail, the greater is the share of the others' responsibility. (c) When the judge grants r.o.r., he has the entire responsibility for releasing the defendant.

The setting of dollar bail implicitly condones the release of the defendant. Even in cases where high bail is set to prevent the release of the accused, it is possible that the bail will somehow be raised. The reluctance expressed by some officials at the thought of granting r.o.r. to a dangerous defendant (hark back to Judge Morrissey's statement) can be easily explained: if such a defendant commits a crime while free on r.o.r., the judge may be pilloried. If, on the other hand, he sets such a defendant free on bail, he cannot be held strictly to account; the responsibility for the defendant's release is not exclusively his.

By permitting different degrees of judicial responsibility to be attached to the release of the defendant, bail setting functions as a protective device for the court. Thus, where the judge has the slightest hesitation about utilizing r.o.r., he can share the responsibility for release by setting minimal bail. And even where he does grant r.o.r., the judge does not assume the full responsibility for releasing the defendant, as might first appear. One function of the Manhattan Bail Project, which formerly operated in the court studied, was to share this responsibility by providing recommendations for good r.o.r. risks. This function continues now under the Office of Probation. Of the 281 cases of r.o.r. falling into the sample, 61 percent were backed by a Probation Office recommendation. Virtually all of the remainder were granted r.o.r. on the recommendation of one of the attorneys. Only eighteen defendants—approximately 1 percent of all cases observed—were given r.o.r. without a recommendation from someone other than the judge. Thus, the judge almost never takes absolute, complete responsibility for releasing a defendant outright. Even in the r.o.r. cases the judge is sharing the responsibility, no matter to how small a degree, with someone else.

The reason why the judge adheres to the same bail standards as the prosecutor now becomes clear. Handing down bail dispositions which fall toward the severe end of the bail-setting scale (much in line with the kinds of dispositions suggested by the prosecutor) more broadly diffuses the responsibility for releasing the defendant. If the judge were to make more frequent use of r.o.r. or set generally lower bail amounts, he would not be sharing the responsibility for the defendant's release quite as much. If, as we assume, the judge is aware of the ever present possibility of negative public response should a case go wrong, it is to his interest to increase others' share in the responsibility for release by being more severe. Thus, he finds himself in the same position as the prosecutor but for different reasons. The prosecutor is supposed to represent the public interest according to the prescriptions of his role; the judge, however, must keep the public in mind because, as the final decision-maker, he is the most vulnerable target of criticism.

Bail setting's latent function of diffusing the responsibility for the release of the accused puts a buffer between the court and the potential outraged response of the public to crimes which may be committed by persons at liberty pending court appearance. As long as the courts need such a buffer, it is doubtful that bail setting as a social practice will entirely disappear.

Judicial Attitudes toward Rape Victims

Carol Bohmer

In criminal proceedings against suspected rapists, there is a tendency to regard the rape victim as just another piece of evidence. The victim's role is to establish a legal case against the offender; little concern is shown for her efforts to adjust to the alleged rape, for the responses of her family and peers, or for the attitudes she encounters in interacting with the criminal justice system. Victims frequently report that their encounters with the police, district attorneys and courtroom personnel were more traumatic than the rape incident itself.

Most observers seem to accept the biases evidenced by police and defense attorneys toward rape victims as inevitable, but feel that the judge will balance any inequities. There is a common assumption that the judge is the objective source of authority and control in courtroom procedures and that his presence assures a balance between these highly charged, goal-oriented factions. His function is presumed to guarantee that an evenhanded justice which serves the best interests of society in punishing offenders and protecting victims will prevail.

In recent interviews with 38 Philadelphia judges who have handled rape cases, I found that judicial attitudes toward rape victims are far less impartial than is frequently supposed. The judges' comments supported the allegation of courtroom victimization of some rape victims and established the need for further inquiry into judicial attitudes.

The basic assumption of this research is that judicial attitudes are correlated with judicial behavior and that the first are the key factor in determining the effects of courtroom experience on rape victims.[1]

SOURCE: *Judicature* 57 (February 1974): 303–7. Reprinted by permission of the author and the American Judicature Society.

NOTE: The research for this article was undertaken while the author was Research Assistant at the Center for Study in Criminology and Criminal Law, under Ford Foundation Socio-Legal Research Grant, and also in her present position as Research Attorney at the Center for Rape Concern under NIMH Grant MH-14773.

[1]There is social-psychological material which provides a theoretical background for this relationship between attitudes and behaviors, making it theoretically acceptable to question judges about their attitudes and from their responses to infer how they would behave in court situations. "An attitude represents both an orientation toward or away from object, concept, or situation and a readiness to respond in a predetermined manner to these or related objects, concepts, or situations." *See:* Hilgard and Atkinson, *Introduction to Psychology* (1967), 583. Additionally, the research on cognitive dissonance provides data which show the need in individuals to bring their attitudes and behavior as close as possible to each other, e.g., Festinger and Carlsmith (1959) in P. F. Secord and C. W. Backman, *Social Psychology* (1964).

It is for this reason that the research focused on an investigation of judicial attitudes toward rape victims.[2]

The 38 judges chosen for study were all judges of the Philadelphia court system (municipal court and common pleas division) who had been involved in trying rape cases. Several of the judges were not interviewed because their experiences in this area were either non-existent or too limited to be of benefit in responding to the inquiries.

The approach of personal interview based on a standardized set of questions was selected for two reasons: (1) since the judges operate under heavy schedules, it seemed more likely that they would grant time for an interview than for responding to a questionnaire, and (2) since the topic of judicial attitudes toward rape victims is a sensitive area of inquiry, the spontaneous remarks and responses of the judges in an interview situation would yield useful information which might not be elicited without personal contact. The interviews were conducted from June to September of 1971.

Possible Defenses

The defenses available in a rape case are limited to three: that the alleged event did not take place, that sexual intercourse between the complainant and the defendant did take place but ... was consensual, or that a rape may have occurred but the defendant is not the rapist i.e., the defense of identity.

The kinds of evidence judges accept have a bearing on the proof of any of these defenses. For example, the scene of the rape may be relevant to the existence of consent. The fact that the alleged rape takes place in a dark alley or a parking lot has very different implications for the judge than if it took place in an apartment or a car. In the latter situations, the judge will want to know how the complainant and defendant arrived at the scene. If the complainant went willingly to the apartment or car in question, she is likely to receive a less sympathetic hearing than if the defendant had broken into her

[2]*See* Hogarth, *Sentencing as a Human Process* (1971). Roger Hood is presently conducting a study in England dealing with the sentencing of serious motor offenders in magistrate courts, referred to in R. Hood and R. Sparks, *Key Issues in Criminology,* (1970), 160 *et seq.*

The influence of attitudes on judicial behavior in general has not, however, been directly studied, although there is presently some material dealing with the influence of attitudes and background factors as the political party of the judge (A. S. Blumberg, *Criminal Justice* (1967), 117 *et seq.*) their social attitudes (S. S. Nagel, "Off the Bench Judicial Attitudes" in *Judicial Decision Making* [1963]. These attitudes are measured by Hans Eysenck's social attitudes questionnaire). Specific beliefs, e.g., religious beliefs (Hogarth, *supra.,* at 368) have been shown to influence the judges' sentencing behavior. John Hogarth also shows that there is an association between a number of factors he isolates through factor analysis and sentencing behavior. (Hogarth, *supra,* at 360–65, where the factors he isolated and their relation to sentencing practices are summarized.) These factors include justice, tolerance, as well as several which relate in different ways to the penal philosophy of the judge.

apartment. In these types of situations, the existence and degree of a prior offender-victim relationship becomes important in determining the likelihood of a consensual situation.

The interviews with the judges revealed that their central orientation in trying rape cases is to evaluate the credibility of the victim's allegation that forcible rape (as defined by the law) occurred. As several of the judges stated: "Rape is the easiest crime to allege, and the hardest to prove." Their recognition of the complexity of legal issues involved in rape cases, coupled with the belief that the worst error the criminal justice system can commit is to convict an innocent man, results in a fairly high level of judicial skepticism toward those who allege rape. Despite these attitudes, the judges' responses also indicated the rights of the defendant and the sensitivities of the victim as they face the trauma of testifying in court.

Genuine Victim

The judges interviewed appear to divide rape cases into three basic types, giving each category a different degree of credibility. The first type includes those women they consider "genuine victims." They give these women sympathetic hearings and react very punitively toward the men who raped them. An evaluation of this sort occurs when the situation is such that the judges have no problem defining the circumstances as those of forcible rape. The suitable paradigm for this category might be the "stranger leaping out of the shadows in the dark alley situation." In such cases, the judges apparently agree with the graphic description of an articulate victim who said, "Who would consent to lying flat on her back in a dark alley in January?" The judges feel that in this type of situation the effects on the woman can be traumatic, and they make an effort to buffer her court experience. As one of them said: "The effect on the average girl is devastating, she will never get over it, the indignities, the knowledge on the part of her associates; rarely do they ever adjust to a full, happy life."

However, judicial attitudes can be very different in cases which may be rape according to law but which they classify as "consensual intercourse." In these situations they see the complainant as "asking for it." An example would be when a woman meets a man in a bar, agrees to let him drive her home, and then alleges he raped her. Judges have several graphic ways of describing this situation: "friendly rape," "felonious gallantry," "assault with failure to please," and "breach of contract."

Vindictive Female

The third type of situation occurs when they see the accusation as marked by "female vindictiveness." In these cases, the judges believe either that the event occurred was totally consensual or that the alleged event did not in fact occur. Therefore, they judge the allegations as reflections of a woman's desire to get even with a man. Several judges described the typical situation in this category as that of a woman who is tired of her husband or boyfriend, wants to get rid of him, and so convinces her daughter to allege the defendant raped her.

The kinds of evidence which a judge allows to be admitted into the trial record and which he weighs in assessing the merits of a rape case can have an important bearing on the atmosphere in the court and on the victim's reactions to her court experiences. For example, the judge controls the amount of evidence the defense attorney can submit as testimony of a female's reputation, which is an area of inquiry that can produce strong emotional and psychological repercussions for the victim.

Table 1 outlines the kinds of evidence the judges indicate they weighed in their evaluations.

Table 1.

What kind of evidence do you place weight on in rape trials?

4	demeanor of complainant
11	medical
23	circumstantial*
3	don't know
10	no information
51	(some of the judges gave more than one response)

* Circumstantial evidence can include the following: enticement; prior history of promiscuity; torn or dishevelled clothing; bruises or physical marks; prior relationship; where, how and when it occurred; drinking in a bar; resistance; immediate outcry; presence of a weapon; time between incident and filing of complaint; whether complaint made without intervening circumstances; confession; flight of defendant; cooperation with identification; age differential (big gap more likely to be rape).

As can be seen from the table, the most important kind of evidence is circumstantial since that is usually the only way to prove the complainant's charge. (The term circumstantial evidence includes all evidence of an indirect nature. It means that the existence of certain facts is only inferred from circumstances rather than deduced by a process in which tangible facts are utilized.) Circumstantial factors which are considered indicators of the good faith of the complainant include the speed with which she filed the complaint, the reasons she decided to file the complaint, and the amount of cooperation she offers legal authorities for the prosecution. Judges often feel that a complainant's indecision about her willingness to testify indicates that she started to doubt her allegation of rape. According to this view, a complainant who does not cooperate in judicial proceedings (usually because she feels that the officials are insensitive or skeptical), must be lying.

Although medical findings can indicate whether intercourse occurred if the examination takes place immediately following the incident, they cannot provide evidence concerning the presence or absence of consent. Indication of physical trauma, however, can provide support to substantiate nonconsent. Similarly, testimony of witnesses who saw the victim in a state of physical disarray or injury soon after the incident lends credence to the allegation of rape.

In the interviews the judges revealed a high level of concern for the effects of the courtroom experience on child victims of rape. In assessing the rape allegations of children, the judges feel protective toward the complainant and to a large extent abandon their category of the "vindictive female." Although the judge may feel antagonistic toward the child victim who alleges rape to assist her mother in getting even with a man, he also tends to view the child as a pawn in an adult world. Several of the judges indicated that in such situations the child is frequently incapable of knowing that she is lying.

The Child Witness

Since the admissibility of a child's testimony depends on her ability to distinguish truth and falsehood and to comprehend the significance of swearing an oath on the Bible, the judge is responsible for assessing the child's understanding of her role as a witness. In Pennsylvania, the determination of a child's ability to testify is the sole responsibility of the judge since there is no minimum age set for the legality of a witness's testimony. Although judges are aware that lengthy questioning about her alleged sexual experience may be traumatic for a child, they are also aware of their responsibility for deciding whether the child qualifies as a witness. Judges feel a great sense of conflict in these situations since they are concerned for the well-being of the child and yet are also charged with the legal responsibility of determining that the child fully understands the seriousness of the proceedings, and with the further responsibility of assuring that the defendant is given a fair trial in open court with the right to cross-examine all witnesses for the prosecution.

Although most judges agree that it can be a very difficult experience for a young child to give evidence, many of them also maintain that there is no way to eliminate the trauma without sacrificing the current system of adversary justice in the U.S. These judges feel that the United States could never adopt the system used in Denmark and

Israel in which a court official questions the child privately for both the prosecution and defense, eliminating the need for her public appearance in an open court. Although several judges expressed a wish to deviate from the adversary procedure, they felt such a change would violate the defendant's essential Constitutional rights. Therefore, those judges who did offer suggestions for alternative methods of introducing the testimony of children formulated their ideas so they could be implemented without any radical changes to the present judicial system. Table 2 lists the distribution of responses to inquiries on this topic.

As Table 2 indicates, judges apparently do try to lessen the frightening aspects of court appearances for children. The effectiveness of the measures they use obviously depends on the sensitivities of the judges and attorneys and the emotional and mental receptiveness of the children to these procedures.

Table 2.

Do you think it is a traumatic experience for children to give evidence?

27	yes
5	depends on the circumstances
3	no
3	no information
38	

If yes, do you think there is anything we can do about it?

17	yes
7	no
2	don't know
9	no information
35	(N = 35: respondents in the affirmation to the first question)

If yes, what?

4	private hearings
3	dispositions rather than adversary proceedings
10	other*
17	(N = 17: respondents in the affirmative to the second question)

* Other suggestions for making a child's experience less traumatic included: Let the child sit on her father's lap while giving evidence; treatment by a psychiatrist; clear courtroom, take over questioning; try to keep them out of court (i.e., guilty pleas); tape record first interview to avoid trauma of repetition; try to get confession; have child in court the shortest possible time; have defense counsel talk to parents to indicate the importance of child's testimony; control defense attorney; try certain cases less rigidly; bring child to side bar.

Racial Overtones

An attempt was made to determine the racial attitudes of the judges interviewed by asking the judges whether any particular types of people make better witnesses than others. Although most responses indicated a differentiation in terms of age (older women being seen as better witnesses than children), several responses definitely reflected racial attitudes which may be presumed to affect judicial behavior. Some judges alluded to the chaotic life styles and attitudes of ghetto dwellers—by which they meant blacks. Several judges indicated that they correlate the category of "vindictive women" with females of the black ghetto. One actually stated: "With the Negro community, you really have to redefine the term rape. You never know about them." (Another possible indication of racial overtones in judicial attitudes might be found in the fact that none of the judges ever used the term "black." Instead they referred to the black population with words such as "Negro," "nigra," or "colored.")

In contrast to responses such as these were those that indicated judicial sensitivity for black rape victims. One judge referred to a specific case involving a black woman who had been raised in a strict religious atmosphere and was therefore experiencing great difficulties in adjusting to her rape experience. Others referred to the prejudices they witnessed in white victims toward black offenders. They pointed out that many white females have difficulty identifying black offenders because all black men look alike to them. Some of the judges also indicated their belief that many interracial rapes may go unreported because some white women find it abhorrent to admit that they were touched by a black man.

The responses given by the judges which reflected social biases and sensitivities illustrate the need for further inquiry into this area of judicial attitudes and their effects on courtroom proceedings.

The process of interviewing judges in Philadelphia to ascertain their attitudes toward the adjudication of rape cases has provided sufficient information to warrant further inquiry into the effects these attitudes might have on the outcome of the trial over which the judge is presiding. A judge can affect the proceedings both directly by his rulings on the evidence presented and indirectly by his demeanor toward the participants in the trial. Furthermore, his attitude toward the victim and her testimony can play a role in determining her adjustment to the effects of the rape.

An important aspect of my further research will be to observe the courtroom interactions experienced by the alleged rape victims and to analyze both the differential attitudes and behaviors of courtroom personnel and the differential responses of the victims. I hope to use

this information to devise ways to assist rape victims to prepare for
and adjust to their experiences in court. I am also hopeful that my
findings will increase the sensitivity and awareness of personnel in
the criminal justice system to the difficulties rape victims experience in taking their cases to court.

Drunk Court
The Adult Parallel to Juvenile Court
Jacqueline P. Wiseman

The distinction that Peterson and Matza (1963:107) draw between two basic types of court procedures—the legalistic court and the so-called socialized court—is especially pertinent to the operation of the drunk court, as will be seen from the following brief outline.

> *Legalistic courts* operate under an adversary system, by which a state attorney and a defense counsel plead a case before a judge and/or jury. The purpose of the trial is to determine whether the defendant in fact committed the crime with which he is charged. Great stress is placed on formal proceedings and rules of evidence, very little on information regarding the defendant's character and background. If he is convicted, the defendant is subject to fine, imprisonment, or execution. The punishment fits the crime, not the particular individual.
>
> *Socialized courts* usually exercise jurisdiction either over juveniles, both neglected or dependent and delinquent or criminal; or over family law or, in some jurisdictions, over both juvenile and domestic problems in one omnibus court. Its methods and procedures have made greatest inroads in the juvenile court. Here, the adversary system in replaced by one or more social workers' reports, which emphasize information regarding the character and background of all parties. Judicial procedure is informal; rules of evidence do not apply. The purpose of the hearing is to determine whether a serious problem exists—whether, for example, a child requires help—and to provide the means to meet the needs of the individuals involved.

Although not officially designated as a socialized court in the statutes, drunk court sessions are almost always operated along the latter lines. However, the drunk court judge faces unusual administrative and decisional problems that have a gross distorting effect on its more informal and humanized ideology.

Unlike other cases in other courts, where guilt or innocence of the defendant is the issue, the judge's decision in drunk court is almost always the sentence alone. ... With but rare exceptions, the men plead guilty. The judge, therefore, has no official reason to assume the men are other than guilty.

233

Sentencing men who plead guilty to a public drunkenness charge, however, presents a real conflict to a judge who wishes to see himself as compassionate, wise, and just. Because of the widespread discussion of alcoholism as a social problem and a physical illness, a judge must take cognizance of both the need for efficient administration of sentences for public drunks and the theoretical causes of alcoholism. As a collateral matter, he is also aware that ordinary male citizens sometimes "tie one on," perhaps do damage to themselves or others, and are arrested by police. Such men usually have jobs and a family. A jail sentence for public drunkenness would be a severe blow, both socially and economically.

In other words, with each man who appears before him the judge must ask himself whether he should view the defendant as merely an "overindulgent social drinker," or as a "chronic drunken bum," or as a "sick alcoholic."

In the first of these possible definitions, the judge must make a decision about whether the defendant is a wayward, but basically solid, citizen. If this is the case, the sentence can be suspended and the person let off with a warning. On the other hand, if the defendant is the type the judge tends to mentally characterize as a "childlike, hedonistic, willful, chronic drunk," he must be dried out for his own good, since he is a menace to himself and society. All the while, the third possible definition creates great decisional pressures, because the judge is aware that he must consider the prevailing public opinion that alcoholism per se is an illness, even if some of the acts of the person who drinks too much may legally be defined as a crime. (See Stem, 1967.) If the judge accepts this latter view, he is forced to consider the possibility he is sentencing a man who may be ill to jail. The implied inhumanity of this act must be explained and justified, even if only self-justification is involved.

This decisional picture is further confused by the fact that the judge must consider not one but two types of illness. The first type is the temporary, acute *physical distress* caused by repeated overindulgence in alcohol which, in cases of continuous heavy drinking, is serious enough to cause death if left unattended. The second type is based on the assumption that some mysterious psychological compulsion forces a man to drink and, like the plea "not guilty by reason of insanity," the chronic alcoholic is not responsible for his excessive drinking. Each type of illness demands a different kind of concern and treatment, although in judicial discussions these are often blurred together.

If a judge were to think aloud, he might explain the chronic drunk sentence dilemma and his solution to it something like this:

> Alcoholism may be an illness or it may be a weakness. Whatever it is, all alcoholics need help to quit drinking. One of the

surest ways to help an alcoholic quit drinking is to separate
him forcibly from any supply of liquor. However, jail is a
drastic penalty for being found drunk and therefore should be
used only after other methods fail. This is because if a man is
sent to jail, he may suffer undesirable social consequences, such
as jeopardizing his job or causing his wife and children great
embarrassment. Some men are so upset about being arrested,
that is all the punishment they need. It serves as adequate
warning. Others should be educated about the dangers of overindulgence through forced attendance at Alcoholism School.
Others need a short sentence to see what jail is like so they don't
want ever to go back; and some repeaters need aid in getting off
the bottle which can be supplied by a longer separation from
it—say 30, 60 or 90 days. The jail is set up to give these men both
medical and psychological therapy through the Jail Branch
Clinic of the Out-Patient Therapy Center, so they are well taken
care of. Transients can be handled by telling them to leave
town.

Matching sentences with men who plead guilty is thus the judge's
true concern. This task must be handled within the pressures
created by restricting drunk court to a morning session in one courtroom, regardless of the number of men scheduled to be seen that day.

Up until last year (when drunk arrests were temporarily reduced
because of the large number of hippies and civil rights demonstra-
tors in jail), 50 to 250 men were often sentenced within a few hours.
Appearance before the judge was handled in platoons of five to 50.
This meant the judge decided the fate of each defendant within a few
short minutes. Thus judicial compassion attained assembly-line organization and speed.

As a court observer noted:

The Court generally disposes of between 50 and 100 cases per
day, but on any Monday there are 200 to 250 and on Monday
mornings after holiday weekends the Court may handle as
many as 350 cases. I would estimate that, on the average, cases
take between 45 seconds and one minute to dispose of [Le-
Clercq, 1966:1].

Later, with drunk arrests drastically curtailed, the court handled
no more than 50 cases in an average morning, and perhaps 125 on the
weekends, according to the observer. Right after a civil rights demonstration that resulted in many arrests, only 33 persons were observed in drunk court. This reduction in the quanity of defendants,
however, did not appear to increase the length of time spent on each
person. Rather, it seemed to reduce it. The observer noted the aver-

age length of time per person was 30 seconds, although the size of platoons was reduced from 50 to 15 or 20.

Sentencing Criteria

How is the judge able to classify and sentence a large, unwieldy group of defendants so quickly? The answer is he utilizes social characteristics as indicators to signify drinking status—just as in an arrest situation the policeman looked for social characteristics to identify alcoholic troublemaking potential, combined with the arrestee's legal impotence. The effect is essentially the same: the men are objectified into social types for easy classification. In the case of the judge, the legal decision process must be more defined than for a policeman's arrest, no-arrest decision. Therefore, the judge's sentencing criteria are more complex, as they must include all possible decision combinations.

From court observations, plus interviews with court officers and judges, three primary criteria for typing defendants in drunk court emerge:

The General Physical Appearance of the Man

Is he shaky and obviously in need of drying out? Here, some of the judges ask the men to extend their hands before sentencing and decide the sentence on the degree of trembling.

Physical appearance may actually be the most potent deciding factor. As one court officer put it, when asked how the judges decide on a sentence: "Primarily by appearance. You can tell what kind of shape they're in. If they're shaking and obviously need drying out, you know some are on the verge of the DTs so these get 10 or 15 days [in jail] to dry out." One of the seasoned judges said that his criteria were as follows: "I rely on his record and also his 'looks.' Their 'looks' are very important. I make them put their hands out—see if they are dirty and bloody in appearance" (LeClercq, 1966:12).

Past Performance

How many times have they been up before the court on a drunk charge before? A record of past arrests is considered to be indicative of the defendant's general attitude toward drinking. The longer and more recent the record, the greater the need for a sentence to aid the defendant to improve his outlook on excessive liquor consumption. (This is in some contradiction to the presumed greater need the man must have for drying out, since previous recent jailings mean that he could not have been drinking for long.)

The previous comment, plus the answer by a court officer to the question "Who gets dismissed?" illustrates this criterion for sentencing:

A person with no previous arrests [gets dismissed]. If they have had no arrests, then the judge hates for them to have a conviction on their record. *The more arrests they've had and the more recently they've had them, the more likely they are to get another sentence.* [Emphasis mine.]

The Man's Social Position

Does he have a job he could go to? Is he married? Does he have a permanent address, or will he literally be on the streets if he receives a dismissal?

For these data, dress is an all-important clue, age a secondary one. A man who looks down-and-out is more likely to receive a sentence than the well-dressed man. According to a court officer:

If they look pretty beat—clothes dirty and in rags, then you figure that they need some help to stop drinking before they kill themselves.

If they're under 21 we usually give them a kick-out. If they are a businessman or a lawyer we have them sign a civil release so they can't sue and let them go.

An observer reports that a judge freed a young man with the following remarks: "I am going to give you a suspended sentence and hope that this experience will be a warning to you. I don't want you to get caught up in this cycle."

Transients form a category of their own and get a special package deal—if they will promise to leave town, they draw a suspended sentence or probation. The parallel between this practice and the police policy of telling some Skid-Row drunks to "take a walk" need only be mentioned. The following interchanges are illustrative:

JUDGE: I thought you told me the last time you were in here that you were going to leave Pacific City.
DEFENDANT: I was supposed to have left town yesterday. I just got through doing time.
JUDGE: Go back to Woodland. Don't let me see you in here again or we are going to put you away. Thirty days suspended.
DEFENDANT: I am supposed to leave with the circus tomorrow. If I don't go, I will be out of work for the whole season.
JUDGE: You promised to leave three times before. Thirty days in the County Jail.

By combining the variables of physical appearance, past performance, and social position, a rough description of the social types expected in drunk court and matching sentences for each type are shown in Table 1.

These first two categories in Table 1, and sometimes the third, have not been, in Garfinkel's terms, "made strange" (1967). They are treated as though they are full-fledged persons who may have over-indulged. The remaining types are stripped-down persons, on the "other side," so far as they are perceived by the judge.

A total of 180 men were observed in drunk court and tabulated according to the social types outlined in the table. Observations were spread over three days. Two different judges presided. The results are shown in Table 2.

Of the total tabulated, the Skid-Row alcoholics category would include the derelict (38 percent), the middle-aged repeater who has not been arrested for some time, probably having been in the loop (11 percent), the out-of-towner (8 percent), and the man who looks gravely ill (2 percent), for a total of 59 percent. This is quite near the usual 40 to 45 percent of Skid-Row men represented in the total arrests for drunkenness in Pacific City.

The detailed pattern of sentencing was also tabulated and is illustrated in Table 3. As can be seen in the table, only 26 percent of the men received sentences to be served in County Jail. This is quite close to the yearly average of 20 to 25 percent.

Most pertinent to this study, however, is the distribution of sentences among social types of defendants. From Table 4, it can be seen that the derelicts who look rough or men who are repeaters (regardless of age or appearance), are most likely to serve time and get the longest sentences. Furthermore, the derelict who looks rough is the least likely of any social type to escape jail.

A word should be said about the suspended sentence. Judges sometimes give exceedingly long suspended sentences to drunk ordinance defendants—often 90 days or more to repeaters. This places a weapon in the hands of the court that is greatly feared. If at any time within the following 90 days (or whatever the length of the sentence), the man is picked up on a drunk charge, he may be sent directly to jail without trial for the entire length of the suspended sentence. Many men, upon receiving a long suspended sentence, and realizing their vulnerability to arrest, will "take out insurance" against being incarcerated for that length of time by seeking admission to another "more desirable" station on the loop. Favorite "hide-outs" while waiting for the suspended sentence to run out are (in approximate rank order): Welfare Home for Homeless Men, State Mental Hospital, and the Christian Missionaries.

Other Sentencing Assistance

Even with the aid of a simplified mental guide, the judge cannot be expected to assemble and assimilate sufficient material on each man,

Table 1. Paradigm of Social Types and Sentences in Drunk Court

Social Type	Probable Sentence
A young man who drank too much: a man under 40, with a job, and perhaps a wife, who has not appeared in court before	A kick-out or a suspended sentence
The young repeater: same as above, but has been before judge several times (may be on way to being an alcoholic)	Suspended sentence or short sentence (5–10 days) to scare him, or possible attendance at Alcoholism School
The repeater who still looks fairly respectable. (Image vacillating between an alcoholic and a drunk)	30-day suspended sentence, with possible attendance at Alcoholism School
Out-of-towner (social characteristics not important as they have nonlocal roots). Therefore not important whether overindulged, a chronic drunk, or an alcoholic	Suspended sentence on condition he leave town. Purpose is to discourage him from getting on local loop and adding to taxpayer's load
The middle-aged repeater who has not been up for some time. (May be an alcoholic who has relapsed)	Suspended sentence with required attendance at Alcoholism School or given to custody of Christian missionaries
The derelict-drunk who looks "rough," i.e., suffering withdrawal, a hangover, has cuts and bruises, may have malnutrition or some diseases connected with heavy drinking and little eating; a chronic drunk; seedy clothing, stubble beard, etc.	30–60–90-day sentence depending on number of prior arrests and physical condition at time of arrest. (Has probably attended Alcoholism School already)
The man who looks gravely ill (probably a chronic alcoholic)	County hospital under suspended sentence

Table 2. Distribution of Drunk Ordinance Social Types in Court

Social Types	Percent (N = 180)
Derelict who looks "rough"	38
Young repeater	15
Recent repeater who looks respectable	15
Middle-aged repeater who has not been arrested for some time	11
Young man with wife, job, first offense	11
Out-of-towner	8
Man who looks gravely ill	2
Total	100

Table 3.   Distribution of Sentences in Drunk Court

Sentences	Percent of Defendants (N = 180)	
Kick-out (no sentence, warned only)	2	
County hospital		
With hold	—	
No hold	2	74
Suspended sentence		(non-jail
10 days or less	—	sentence)
11 to 30 days	23	
31 to 60 days	28	
61 to 90 days	19	
Over 90 days	—	
Sentence to County Jail		
10 days or less	1	
11 to 30 days	23	26
31 to 60 days	2	(jail
61 to 90 days	—	sentence)
Over 90 days	—	
Total	100	

review it, mentally type the man, and then make a sentencing decision in less than a minute. Thus, it is not surprising that almost all drunk court judges employ the aid of one assistant and sometimes two court attaches who are familiar with the Row and its inhabitants. These men are known as court liaison officers. Because of personal familiarity with chronic drunkenness offenders, the liaison officers are able to answer questions about each accused person quickly and to recommend a case disposition. Such persons obviously operate as an informal screening board.

The most important court helper in Pacific City is a man who knows most of the Row men by sight and claims also to know their general outlook on alcohol and life. Known to the defendants as "the Rapper," this man often sits behind the judge and suggests informally who would benefit most from probation and assignment to Alcoholism School, and who might need the "shaking-up" that jail provides, and who ought to be sent to alcoholic screening at City Hospital and perhaps on to State Mental Hospital. As each man is named, the Rapper whispers to the judge, who then passes sentence. (See Bogue, 1963:414.)

In Pacific City, the man who was the Rapper for a period of time was an ex-alcoholic who could claim intimate knowledge of the chronic drunkenness offender because he had drunk with them. A relative of the Rapper was highly placed in city politics, and the Rapper made no secret of the fact that his appointment was politically engineered. During the course of the study (several times in

Table 4. Distribution of Sentences Among Social Types of Defendants in Drunk Court

Sentences	Percent of Defendants by Social Types						
	Young Man with Job, Wife, 1st Offense (N = 19)	Young Repeater (N = 27)	Middle-aged Respectable Repeater (N = 26)	Out-of-towner (N = 15)	Middle-aged Repeater, Not Recent (N = 20)	Derelict Who Looks Rough (N = 69)	Man Looking Gravely Ill (N = 4)
Kick-out (no sentence, warned only)	21	—	—	—	—	—	—
County hospital							
With hold	—	—	—	—	—	—	—
No hold	—	—	—	—	—	—	75
Suspended sentence							
10 days or less	59	22	11	60	15	13	25
11 to 30 days	10	22	35	—	60	30	—
31 to 60 days	10	37	35	33	25	3	—
61 to 90 days	—	—	—	—	—	—	—
Over 90 days	—	—	—	—	—	—	—
Sentenced to County Jail							
10 days or less	—	4	4	7	—	54	—
11 to 30 days	—	15	—	—	—	—	—
31 to 60 days	—	—	15	—	—	—	—
61 to 90 days	—	—	—	—	—	—	—
Over 90 days	—	—	—	—	—	—	—
Totals	100	100	100	100	100	100	100

fact), the Rapper himself "fell off the wagon" and underwent treatment at Northern State Mental Hospital, one of the stations on the loop. While there, the Rapper told about his recent job with the court and how he helped the judge:

> Each man arrested has a card with the whole record on it. We would go over the cards before the case came up. We see how many times he's been arrested. I could advise the judge to give them probation or a sentence. Many times, the family would call and request a sentence. I would often arrange for them to get probation plus clothes and a place to stay at one of the halfway houses. Oh, I'll help and help, but when they keep falling off—I get disgusted.

The Christian Missionaries also send a liaison man to the drunk court sessions. He acts as Rapper at special times and thereby also serves in an informal screening capacity. Sponsorship by this organization appears to guarantee that the defendant will get a suspended sentence. For instance, this interchange was observed in court several times:

> JUDGE (*turning to Missionary representative*): "Do you want him [this defendant]?" (*Meaning,* "Will you take him at one of your facilities?")
> MISSIONARY: (*Nods* "Yes.")
> JUDGE: Suspended sentence.

Another observer discussed this arrangement with a veteran judge:

> INTERVIEWER: "Isn't there any attempt made to consider the men for rehabilitation?"
> "The men are screened by the Christian Missionaries usually. The Christian Missionaries send someone down to the jail who tries to help them. They talk with the men and screen them. Nobody does the job that the Christian Missionaries do in the jail."
> INTERVIEWER: "The Court abdicates the screening of defendants to the Christian Missionaries, then?"
> "Not completely. We try to keep a record. Some of these men we can help, but most we can't. I know by heart all of their alibis and stories" [LeClercq, 1966:11].

Another important informal court post is filled by an employee who is known to some of the men as "the Knocker." The job of the Knocker is to maintain the personal records of the men who appear before drunk court and to supply the judge with this information. A court observer reported the following:

The Knocker spoke to the judge in just about every case. However, I do not know what he said. He may just be reading to the judge the official records, or he may be giving his personal judgment about the possibility of the defendant being picked up again in the near future. One thing seems clear: the judge receives his information from the Knocker just before he hands out the sentence.

Sometimes it is difficult to distinguish the Knocker (who merely gives information to the judge) from the Rapper (who "suggests" the proper sentence). In 1963, two of these court liaison officers worked together. An interview with one partner is quoted below:

> INTERVIEWER: "What do you do?"
> "Up here we act as a *combination district attorney and public defender* [emphasis mine]. We are more familiar with these guys than the judges are. The judges alternate. We have the previous arrest records. A lot of times, guys will give phony names. It may take us a while to catch up with them. We try to remember if we have seen a guy before."
> INTERVIEWER: "How does a judge decide whether to sentence the men and if so, for how long?"
> "We help him out on that. If a guy has been in three times in four weeks, they should get a minimum of 30 days. They need to dry out. You know, if a man has been arrested three times in four weeks, you ask yourself the question: 'How many times has he been drunk that he wasn't arrested?' Also, you look at the condition of a man—he may even need hospitalization."
> INTERVIEWER: "You mean you can tell whether a man ought to be sent to jail by looking at him?"
> "Some of them look a lot more rough looking than others. You can tell they have been on a drunk for more than one day. They are heavily bearded. They have probably been sleeping in doorways or on the street. You can tell they have been on a long drunk" [LeClercq, 1966:6–7].

Thus perhaps the most revealing aspect of the sentencing procedure is the virtual absence of interest in the *charge* and the judge's role as spokesman for the court officer's decision. This may account for the fact the judge seldom discusses the case with the defendant, except in a jocular, disparaging way. The following interchanges, which illustrate this attitude, were witnessed by observers:

> DEFENDANT: I was sleeping in a basement when a man attacked me with a can opener.
> JUDGE: Did you also see elephants?

JUDGE: What is your story this time?
DEFENDANT: (*As he begins to speak, Judge interrupts.*)
JUDGE: You gave me that line yesterday; 30 days in the County Jail.

Court Atmosphere

The above exchanges between the judge and the defendant would seem to suggest the atmosphere of drunk court is more informal than most courts of law. From the reports obtained from all observers, this is true. Drunk court is not taken as seriously as other sessions of the municipal court, or other departments, and a great deal of levity and antic behavior is tolerated (in full view of defendants), an attitude not allowed in other Pacific City courts. Excerpts from observers' notes illustrate this unserious aspect of drunk court:

> Bailiff came in today and asked other court officers in voice audible to all, "When does the parade [of defendants] begin?"
>
> There is open flirting between a police matron and police before court starts.
>
> The Knocker and bailiff put a sign, "The Flying Nun," over the judge's name before court started. Removed it when judge appeared.
>
> Judge comes in the front door of the court, walks very casually, often presides without robe. Unlike other courts, bailiff asks everyone to remain seated when judge appears. Judge is always five to ten minutes late.
>
> Just as the judge was about ready to start, there was a gasp and a thud. (This didn't seem to shake anyone except me.) One of the defendants had fallen over near the front of the line, and the other defendants stood there like this wasn't anything to get upset about.
>
> The judge asked, "What was his number?" and the Knocker told him. Then one of the court policemen said that he thought the guy was dead. "This man has had an alcoholic seizure. We're going to take him to the hospital," the judge said.
>
> The bailiff asked what should be done about the man's case. The judge dismissed it. It was the only kick-out that day.

From this it can be seen that the operational ideology of the judge in drunk court, although much like that of juvenile court, is lacking in the compassion often shown for juveniles. An attempt is made to sentence the man in terms of his characteristics and not the criminal act he is accused of. Extenuating circumstances of all types are used in arriving at decisions. There is no lawyer or advocacy system in operation. The defendant may be discharged to "responsible" persons in the community (this means some member of his family if he has one, or the Christian Missionaries if they exhibit an interest in him).

Far from freeing the judge to make idiosyncratic personalized decisions, the result of the drunk court system is to standardize drunks on the basis of social types and then with the assistance of court aides objectify them in such a way as to fit the predetermined types. Thus the decision of the patrolman in typification of the Skid-Row drinker is not only accepted in the court without question —it is reinforced and embellished.

Justifying the Sentencing Process

How does the municipal court judge, serving in drunk court sessions, allow himself to be a party to such extralegal activities as platoon sentencing, the heavy reliance on advice from "friends of the court," and the utilization of extraneous social characteristics in setting the sentence? Why is there not a conflict with his self-image of judicial compassion for the individual and scrupulous attention to legal niceties?

For some judges, the conflict is resolved by falling back on the alcoholism-as-an-illness view of drunkenness, and by redefining many of the men who appear before him as patients rather than defendants. Thus, when asked to describe their duties, drunk court judges often sound like physicians dealing with troublesome patients for whom they must prescribe unpleasant but necessary medicine, rather than judges punishing men for being a public annoyance. As an example of this:

> I know that jail isn't the best place for these men, but we have to do something for them. We need to put them someplace where they can dry out. You can't just let a man go out and kill himself.

> This is a grave and almost hopeless problem. But you have to try some kind of treatment. Often they are better off in jail than out on the street.

The drunk court judges sometimes add the wish that the city provided a more palatable alternative to the County Jail, but then reiterate the view that it is better than no help at all.

Court attachés have essentially the same attitude:

> Some of these guys are so loaded that they will fall and break their skull if you don't lock them up. Half of these guys have no place to stay anyway except a dingy heap. They are better off in jail.

The whole purpose of the law is to try to help them. It's for the protection of themselves and for others, that's the way the law reads. For example, say you're driving through here [Skid-Row] and you hit a drunk. He could get killed and if you don't stop and render aid, you could become a criminal.

Giving them 30 days in County Jail is sometimes a kindness. *You are doing them a favor, like a diabetic who won't take his insulin.* Sometimes you must hurt him to help him. [Emphasis mine.]

Like the Skid-Row police, the officers, the judge and his coterie are reinforced in their definition of the situation as clinical, and of themselves as diagnosticians and social internists, by the fact that relatives often call the court and ask that a man be given time in jail for his own good. The judge usually complies. Furthermore, as has been mentioned, there is at the jail a branch of the Out-Patient Therapy Center that was originally established to work for the rehabilitation of alcoholics. Having this jail clinic allows the drunk court judge to say: "I sentence you to 30 days and I will get in touch with the social worker at the County Jail and she will help you." Or, "I sentence you to therapy with the psychologists at the County Jail" (also reported by court observers).

Creation of the Pacific City Alcoholism School also allows the judge to feel that he is fulfilling both judicial and therapeutic duties, giving the defendant a suspended sentence on the condition that he will attend the lecture sessions.

Where the name of the social worker or psychologist of Alcoholism School is not invoked as part of the sentence, an awareness of alcoholism as an illness is frequently used as an introductory statement to indicate the reasoning of the courts for giving a jail sentence: "We realize that you men are sick and need help. Any action I might take, therefore, should not in any sense be construed as punishment. Jail in this case is not a punitive measure, but to help you with your alcoholism problem."

However, the uneasiness of the judge with the jailing of alcoholics has other indicators. The captain of the County Jail, for instance, reports that inmates serving time for public drunkenness have only to write a letter requesting modification and it is almost automatically forthcoming, something not true for modification requests of of prisoners convicted of other misdemeanors.

That drunk court's methods and procedures of handling the Row men go against the judicial grain also seems to be indicated by the fact court officers claims a new judge must be "broken in" to drunk court before he operates efficiently. When the judge first arrives, he will sentence differently from an experienced judge and in the direction of greater leniency. This upsets the established pattern.

The result is he is taken in hand and guided to do "the right thing" by the veteran court aides. As one court aide put it:

> Most of the judges are pretty good—they rely on us. Sometimes you get a new judge who wants to do things his way. We have to break them in, train them. This court is very different. We have to break new judges in. It takes some of them some time to get adjusted to the way we do things.

The high rate of recidivism of chronic drunkenness offenders leads some experts to question the value of jail as a cure for alcoholism or chronic drunkenness. Publicly, at least, the judges appear to hold to the view that the current arrest and incarceration process *can* be helpful, but that often the alcoholic simply does not respond to "treatment" permanently and needs periodic "doses" of jail-therapy. As one judge put it: "Some men have simply gone so far that you can't do anything for them. They are hopeless. All we can do is send them to jail to dry out from time to time."

Sentencing as an Assembly-Line Outrage

Although the chronic drunkenness offender makes many trips through drunk court, it is not too surprising that he never becomes completely accustomed to the way he is treated there. The mass sentencing, the arbitrariness of the judge, the extraneous factors that seem to go into sentencing decisions, all these shock and embitter him.

Of the group-sentencing procedures, the Row men have this to say:

> It's law on the assembly line. That's how it really is. No judge would admit it, though. He's got a nice, soft, plush $15,000 or $18,000 job which hinges on this.
>
> I mean there's no concept on the part of anybody that goes into drunk court, that this is a court of law, that the judge is going to weigh the pros and cons. . . .
>
> Let me tell you, he's handling 50 guys in a period of an hour or less. Do you think he has time to, uh, to say, "Well now, why do you drink?" and like that?
>
> The situation here [in jail] could stand a lot of improvement, but the court situation is much worse. When you go down there to court each individual in the courts of the United States is entitled to individual and separate trial. You go down there

and they run you into these courts, 30 or 40 at a time, and they
sentence you accordingly. The front row first.

I was in there one time, I don't remember who the judge was,
when we got in he ran off about seven or eight names, "You
people have 30 days in the County Jail." Then he says, "The rest
of you in the front row can plead guilty, not guilty, trial by
court, trial by jury."

Here is how they describe the seemingly unrelated factors that
appear to go into the judge's decision:

If you haven't been picked up for a long time and you've been
in town all that time, you'll get a kick-out; but if you've been
out of town, you get a sentence, because they figure you were
probably drinking all the time.

. . . If you've been [picked up], say, a couple of times in a week
or more, why you're subject to be sent to County Jail.

On Monday before court, we all 15 of us shaved on one razor
after being picked up on Friday because we knew that if we
were whiskery we'd go to County Jail for sure.

Of those arrested before Christmas, everyone who had an
address other than Skid-Row—even a Beatnik area—got a kick-
out. Others like us went to County Jail.

Judge Darlington is a no good son-of-a-bitch. He says to us,
"Hold your hands out." They have been holding you in the
drunk tank for about eight hours, no beds there, just concrete.
After that you go to a holding cell. They line them up ten at
a time in front and ten in back. After three days in there,
worrying what's going to happen to you, you shake a bit. If you
do, Judge Darlington says, "Sixty days."

The fact the judge acts on advice from an ex-alcoholic, a nonprofessional who clearly is drawing his views from personal (and possibly
petty) recollections of the men, further confirms the picture of totally arbitrary power with little concern for justice.

There's this guy they call "the Rapper" and he has the ear of
the judge. He actually sets the sentence whenever he's there.
I'd like to get my hands on him sometime.

We call him "the Rapper." He has the power of life and death
for the men. He sat up next to the judge and would say, "probation," "30 days," "90 days," and that's what you'd get. Is that
legal? I don't think anyone should be allowed to play God like
that.

We were all glad when he slipped. He looked for the worst
of himself in others. [Comment on the fact that the Rapper had
recently fallen off the wagon himself and was at State Mental
Hospital.]

The Christian Missionary Rapper was no more popular with the men:

> Jim Brown, a reformed alcoholic who has no use for another alcoholic, is the Rapper. He will hang a man if he doesn't like him. I was at Barabas Abode and Beacon in the Darkness. We speak to each other, but he's a double-crossing, no-good son-of-a-bitch. Absolutely no good! At 6 A.M. he and the court liaison officer go through the records and *they* decide what each man shall get. They see my name and say, "Give that bastard 60 days!"

The Row men are also aware that there are sometimes drastic differences between the sentences received one day in court and those received another. Empirical evidence of this can be seen in Table 5, where sentences received during a time when County Jail was normally full, and during a time when it was beyond normal capacity because of a recent demonstration, are compared. (Arrests were also below average for that day, as well.)

Table 5. Comparison of Sentences Given in Drunk Court When Jail Was Full and When It Was Beyond Capacity

Sentences	State of County Jail	
	Full (N = 180) Percent	Beyond Capacity (N = 36) Percent
Kick-out (no sentence, warned only)	2	8
County Hospital		
With hold	—	—
No hold	2	—
Suspended sentence	} 74	} 91
10 days or less	—	5
11 to 30 days	23	70
31 to 60 days	28	8
61 to 90 days	19	—
Over 90 days	—	—
Sentenced to County Jail		
10 days or less	1	3
11 to 30 days	23	6
31 to 60 days	2 } 26	— } 9
61 to 90 days	—	—
Over 90 days	—	—
Total	100	100

As shown in Table 5, only 9 percent of the men received a County Jail sentence when the jail was beyond capacity (as compared to 26 percent when it was merely very full).

Skid-Row drunks explain such disparity not as a function of jail capacity but as evidence of graft among agents of social control. Collusion is assumed to exist among the police, City Hospital, the Christian Missionaries, the jailers, and the judges in the Municipal Court, and among the judges, the police, the jailers, and the social workers in the Superior Courts. This reinforces the idea of a powerful system beyond the control of a penniless individual. The Row men cite the following evidence (so far as they are concerned) as proof of this.

Sometimes, if you get smart with the policeman, he tells the judge and you get a bigger sentence.

When I was arrested for drunk, they took me first to the hospital. A social worker came around, and she had a folder, and she said, "Let's see now, uh, you won't have any way to pay for your stay here." I'd only been there [in the hospital] a day and a half, and I says, "Well, how do you know?" And she said, "Well, where you're going, you won't be able to pay anyway." So I says, "Well, how do you know where I'm goin'?" She says, "Well, you're goin' to County Jail for 60 days." I says, "Well, how do you know? I haven't even been before the judge yet!" She said, "Oh, it's right here in your folder." I hadn't been to court yet, see, and sure enough, as soon as I went before the judge—60 days at County Jail. I told the judge about it after he sentenced me and he said, "You're being irrelevant," or something like that. In other words you're going for 60 days, and you just don't argue. He said also, "Well, sometimes that's court procedure."

This cooperation is oftentimes suspected by embittered Row men to serve the purpose of enriching unscrupulous agents of social control or at the very least maintain them in their jobs by keeping the jail population at an assigned level:

The key to the whole situation is the cut on the food taken by Sheriff Smith and Captain Jackson and the judges. They are all getting their cut by stealing from the food appropriations to the jail. They make $1.50 a day on each one of us. I think they have a quota at County Jail. If they are down 50 men, you can bet that 50 will go out on the next bus.

What a lot of people don't realize is that this institution and most jails need labor and the alcoholic furnishes that. When I was a trusty in Minneapolis, I'd hear the superintendent call the judge and say, "We are short 150 men here"—and in three days the courts would send us our 150 men [Bittner, 1967].

Maneuvers to Escape County Jail

Lacking the power to fight a drunk charge legally or by means of forfeiting bail, the Skid-Row alcoholic has developed other ways of avoiding the County Jail, which is hated more than any other locale on the loop. It should be emphasized that if such avoidance tactics are successful the Row man is still incarcerated, but in another (and more desirable) area.

For instance, a "regular" (i.e., chronic drunkenness offender) may get a job at the City Jail as trusty if he is known to be a good worker and is popular with guards: "After you're sentenced, then you go see the head man there [at City Jail], and if you've been there before, which most of 'em have, then he'll say, 'Yeah, you can stay here and work for me.' It's who you know that counts."

A second means of avoiding County Jail is for a man to act psychotic so that he is referred to the City Screening Facility at the hospital, and perhaps even to the psychiatric ward there. Often this results in a five-day hospitalization or a sojourn in the Northern State Mental Hospital rather than a jail sentence. As one man put it: "One good way is to act or talk suicidal. That scares them sometimes. Do a lot of yelling and pretend to hear voices. This will often break them [the jailers] down and you'll get to go to City Hospital."

The Feeling of Unfairness

The judge may feel righteous because he is saving a man from drinking himself to death by sending him to jail to dry out, but the Skid-Row alcoholic is neither convinced this alleged judicial "good will" exists, nor is he grateful even if it does. With the exception of those Row men who have settled on the jail as a second home, most believe there is great inequity in the way Pacific City courts are operated. They point to other state jurisdictions that deal with the drunk far less harshly:

> You take Alabama, Georgia, any place, they'll give you a ten dollar fine. Texas, you get two days in jail. You can get in jail ten times and you'll still only get two days and more chance the judge'll let you go.
> Chicago doesn't treat its alcoholics like this city, neither does New York. Most of the time they keep you overnight or a couple of days. They don't send you to jail for a month or more.

The alcoholics' opinion of being sent to jail for drunkenness is perhaps best summed up in this quote:

> As far as the jail goes, all jails are the same. Nobody likes to be in 'em regardless of whether they give you steak or, uh, filet

mignons, or whatever it is, nobody likes to be in jail. They don't beat you or nothin' like that. Like any place, it's a place of detention; that's their job, that's what the judge said; we're just taken away from the public. As far as gettin' here, it's for drunk, and as far as the sentence goes I believe that's quite a price to pay. Even if it's ten days, I think it's too much myself—even ten days, takin' ten days away from your life for gettin' drunk.

References

Bittner, Egon. 1967. The Police on Skid Row: A Study of Peace-Keeping. *American Sociological Review* 32 (October).

Bogue, Donald J. 1963. *Skid Row in American Cities.* Chicago: Univ. of Chicago Press.

Garfinkel, Harold. 1956. Conditions of a Successful Degradation Ceremony. *American Journal of Sociology* 61 (March): 420–22.

LeClercq, Frederic S. 1966. Field Observations in Drunk Court of the Pacific Municipal Court, p. 1. Unpublished memorandum.

Petersen, William, and David Matza. 1963. Does the Juvenile Court Exercise Justice? In *Social Controversy,* ed. Petersen and Matza. Belmont, Calif.: Wadsworth.

Stem, Gerald. 1967. Public Drunkenness: Crime or Health Problem? *Annals of American Academy of Political and Social Science* 374 (November): 147–56.

Some Factors in Sentencing Policy

Robert M. Carter and Leslie T. Wilkins

The probation officer as a member of the court staff has two major functions to fulfill. The first is to conduct an investigation of an offender which culminates in a presentence or probation report. This report is frequently accompanied by a recommendation to the court as to the selection of an appropriate sentence. The second function is to provide supervision for offenders placed on probation or some other form of conditional liberty. Despite the recent focus of correctional interest and attention, and a considerable volume of literature, the terms and conditions of these functions remain relatively vague. It is proposed to examine here a segment of one of these, namely the presentence report recommendation and its relationship to the court disposition. Our purpose is not so much to provide data, but to make explicit some questions about presentence report recommendations and their relation to court dispositions.

Even though corrections is a relatively new field in the United States, some of its components have already become so institutionalized that they form a cornerstone for the development of a correctional folklore or mythology. In essence, it appears that the increasing problem of crime and delinquency is being addressed by the application of principles and practices which have not been substantially modified, or even questioned, since their inception. Yet the correctional systems must change if for no other reason than that of the increasing number of offenders processed. Tradition would have it that the changes be in the direction of increased probation and parole staff, prison personnel, new institutions, and related services. If these be the sole nature of the changes—more of what already exists—there will be a reliance upon a view of the past without a realistic vision of the future.

Caseload

The fifty-unit workload as the standard for probation and parole supervision is an example of one of the myths. Where did this number come from? On what empirical data is it based? Is it an appropriate limitation of caseload size? If it is not appropriate, what should be the workload for corrections? A search of the literature dates the fifty-unit concept back to at least 1922, when Charles L.

SOURCE: *Journal of Criminal Law, Criminology, and Police Science* 58, no. 4 (1967): 505–14. Copyright © 1967 by Northwestern University School of Law. Reprinted by special permission of the journal.

Chute, then President of the National Probation Association, observed: "To this end fifty cases is as many as any probation officer ought to carry."[1] The fifty-unit concept found its way in the prestigious academic literature when Sutherland[2] in 1934, and Tannenbaum[3] in 1938, suggested that fifty cases "is generally regarded as the maximum number" and "the best practice would limit the caseload of a probation officer to fifty cases." The concept of fifty entered the professional literature when the American Prison Association in 1946 indicated that a probation officer "should not have more than fifty cases under continuous supervision."[4] An almost identical statement appears in the 1954 revision of the Manual of Correctional Standards.[5] Not until 1966 (while still suggesting a fifty-unit workload) did the American Correctional Association indicate that "where methods of classification for caseloads have been developed through research varying standards of workloads may prevail."[6]

The institutionalization of the fifty-unit concept is now firmly entrenched. Budgets for operating agencies, testimony before legislative bodies, standards of practice, and protections for future operational needs all center about this number. There is no evidence of any empirical justification for fifty, nor for that matter any other number.

The following discussion relates mainly to the federal probation system, and we are indebted to the Administrative Office of the United States Courts for furnishing pertinent data. Information has also been drawn from the San Francisco Project, a study of the federal probation system, supported by the National Institute of Mental Health.[7] It should be noted that these data cover different populations over different periods of time and are not to be seen as interesting in themselves, but as throwing light on the presentence report recommendation and court dispositions.

Recommendations and Dispositions: The Relationship

The presentence report is a document basic to the functioning of both judicial and correctional administrations. The contents of the

[1]Chute, "Probation and Suspended Sentence," *J. Crim. L. & Co.* 12 (1922), 562.

[2]Sutherland, *Principles of Criminology* (1934), 359.

[3]Tannenbaum, *Crime and the Community* (1938), 462.

[4]*Manual of Suggested Standards for a State Correctional System*, Am. Pris. Assn. (1946), 13.

[5]*Manual of Correctional Standards*, Am. Corr. Assn. (1954), 43.

[6]*Ibid.* (1966), 109.

[7]See Lohman, Wahl, and Carter, *A Non-Technical Description of the San Francisco Project,* The San Francisco Project series (April 1965).

report, including the recommendation, assist the court in making a judgment consistent with its dual responsibilities to society and the defendant. Within the federal system that report aids the institutions within the Bureau of Prisons in determining classification and treatment programs and also in planning for subsequent release. The report provides information to the Board of Parole, furnishing information believed to be pertinent to its deliberations. Furthermore, the report contributes to the probation officer's rehabilitative efforts while an offender is under his supervision.[8]

In February 1965, with the publication of a 39-page monograph entitled *The Presentence Investigation Report,* a standard outline and format were adopted for the preparation of presentence reports in the federal courts.[9] The final paragraph headings of the report are "Evaluative Summary" and "Recommendation." The importance of these paragraphs is recognized by the American Correctional Association, which includes among its standards for the preparation of presentence reports a "recommendation for or against probation, or for other disposition according to court policy."[10]

The fact that there is a substantial number of sentencing alternatives available to federal judges also means that an equal number of possible recommendations may be considered by the probation officer. The selection ranges, of course, from probation with or without a fine or restitution, and/or a jail sentence, and imprisonment under various statutes which determine parole eligibility, to other dispositions which include commitment for observation and study and continuances for community observation.

Because of this variety of available disposals, the relationship between a recommendation and a disposition may be more simply considered from one of two directions. The first method would be to contrast recommendations for probation made by probation officers with actual court dispositions resulting in probation. The second would be from an opposite direction, viewing recommendations against probation (or for imprisonment) with actual court dispositions for probation.

Data developed during the San Francisco Project contrast recommendations and dispositions for 500 consecutive cases processed through the United States District Court in the Northern District of California between September 1964 and August 1965.[11] These data indicate that:

[8]The federal probation officer supervises persons released on parole or mandatory release from federal correctional institutions or the United States Disciplinary Barracks.

[9]*The Presentence Investigation Report,* Adm. Off. U.S. Cts. (1965).

[10]*Manual of Correctional Standards,* Am. Corr. Assn. (2d ed. 1959), 521.

[11]Carter, *It Is Respectfully Recommended. . . .,* 30 Fed. Prob. 2 (1966).

... there is a close relationship between the recommendation of probation and the actual granting of probation. Probation was recommended in 227 cases and was granted in 212 of those cases. If the 7 cases of "observation and study" are not included, probation was granted, when recommended, in 212 of the 220 cases or in 96 percent of the cases. In only 2 of the 227 cases was there a substantial difference between the probation officer's recommendation and the court's disposition of the cases. In these instances, prison sentences were ordered where probation had been recommended.[12]

These data closely parallel the California data. The percentages of probation officer recommendations for probation followed by California Superior Courts, for the years cited, are shown in Table 1.

Data on the federal system, arranged by the ten judicial circuits, indicate the relationship, shown in Table 2, between probation officer recommendations for probation and such dispositions in court for fiscal year 1964.

The patterns in these first two tables exhibit almost total agreement between a probation officer's recommendation for probation and an actual disposition of probation. However, this trend appears less stable when viewed from the opposite perspective—the relationship between recommendations against probation (or for imprisonment) and court dispositions of probation. California data reveal, in Table 3, the percentages of "against probation" recommendations and probation disposition in court.

It is noteworthy that California authorities indicate the "superior court judges are more lenient than probation officers as to who should be granted probation."[13] This pattern has already been observed by one of the authors,[14] and by others,[15] in respect to the federal probation officer. Further confirmation of this pattern is found throughout the federal system as indicated by a review, in Table 4, of "against probation" recommendations and probation dispositions according to the ten judicial circuits for fiscal year 1964.

As already indicated, the probation officer has a wide latitude in his choice of a recommendation. Table 5 presents data on the specific recommendations of probation officers in the Northern District of California between September 1964 and February 1967, and shows the wide variety of possible recommendations.

---

[12] *Ibid,* 41.

[13] *Delinquency and Probation in California,* 1964, Calif. Dept. of Justice (1964), 166.

[14] Carter, *supra* note 11.

[15] Lohman, Wahl, and Carter, *San Francisco Project* series (Report No. 2), Berkeley (June 1965), 8.

Table 1. Percentage of Probation Officer Recommendations
for Probation Followed by California Superior Courts

1959	95.6
1960	96.4
1961	96.0
1962	96.5
1963	97.2
1964	97.3
1965	96.7

Source: State of California, Department of Justice. *Delinquency and Probation in California,* 1964, p. 168; and *Crime and Delinquency in California,* 1965, pp. 98–99.

Table 2. Percentage of Probation Officer Recommendations
for Probation Followed by Ten Judicial Circuits, Fiscal Year 1964

First Circuit	99.4
Second Circuit	96.0
Third Circuit	93.2
Fourth Circuit	93.3
Fifth Circuit	95.2
Sixth Circuit	93.9
Seventh Circuit	89.9
Eighth Circuit	95.0
Ninth Circuit	93.5
Tenth Circuit	97.8
Overall	94.1

Source: Data furnished by the Administrative Office of the United States Courts.

Table 3. Percentage of Probation Officer Recommendations
Against Probation Not Followed by California Superior Courts

1959	13.5
1960	12.8
1961	14.8
1962	17.4
1963	21.6
1964	21.1
1965	19.9

Source: State of California, Department of Justice. *Delinquency and Probation in California,* 1964, p. 168; and *Crime and Delinquency in California,* 1965, pp. 98–99.

Table 4. Percentage of Probation Officer Recommendations
Against Probation Not Followed by Ten Judicial Circuits,
Fiscal Year 1964

First Circuit	7.3
Second Circuit	9.5
Third Circuit	27.4
Fourth Circuit	31.8
Fifth Circuit	11.5
Sixth Circuit	19.3
Seventh Circuit	15.9
Eighth Circuit	16.5
Ninth Circuit	23.3
Tenth Circuit	9.2
Overall	19.7

Source: Data furnished by the Administrative Office of the United States Courts.

Table 5. Probation Officers' Recommendations as to Sentence
(Northern District of California, September 1964 to February 1967)

Recommendation	Total	Percent of Total
All Cases	1,232	100.0
No recommendation	67	5.4
Mandatory sentence (Under certain narcotic law violations)	45	3.6
Probation	601	48.9
Regular	(284)	(23.1)
With Fine and/or Restitution	(197)	(16.0)
Split Sentence (Imprisonment up to Six Months Followed by Probation)	(49)	(4.0)
Under Youth Corrections Act	(71)	(5.8)
Fine only	38	3.1
Jail only	35	2.8
Imprisonment	334	27.1
Parole Eligibility After 1/3 Sentence	(234)	(19.0)
Parole Eligibility At Any Time	(64)	(5.2)
Under Youth Corrections Act	(36)	(2.9)
Observation and study	51	4.2
Adult	(39)	(3.2)
Youth	(12)	(1.0)
Continuance for 90 days observation	16	1.3
Deferred prosecution	3	.2
Commitment under federal juvenile delinquency act	2	.2
Other recommendations	40	3.3

Source: Unpublished San Francisco Project data.

Table 6 presents overall data on the relationship between recommendations and dispositions of 1,232 cases processed through the District Court in Northern California. The reader will note that of 601 cases recommended for probation, 15 were ordered imprisoned; of 334 cases recommended for imprisonment, 31 were placed on probation.

These data seem to support certain generalizations about the nature of the relationship between probation officer recommendations and court dispositions. We have seen that there is a very strong relationship between recommendations *for probation* and court dispositions of probation, an average agreement of about 95 percent. It has also been observed that the strength of the relationship diminishes slightly when recommendations *against probation* (or for imprisonment) are contrasted with court dispositions of probation. Thus, it may be concluded that where disagreements exist between recommendations and dispositions, they occur when the officer recommends imprisonment. In a sense, if this relationship measures "punitiveness," then it may be concluded that the probation officer is more punitive than the judge.

Outcome of Supervision According to the Recommendation

Very limited data are available on the outcome of supervision, i.e., the violation rate, according to recommendations of probation officers. The 1964 cohort study of Davis[16] examined the violation status of 11,638 adult defendants granted probation in California Superior Courts between 1956 and 1958. Davis showed that 27.1 percent of the defendants recommended for and placed on probation were "revoked," while 36.7 percent of the defendants placed on probation against the recommendation of the probation officer were revoked. Davis concluded that the "difference in revocation rates was very significant and indicates that the two groups were not alike in their tendency to recidivism."

It is questionable that this single explanation for the 10 percent differential in revocation rates occurs simply because of differences in the two groups. There are other possible explanations for this. One explanation may be that subtle differences exist in the supervision provided by a probation officer who may feel "resentful" in having an individual placed on probation against his recommendation. The second possibility is that the defendant's attitude toward a probation officer who recommended that he be imprisoned instead of placed on

[16]Davis, "A Study of Adult Probation Violation Rates by Means of the Cohort Approach," *J. Crim. L., C. & P. S.,* 55 (1964), 70.

Table 6. Probation Officers' Recommendation and Subsequent Court Dispositions (Northern District of California, September 1964 to February 1967)

Recommendation	Total	Disposition								
		Mandatory	Probation	Fine Only	Jail Only	Imprisonment	Observation and Study	Continuances	Deferred Prosecution	Other
All Cases	1,232	45	671	30	27	337	73	18	2	29
No recommendation	67	—	44	2	2	14	1	—	—	4
Mandatory	45	45	—	—	—	—	—	—	—	—
Probation	601	—	551	5	3	15	17	2	—	8
Fine only	38	—	14	22	—	1	—	—	—	1
Jail only	35	—	5	1	19	8	2	—	—	—
Imprisonment	334	—	31	—	2	281	13	5	—	2
Observation and study	51	—	3	—	—	9	38	1	—	—
Continuances	16	—	6	—	—	—	—	10	—	—
Deferred prosecution	3	—	—	—	—	—	—	—	2	1
Federal Juvenile Delinquency Act	2	—	1	—	—	—	—	—	—	1
Other	40	—	16	—	1	9	2	—	—	12

Source: Unpublished San Francisco Project data.

probation may affect the outcome of supervision. While there are no measures of these two negative factors, it is possible that they account for a large portion of the observed differential. There are other interesting studies which support the hypothesis of self-fulfilling prophecies.

Another way of viewing Davis's data is to emphasize that 63.3 percent of those who received an unfavorable probation recommendation but were placed on probation completed their probation without revocation. Thus, to deny probation to all those with negative recommendations from probation officers would suggest that approximately two out of every three defendants with such recommendations would be denied the opportunity to complete probation successfully. Davis inquired as to the number of defendants who, denied probation on unfavorable recommendations, would have succeeded on probation if given the opportunity. There are, at this time, no data to answer this question.[17]

Other data are available from the Administrative Office of the United States Courts which indicate that despite considerable variation in the use of probation, the overall violation rates, or the rates broken down by "major," "minor," or "technical" are almost identical. Table 7 of the Administrative Office report is reproduced here to show probation violation rates for 1965, according to the actual percentage of persons placed on probation by the 88 U.S. District Courts, arranged by quartiles.

The data in Table 7 reveal that approximately 19 percent of those placed under probation supervision violate the terms of this conditional liberty, regardless of the percentage of the offender population on probation.

Factors Affecting the Agreement between Recommendations and Dispositions

Reverting to the possible explanations for the high degree of agreement between probation officer recommendations and court dispositions, it is possible that four factors, operating independently, but more probably simultaneously, account for this relationship:

1. The court having such high regard for the professional qualities and competence of its probation staff, "follows" the probation recommendation—a recommendation made by the person (probation officer) who best knows the defendant by reason of the presentence investigation.
2. There are many offenders who are "obviously" probation or prison cases.

[17]Wilkins, "A Small Comparative Study of the Results of Probation," *British J. Crimino.* 8 (1958), 201.

Table 7. Comparison of the Use of Probation in District Courts,
by Type of Violation, Fiscal Year 1965

(Table A 18 of the Administrative Office of the U.S. Courts covering 88 United States District Courts)
(*Excludes violators of immigration laws, wagering tax laws and violators of federal regulatory acts*)

Item	88 District Courts	Quartile Groups of District Courts			
		First 22 District Courts	Second 22 District Courts	Third 22 District Courts	Fourth 22 District Courts
Average					
Actual percent placed on probation	49.0	65.9	53.8	47.2	36.9
Total removed	11,259	2,263	2,759	3,678	2,559
No violations	9,157	1,843	2,267	2,973	2,074
Violated probation	2,102	420	492	705	485
Technical violation	344	78	85	106	75
Minor violation	577	111	120	216	130
Major violation	1,181	231	287	383	280
Percent					
Violated Probation	18.7	18.5	17.8	19.2	18.9
Technical violation	3.1	3.4	3.1	2.9	2.9
Minor violation	5.1	4.9	4.3	5.9	5.1
Major violation	10.5	10.2	10.4	10.4	10.9

Source: Administrative Office of the United States Courts, *Persons Under the Supervision of the Federal Probation System* (Washington, D.C.: 1965), p. 33.

3.   Probation officers write their reports and make recommendations anticipating the recommendation the court desires to receive. (In this situation, the probation officer is quite accurately "second-guessing" the court disposition.)
4.   Probation officers in making their recommendations place great emphasis on the same factors as does the court in selecting a sentencing alternative.

Data from the San Francisco Project confirm the fact that probation officers and judges apply approximately equal significance to similar factors.[18] Examination of 500 probation officer recommendations according to the major categories of recommendations for probation and recommendations for imprisonment (or against probation), produced data on the legal and demographic characteristics of the offender population which had an important effect upon the recommendation selected. In general terms, the proportion of recommendations for probation increased with the number of years of education, average monthly income, higher occupational levels, residence, marital and employment stability, participation in church activities, and a good military record. Recommendations for imprisonment (or against probation) increased proportionately when offenders exhibited such characteristics as homosexuality, alcoholic involvement, the use of weapons or violence in the commission of the offense, the existence of family criminality, and drug usage. Age (in the range examined) did not significantly distinguish between the two recommendations, and racial and religious affiliation differences were absent. The female, however, was more likely to be recommended for probation than the male offender.

Certain offense categories (e.g., embezzlement, theft from interstate shipments or theft of government property, and false statement) usually produced recommendations for probation, while other offense categories (e.g., bank robbery, the interstate transportation of stolen motor vehicles [Dyer Act], and National Defense law violation) usually resulted in recommendations for imprisonment. Offenders who entered a plea of guilty, retained their own attorneys, or were released to the community on bail, bond, or personal recognizance while the presentence investigation was being conducted had significantly greater chances of being recommended for probation. It is recognized, of course, that a recommendation for or against probation is generally based upon some combination of characteristics—some obvious, others subtle—rather than upon any single characteristic or piece of information.

[18]See Lohman, Wahl, and Carter, *San Francisco Project* series (Reports 4 and 5), Berkeley (December 1965, February 1966).

It is apparent that not all factors are of equal significance in determining the probation officer's recommendation. Accordingly, statistical computations produced a general ranking of the significance or importance of various factors.[19]

A further examination of the 500 cases was made, reviewing the selection of the sentencing alternative by the court. Again, statistical computations were completed and a second rank order of the significant or important factors was produced.

These two sets of data—one relating to the recommendation, the other to the disposition—are summarized in Table 8. The rankings were based on probability and contingency coefficient values. A correlation was computed and a significant value of .90 was obtained. These data indicate that there is considerable agreement between probation officers and judges as to the significance of certain factors and characteristics for decisions relating to probation or imprisonment recommendations and dispositions.

Another possible explanation of the close agreement between recommendations and dispositions is certainly that some cases are clearly probation or imprisonment cases. However, there are no "hard" data to identify which cases are "clearly" probation or prison cases. An actual, but extreme, example of an "imprisonment case" is the bank robber who, armed with an automatic pistol and with an accomplice waiting in a stolen automobile, robbed a bank of $35,000, pistol-whipped a teller, and, in the flight from the scene, engaged in a gun battle with pursuing police. It is doubtful that probation officers or judges would be inclined to see probation as a suitable disposition for such a case, regardless of any other factors involved. An example of the "probation case" is the young married offender, who, unemployed prior to the Christmas season, made a false statement to the Post Office for employment, concealing a prior misdemeanor arrest. In general terms, this type of offender would normally be seen as a suitable candidate for probation.

From observation and conversations with judges and probation officers during the past years, it appears that judges do indeed have a high regard for their probation staff and value their professional judgment as to the disposition of a case. It is suspected that this is especially true in the federal system in which probation officers are appointed by the court and serve at its pleasure. This esteem for probation officers and their services by the court may also contribute to the high agreement between recommendations and dispositions, even though there are no statistical data to support this.

The fourth potential explanation for the close agreement between recommendations and dispositions—probation officers anticipating the recommendation the court desires—is now to be discussed.

[19] *Ibid.*

Table 8.   Rank of Demographic Factors Utilized by Probation Officers
for Recommendations and District Court Judges for Sentencing Alternatives,
According to Probability and Contingency Coefficient Values
(500 Federal Offenders, Northern District of California,
September 1964 to August 1965)

Demographic Factors	Probation Officers' Ranking	District Court Judge's Ranking
Prior record	1	3
Confinement status	2	2
Number of arrests	3	4
Offense	4	1
Longest employment	5	5
Occupation	6	8
Number of months employed	7	6
Income	8	10
Longest residence	9	7
Military history	10	9
Number of residence changes	11	17
Distance to offense	12	14
Number of aliases	13	24
Marital status	14	11
Legal representation	15	13
Weapons and violence	16	15
Family criminality	17	21
Plea	18	18
Education	19	12
Church attendance	20	16
Narcotics usage	21	23
Sex	22	19
Alcoholic involvement	23	25
Crime partners	24	20
Homosexuality	25	26
Race	26	28
Age	27	22
Religion	28	27

Source: Joseph D. Lohman, Albert Wahl, and Robert M. Carter. *San Francisco Project*
series, Report 5, Berkeley (February 1966), p. 68.
   Spearman's p = .90

Variation among Probation Officers and Probation Offices

Disparities in sentencing have been of considerable interest in recent
years and attempts to reduce these frequently observed differentials
have normally been focused on judges. For example, sentencing
institutes for judges have been developed at the federal and state
level, as well as training programs for newly appointed or elected
judges. That attention should be directed toward judges—for they

impose the sentences—is certainly normal and, on the surface, a logical approach to resolving disparities. However, this pattern ignores one of the facts of community life—in this case the judicial community and its social system—that many persons play a part in the functioning of the community. Included in the judicial community are probation officers, prosecutors, defense attorneys, perhaps to a lesser extent the law enforcement agencies, and other judges on the same bench.

It seems to have been generally assumed that the judges are solely responsible for the disparities and that the remainder of the judicial community plays only a minor role which remains constant, neither supporting nor contributing to the disparities. Although we do not have complete data upon which a judicial "community-effect" can be shown to be a basis for disparities, there are data available which demonstrate the supporting role of at least one member, namely the probation officer.

If we assume that probation officers are "constant" and that judges are "variable," we would expect to find significant differences in the relationship between officer recommendations and court dispositions as we move toward extremes in the use of probation or imprisonment. We would not, in the federal system for example, expect to find the more than 94 percent agreement between recommendations and dispositions spread uniformly throughout the system, for some courts use probation frequently, others infrequently. In fiscal year 1965, individual federal courts had a range of probation usage in excess of 50 percent, with one court using probation for 23.8 percent of its cases, another for 75.7 percent of its cases. The percentage of defendants on probation in fiscal year 1965 by the ten judicial circuits is shown in Table 9.

Table 9.   Percentage Use of Probation in Ten Federal
Judicial Courts

First Circuit	53.0
Second Circuit	45.2
Third Circuit	63.8
Fourth Circuit	60.8
Fifth Circuit	44.8
Sixth Circuit	44.3
Seventh Circuit	44.4
Eighth Circuit	49.9
Ninth Circuit	49.0
Tenth Circuit	43.7
Overall	49.0

Source: Administrative Office of the United States Courts, *Persons Under the Supervision of the Federal Probation System, Fiscal Year 1965,* pp. 103–5.

Thus, on a circuit-wide basis, there is a high of 63.8 percent in the usage of probation ranging to a low of 43.7 percent, an overall spread of 20 percent, and as noted above the variation is even more marked among individual courts. Six of the 88 district courts used probation in excess of 70 percent for their defendants; 12 courts used probation for less than 40 percent of their defendants.

Despite the variation among courts, individually or circuit-wide, the relationship between probation officer recommendations and court dispositions is generally quite constant, whether there is high, moderate, or low usage of probation. This may be seen more precisely in Table 10, which provides data for fiscal year 1964 on sixteen selected federal courts: the five with the highest usage of probation, the five with the lowest use of probation and the six courts which were within 1 percent of the national average for use of probation.

It will be seen, for example, that in District A, probation was recommended for approximately three of each four defendants (147–55); in District H, the recommendations are about equal (152–149), while District N, probation is recommended for about one defendant in three (148–310). However, the "agreement" rate between probation recommendations and dispositions in District A is 97.3 percent, in District H, 95.4 percent, and in District N, 93.7 percent.

These data indicate clearly that the recommendation-disposition relationship does not vary greatly from court to court, and that disparities in sentencing are supported, at least in terms of recommendations, by the probation officer member of the judicial "influence group." To be sure, there may be differences in the Districts which justify high or low use of probation, but thus far these have not been demonstrated. These data raise some interesting and important questions regarding the utility of sentencing institutes for judges, by themselves, as the solution to disparities, and suggest that probation officers, and perhaps prosecuting and defense attorneys, be included in such institutes.

The data in Table 10 have indicated that there is considerable variation in officer recommendations for or against probation in different Districts, but that rate of agreement between recommendations and dispositions is relatively constant between Districts. Accordingly, we would expect to find a common frame of mind, or "influence group set," among officers in a single District which leads to the agreement in that District, regardless of the frequency of probation or imprisonment dispositions. Thus, where probation is used frequently, we would expect the officers in that court to be sympathetic to such usage and we would anticipate that little variation would exist among officers. If this is the case, we would not expect to find such significant variation among probation officers in a single District. We would not expect to find large differences

Table 10. Use of Probation and Recommendations for and Against Probation by Selected United States District Courts, Fiscal Year 1964

	Percentage Use of Probation	Recommended for Probation			Recommended Against Probation			Recommendations Given by Probation Officers: Percent of Total Cases
		Number of Defendants	Number Granted Probation	Percentage Granted Probation	Number of Defendants	Number Granted Probation	Percentage Granted Probation	
A	78.3	147	143	97.3	55	20	36.4	73.2
B	71.4	144	137	95.1	90	31	34.4	88.0
C	70.7	27	26	96.3	7	0	—	82.9
D	70.4	20	19	95.0	11	2	18.2	43.7
E	70.2	125	125	100.0	28	1	3.6	77.3
F	50.8	106	100	94.3	112	17	15.2	89.3
G	50.0	16	16	100.0	17	1	5.9	82.5
H	50.0	152	145	95.4	149	19	12.8	80.9
I	50.0	14	13	92.9	9	0	—	60.5
J	49.7	12	12	100.0	36	6	16.7	15.4
K	49.6	29	28	96.6	36	0	—	47.4
L	36.8	28	28	100.0	19	0	—	13.6
M	36.5	61	61	100.0	117	14	12.0	73.0
N	35.6	158	148	93.7	310	21	6.8	87.8
O	28.5	92	82	89.1	74	25	33.8	35.1
P	26.3	44	38	86.4	174	24	13.8	90.8
Total for all District courts	50.2	6868	6463	94.1	7691	1518	19.7	63.1

Source: Data furnished by the Administrative Office of the United States Courts.

among colleagues appointed by the same court, operating in a similar fashion as regards court and office policies and directives, appointed under uniform standards, paid identical salaries, and theoretically sharing similar views of the correctional process.

Let us return to our data on the 1,232 recommendations made by the probation officers in the Northern District of California as shown in Table 5. By restricting ourselves to a probation-imprisonment dichotomy, we observe that probation was recommended 64.3 percent of the time (601 of 935 cases) and that imprisonment was recommended 35.7 percent (334 of 935 cases). The recommendations of 19 probation officers in Northern California for probation or imprisonment are presented in Table 11. (Officers who made less than 15 recommendations are excluded.)

Table 11. Individual Probation Officer Recommendations for Probation and Imprisonment (Northern District of California, September 1964 to February 1967)

Probation Officer	Number of Recommendations	Number of Probation Recommendations	Number of Prison Recommendations	Percentage of Probation Recommendations
1	55	40	15	72.7
2	39	25	14	64.1
3	46	21	25	45.7
4	57	35	22	61.4
5	16	14	2	87.5
6	20	13	7	65.0
7	55	22	33	40.0
8	38	22	16	57.9
9	22	17	5	77.3
10	58	46	12	79.3
11	59	32	27	54.2
12	57	35	22	61.4
13	54	42	12	77.8
14	36	17	19	47.2
15	56	34	22	60.7
16	46	31	15	67.4
17	60	43	17	71.7
18	18	16	2	88.9
19	42	24	18	57.1

Source: Unpublished San Francisco Project data.

The percentage of recommendations for probation is almost 50 percent—from a low of 40.0 to a high of 88.9 percent. Three officers recommended probation for less than 50 percent of their cases; three officers between 50 and 60 percent, six between 60 and 70 percent, five between 70 and 80 percent, and two in excess of 80 percent.

While this individual variation may be attributed, in part, to the geographic basis for assignment of cases or to other administrative reasons, it is statistically significant and suggests that probation officers, even in the same District, do not view the correctional process from identical perspectives.

What accounts for this variation among officers? In part, administrative and geographic considerations may be an explanation. There may be differences in probation-suitability among persons from metropolitan areas (e.g., San Francisco-Oakland) and less developed or rural areas such as the northern coast or central valleys of California. But it is equally possible that these variations are due to personal characteristics, including academic training, age, and vocational background. Some general, but not conclusive, observations can be made based on the probation officers in Northern California. For example, probation officers with graduate training or graduate degrees in social work or social welfare recommended probation for 56.3 percent of their cases; officers with graduate work or graduate degrees in criminology in 69.6 percent of their cases, and officers with graduate work or graduate degrees in sociology in 67.7 percent of their cases. Officers with the longest service recommended probation for 54.0 percent of their cases, while the "newer" officers recommended probation for 68.4 percent. Three hypotheses are suggested by these and other data:

1. Some of the variation in probation officer recommendations is a product of the individual background of the officer and includes vocational experience and academic training.
2. The differences or variations tend to diminish with the period of employment; that is, officers with different backgrounds are far more dissimilar upon entering the probation service than after exposure to the agency.
3. With an increase in the period of service (i.e., more experience) there is a decrease in recommendations for probation. This may represent a more "realistic" or less "optimistic" view of the benefits of probation treatment for a greater number of offenders, than was the view held by the officer earlier in his professional career.

"Second-Guessing" or "Following"

There is, in our search for variation, the possibility that the probation officer attempts to second-guess the court by making recommendations which are anticipated to be those desired by the court. If this were the case, one measure of this factor would be that different judges receive different rates or percentages of probation or imprisonment recommendations. Thus, properly "second-guessing" a puni-

Table 12. Recommendations For and Against Probation According to United States District Court Judges (Northern District of California, September 1964 to February 1967)

Judge	Number of Cases Disposed of in Court	Number of Recommendations for Probation	Number of Recommendations Against Probation	Percentage of Cases Recommended for Probation	Number of Cases Granted Probation	Number of Cases Denied Probation	Percentage Agreement between Probation Recommendations and Dispositions
Total	831	527	304	63.4	512	278	97.2
1	64	40	24	62.5	38	23	95.0
2	58	30	28	51.7	29	23	96.7
3	160	103	57	64.4	99	53	96.1
4	156	114	42	73.1	111	38	97.4
5	88	57	31	64.8	57	30	100.0
6	100	58	42	58.0	56	36	96.6
7	60	39	21	65.0	38	18	97.4
8	73	46	27	63.0	44	26	95.7
9	72	40	32	55.6	40	31	100.0

Source: Unpublished San Francisco Project data.

tive judge would require a larger proportion of imprisonment recommendations; second-guessing a "lenient" judge would require more probation recommendations. Returning to the data on the 1,232 cases in the Norther District of California, and again restricting ourselves to a probation-imprisonment dichotomy, we find some, but not significant variation in the percentage of probation recommendations to individual judges. These data are in Table 12. Since none of these judges has a reputation of being punitive or lenient, we can only surmise that in this District, there is little if any second-guessing.

A review of Table 12 will also indicate that individual judges are equally receptive to recommendations for probation; the relationship between recommendations for probation and such dispositions being 97.2 percent overall and constant between judges.

It appears that judges "follow" probation officer recommendations; there is no other ready explanation of the individual officer variation in probation recommendations and the high overall relationship between recommendations and dispositions. This also tends to confirm the observation that probation officers contribute to the problems of disparities in sentencing. From these data, all four previously suggested explanations of the close agreement between recommendation and disposition (probation officers and judges giving approximately equal weight to similar factors, the "following" of recommendations by the court, the presence of "obvious" probation or imprisonment cases, and some "second—guessing") appear appropriate.

Summary

In this paper, some of the dangers of continued reliance on tradition and the development of a body of correctional folklore have been pointed out. It has been determined that the relationship between recommendations for and dispositions of probation are high and that the relationship diminishes when viewed from the recommendations against and the subsequent grant of probation perspective. Limited data on the outcome of supervision by recommendation and by percentage use of probation are provided. We have inquired into the reasons for the close agreement between recommendation and disposition and suggest that four factors, in varying degrees, account for it. We have observed that the overall relationship between recommendation and disposition does not vary from District Court to District Court, but rather remains relatively constant, regardless of the percentage use of probation. We suggest that disparities in sentencing are supported by the probation officer and it appears that these differences, in part, are a reflection of the officer's individual academic training and experience. Length of service brings about a trend toward conformity with colleagues and the development of a more conservative perspective toward the use of probation.

There are other segments of the presentence report process to which questions should be addressed. These include operational and administrative considerations, the decision-making processes of probation officers, and an examination of the nature and impact of the social system of correctional agencies. Within the operational considerations would be inquiries as to the role of subprofessionals in presentence investigations, the rearrangement of the standard presentence format to provide a developmental sketch instead of the current segmented report, a determination as to the appropriateness of "confidential" presentence reports, the collection of presentence data in a fashion which allows computer analysis, and the separation of the investigation and supervision functions. Although some examination has been made of the decision-making process,[20] we need additional information about the sequence of data collection, the relative importance of certain kinds of data, and the eventual use of the data for decision-making within the correctional system. We find almost a complete void in knowledge on the social systems of correctional agencies, although available data indicate that the system itself has a profound influence on job behavior, beliefs, values, and the definition and achievement of correctional goals. Indeed, we know more about the social systems of the offenders with whom we deal than about the systems of the agencies which provide correctional services.

There are vast gaps in our knowledge about the entire correctional process, but these gaps may be closed by imaginative, innovative, and creative research and operational designs and programs. This requires a willingness to subject our current traditional, correctional models to scrutiny and a willingness to set aside those features, cherished though they may be, which are inefficient and ineffective.

[20] *Ibid.*

Juvenile Court Process
The Case of Robert

Aaron Cicourel

The case of Robert is of interest because the family mobilized considerable resources to prevent the boy being sent away from home to the Youth Authority or a state mental hospital. The family is described as a "middle-income" home. The mother has remarried, and the natural father has provided some support since the divorce eight years prior to the present incident. The natural father lives nearby. The P.O. was aware of many incidents at school in which Robert was considered to be "incorrigible." The probation file contains information from the school on fifteen incidents prior to Robert's court appearance. The incidents including "smoking," "continual talking even though he has been asked to keep quiet several different times," leaving "his speech class without permission," interrupting other classes, exposing a "switch blade knife" before other students, "continued defiance," and the like. I was unable to attend the P.O.'s interview with the parents and the boy. At the time the P.O. wrote up her report for the court hearing, she indicated there was no attorney for the minor and parents. Robert was detained at Juvenile Hall until the first hearing. The P.O.'s report contains remarks of the following type:

> According to both husbands, Mrs. Bean has periods of quite severe depression, not talking for a day or so at a time. She also is reported to be disturbed by windstorms, which are frequent in this area, and calls her mother to come and get her or to come and stay with her. Mrs. Bean also will not listen to news broadcasts because, if the news is pessimistic, it causes her a great deal of emotional stress. The overall impression of this woman would be one of great instability and running away from reality. . . .
>
> The marriage of Penny and Ralph Bean took place [date], and according to Mr. Bean, it has been relatively stable except for these periods of depression that Mrs. Bean gets into, and that Robert has seemed to have been the thorn in the side of their present marriage. . . .
>
> His [Robert] attitudes are generally hostile, with a plea for leniency when caught and a promise to do better. Robert is not too happy about placement away from home but, seemingly, is coming around to acceptance. Robert's behavior has been one

SOURCE: Aaron Cicourel, *The Social Organization of Juvenile Justice* (New York: Wiley, 1968), pp. 319–27. Reprinted by permission of the author.

of complete lack of responsibility toward society. He will steal, lie, hit, use various objects to prod or jam into people with no forethought as to the danger or harm that might be brought about [I.Q. given as 75.] . . .

At the present time, Robert's principal at [junior high] is asking for expulsion due to numerous infractions of school regulations. . . . He disrupts classes and refuses or is unable to cooperate. . . . Robert has also showed signs of deep emotional disturbance by spitting great wads of phlegm on the clothing and faces of the students for no apparent reason. According to his natural father, [name], Robert has never gotten along in any school he has ever been in, Mr. [natural father] tried to get Mrs. Bean, Robert's mother, to get psychological help three or four years ago but she refused, saying he doesn't need help.

The officer recommends that Robert be placed in a school or state hospital, as the psychologicals indicate. The psychological tests have been ordered and will be administered on [date].

The P.O. establishes a condition of "severe depression" for the mother; several types of conduct are included presumably because the reader would take them to be documentary evidence of the mentioned "depression." Thus the mother is "disturbed by wind-storms," "will not listen to news broadcasts because, if the news is pessimistic, it causes her a great deal of emotional stress." To say the mother suffers from "great instability and [is] running away from reality" establishes the home as a locus of "difficulties" for the juvenile. The previously mentioned divorce was the first negative home condition. The vague use of the term "home," to include also categories like "unstable mother" or "unstable marriage," provides the reader with implications not clearly spelled out by the P.O., so that the reader "fills in" what appears to be an "obvious" "negative" or "positive" or "whatever" state of affairs. The P.O.'s use of categories to describe Mrs. Bean could, if employed by a psychiatrist, terminate with some explicit diagnosis of mental illness, complete with documentary evidence of same. Insofar as the court decides a case on such information, the formal validation of a psychiatrist is not necessary for the various personnel at probation to base their recommendations on a juvenile by reference to implied allegations of mental illness on the part of the mother or father or guardian. When the P.O. states the present marriage of Mr. and Mrs. Bean "has been relatively stable except for these periods of depression . . . and that Robert . . . [had] been the thorn in the side of their present marriage," the reader can hardly give serious consideration to this marriage as something "stable." The P.O.'s remarks continually provide apparent "positive" qualities about the boy or the mother or the home, but the reader's credibility is taxed before completing the sentence, or is undermined by subsequent sentences.

The P.O. shifts to Robert by noting the juvenile's "attitudes are generally hostile" and then provides an interesting generalization about his character—"a plea for leniency when caught and a promise to do better." The reader could interpret the P.O.'s remark to mean the boy manipulates or tries to manipulate others when in "trouble," with the hint of insincerity to the declaration "to do better." Other interpretations are possible obviously, but I want to stress how the ambiguous or vague remarks (whose appearance may at first glance seem clear) form a collection of suggested thoughts or depictions offered as "clear" to the reader, yet it is for the reader to "close" the collection, thereby creating a "set" of elements that would enable a reader to classify the juvenile's behavior as "psychopathic," "prepsychotic," "immature personality," and the like. The P.O. occasionally employs terms to pinpoint an apparent lack of parental "responsibility," a defect in the juvenile's "character," and so on, but most of the report is devoted to categories whose import for a reader is not explicit, but require a "filling in," a "closing" to create unambiguous sets in which objects and events can be counted and placed. But the "rules" for assignment, closing, counting are not always given clarity by language usage (e.g., the mother suffers from "severe depression" and is often "disturbed by windstorms," "pessimistic" news broadcasts, etc.), but juxtaposed in sentences where seemingly positive and negative elements are included, but no further explication is given. Vague sentences are also presented, hinting at "mental states" in the object but where it is difficult for the reader to assess the hints: "Robert is not too happy about placement away from home but, seemingly, is coming around to acceptance." The reader must fill in remarks attributable to the juvenile to understand the meaning of "not too happy," or "coming around to acceptance." Thus if the referee asks himself "how does the boy feel about placement outside of the home," and the report is being consulted, then he might easily conclude the boy is not that opposed. But the problem is quite serious in the case of the allegations against the mother, for the referee can easily ask the boy himself about his feelings on placement away from home, but is not as likely to ask the mother to verify the P.O.'s remarks about her "severe depression." (In the present case, a lawyer representing the Bean family used the mother's problems to advantage. See below.) But then it is difficult to imagine a situation where adversary rules could be enforced so strictly that leading questions and decisions would expose the tacit knowledge and information exchanged unofficially, but integral to evaluations and recommendations.

The P.O. does not leave much room for doubt vis-à-vis her view of Robert when she states the juvenile's "behavior has been one of complete lack of responsibility toward society." There is little of an equivocal nature in the sentence "He will steal, lie, hit, use various objects to prod or jam into people with no forethought as to the danger or harm that might be brought about." When the boy's I.Q. and test scores are given in the following paragraph, they are not connected to any of the previous material. The reader is confronted with direct statements "convincing" him of how "bad" Robert is, then is exposed to low test scores and a low I.Q. Does the reader conclude the boy's behavior is to be accounted for by divorced parents, a depressed mother, an unstable marriage to which he has contributed, and low native abilities for comprehending his environment? Notice how the sociological researcher could easily code each of the above statements so as to produce numerical representations of the "factors" associated with the juvenile's "problems." The sociologist's measurement would bear a striking resemblance to the P.O's reasoning, but objectification and the P.O.'s method of verification are seldom problematic issues in conventional usage of official records. If we add the P.O.'s remarks about the school problems, we have one more "variable" or "factor" to explain the juvenile's behavior. But such a line of reasoning misses the practical reasoning of the P.O. and those with whom he talks, and does not address the properties of the objects and events the P.O. and other actors attend when making decisions. The attributes the sociologist wishes to "freeze" for measurement and cross-tabulation are being transformed by the actions of the members involved in the social organization under study.

The case of Robert suggests how the P.O. depicts the boy's family —divorced, the mother depressed, the juvenile as having a generally "hostile" attitude and "complete lack of responsibility toward society," "deep emotional disturbance by spitting great wads of phlegm on the clothing and faces of the students for no apparent reason," continual trouble in school, and a mother who refuses to acknowledge the natural father's advice "to get psychological help three or four years ago." The P.O. clearly indicates placement outside of the home is necessary and indicates she has spoken to the boy about this.

A few days before the court hearing I was at the police station in City B, speaking with the juvenile sergeant about the Bean case. I was told the family had retained the services of a young lawyer and that the police department of a nearby suburb had furnished the Probation Department with information about three prior burglaries by Robert. The lawyer had apparently been to the City B police station inquiring about the possibility of further incidents. The sergeant described the lawyer as "quite annoyed" with the Bean family for not informing him of the burglaries. I went to see the P.O. on the case and she informed me the case took on "new light" because of the burglaries. She now felt the boy should go to the Youth Authority rather than a boys' ranch or the state mental hospital.

The lawyer had been very busy building up his case and had obtained several letters from neighbors and one of the juvenile's teachers to support his contention the family was a "good one." Consider the following excerpts:

> SCIENCE TEACHER: I have, on several occasions, had the opportunity to visit with Bob's parents, Mr. and Mrs. Bean. In my opinion, Bob has a wonderful mother and father. They were of great assitance to me in helping orient Bob at the first school. I am not saying that Mr. and Mrs. Bean are not capable of making a mistake. However, I am saying there has been mistakes made by many, including Bob, which can be amended.
>
> FRIEND: I have been a friend of Penny Bean for about two years and have known her much longer. The Beans have a very lovely home always neat and clean. The children are well behaved and mannerly. Penny and Ralph are very good parents and very concerned about the welfare of their children. Robert has always been very polite. He is especially considerate of his sister. My neighbor of the same age as Tina told me she wished her brother was that nice to her.
>
> FRIEND: Robert has always conducted himself as any other child would at his age. I cannot say that this is a calm, quite polite child who never has any outbursts of anger or self pity but then no normal young boy is placid at all times. . . .
>
> I have noticed Robert being hi strung and sometimes things are said and done before thought, but this has never reached any level to cause any trouble at home that has been out of the norm. Just being a boy seems to be most of Robert's trouble.

The science teacher seemed interested in making the point of "mistakes" by both the family and the juvenile, but trying to balance this with strong assurances of the "goodness" of the family and the boy, and the assertion things "can be amended." The first friend was positive from beginning to end. The second friend acknowledges "anger," "self pity," "hi strung," but seeks to establish such difficulties as what any child of Robert's age would do. "Just being a boy seems to be most of Robert's trouble," according to this friend. The psychologist at Juvenile Hall tested Robert, and the P.O. summarized the report as follows:

> The test results show that he had a full I.Q. of 101 on the Wechsler Bellview, a verbal score of 101, and a nonverbal of

100. He has a moderate scatter which suggests academic retar-
dation. The Rorschach shows aggressiveness with a potential
for explosive behavior and a great deal of anxiety.

The statement on the I.Q. contradicts the earlier cited report from the
school records by the P.O. The testing occurred after the P.O.'s report
was written.

The P.O. and referee were surprised at the retention of a lawyer,
and my impression was that the lawyer was viewed with some
amusement, as if to say he had been retained "for nothing." The case
was viewed as "clear," and the referee seemed convinced of placement outside of the home and seemed responsive to the P.O.'s changing her recommendation to Youth Authority incarceration. When
the hearing opened I sensed the lawyer was uneasy about the proceedings. Prior to their beginning he tried to elicit from the referee
some statement about how the hearing would proceed. The referee
treated the matter as "life as usual," implying it would be routine
and straightforward. The lawyer apparently had never attended a
juvenile court hearing and did not appreciate the referee's "explanation." The referee went over how "serious" the case was, and emphasized the three burglaries and the continued difficulty at school. The
exchanges were rather quick and I could not record much of it. The
lawyer introduced the letters (cited earlier) as supportive material
for his client. The referee suggested the boy would have to be placed
outside of the home because of the "seriousness" of the present incident, the past burglaries, and school record. The lawyer began to
protest, and the referee seemed surprised. There were some awk-
ward silences in which both the referee and the lawyer seemed to
be thinking about their next move. I was able to record the following:

> LAWYER: Now just a minute here. It is my understanding that
> all parties being helped here have been aided by psychological
> tests. I feel my client should be exposed to the same help. I
> would like a continuance on the case.
> REFEREE: Now you understand that there is a question of
> establishing the jurisdiction of the court and then there is the
> problem of disposition. First there is the question of evidence.
> Now if you want the boy to remain silent, then we could sub-
> poena witnesses.
> LAWYER: Now the psychologicals could affect the evidence of
> the case and therefore the disposition.
> REFEREE: As far as the jurisdictional part of it is concerned,
> I [pause], the court will have to deny it.
> LAWYER: Is the court ready to present evidence?
> REFEREE: We can continue it for a week. Then have witnesses
> if you dispute the jurisdictional side.

LAWYER: Well, I will have to ask for that.

REFEREE: Well, now you are concerned with whether the boy will be placed outside of the home. What is it you want? Can you clarify it?

LAWYER: Well, the whole case may change depending upon the psychologicals.

REFEREE: You realize Robert will have to be detained [in Juvenile Hall].

LAWYER: I will have to go along with that.

REFEREE: I still can't see how things are going to be helped.

LAWYER: If you let me speak to Mr. [natural father] and the others for a minute maybe we could speed things up some since I have delayed things.

After the conference, the lawyer asked for a continuance and received a two-week delay. My interpretation of the dialogue and the accompanying nonverbal behavior suggested the referee was confident he could clearly establish Robert as the "leader" of the incident and the principal offender. The other juveniles involved were all handled in a less severe way and were readily available. I felt the lawyer was not about to contest "what happened." The demand for psychological tests was an expression of dissatisfaction with the court psychologist's report. The Peters girl obtained the services of two psychiatrists paid for by the parents. The lawyer knew (in my opinion) the court was not prepared to present its evidence and, therefore, did not have to ask for a continuance on the basis of wanting the psychological examination. The referee calls explicit attention to the problem of placement outside of the home and seeks to elicit the lawyer's view ("what is it you want?") about disposition. The lawyer does not state his view, but refers to the "psychologicals" again. The referee does not push for an answer to his question about "what is it you want?" The mention of detention produced noticeable (to me) grimaces from the juvenile and his mother. The referee continued to push for some kind of clarification from the lawyer as to his view with the remark: "I still can't see how things are going to be helped." The implication of the last remark seems to be that the referee cannot see how further psychological evaluation will influence the disposition of the case or the evidence to be presented.

Before the subsequent hearing, the lawyer spoke to the referee and apparently agreed the evidence in the case was not something he could or should contest. But the lawyer went ahead and arranged for a psychiatric examination. My understanding of the referee-lawyer discussion was an agreement to accept the referee's view on the jurisdictional elements of the case and to decide the disposition after considering the psychiatric examination. The second hearing established the "seriousness" of the charges and the necessity of firm action. The psychiatric examination was obtained prior to the third hearing. The psychiatrist's report is fairly routine:

> It is my conclusion that Robert has repressed earlier in life a considerable amount of hostility and anxiety and that this has lead to the development of an emotional unstable personality and that coupled with his lack of judgment and control have lead to his aggressive behavior. There also appear to be many other mechanisms involved such as a rather low self-image with overcompensatory strivings for attention and/or approval of his peer group. Contributing to this has been lack of consistent discipline and proper manifestation of the authoritarian role of the stepfather.

The psychiatrist acknowledges speaking to, and examining the reports of, the P.O. and the psychologist who tested Robert. He also spoke to the parents. The report provides all of the necessary validation necessary for a psychiatric gloss to the material from the P.O. and the psychological testing. The psychiatric pitch is unequivocal in saying "something is wrong," but equivocal as far as knowing what one is to make of the abstract language unless the reader "fills in" and "knows" the boy's "history." The psychiatrist recommends therapy for the entire family.

During the third hearing I felt the lawyer made a brilliant defense. He carefully reviewed each of the allegations, along with the various incidents said to have contributed to a picture of "complete incorrigibility," and suggested the court was imputing motivated connections between each difficulty, but he argued the incidents could also be seen as independent events arbitrarily connected by the court. The lawyer pointed out there were no explicit references to occasions between incidents when the juvenile presumably was "doing well." The referee was not swayed by the lawyer's arguments, and insisted there "was too much" evidence to make such an argument. Finally, the lawyer argued the case would best be settled if the boy changed schools, the family moved to another neighborhood, and the entire family participated in a therapy program as suggested by the psychiatrist. The lawyer sought to convince the referee the course of action suggested by him was covered by the juvenile court law. The referee seemed to hesitate, but could not muster an argument to refute the lawyer's calculated appeal to those elements of the court often forgotten when it has been decided tacitly (by adopting a criminal view of the case) that the juvenile should be "sent away" for "his own good." I interpret the referee's and P.O.'s perspective to be the one which included some form of punishment in their insistence that the boy be sent away, particularly to the Youth Authority. The disposition suggested by the lawyer was agreed to by the referee and arrangements were made for the family to begin therapy sessions with the psychiatrist.

The P.O.'s supplemental report anticipated the lawyer's suggestion for keeping the boy at home (with the family in therapy) because she spoke to the psychiatrist three days before the third court hearing. But the P.O. notes Robert had difficulties during his stay in Juvenile Hall leading to three occasions in which the boy had to be isolated because of "his attitude and overacting out. The officer is of the opinion that Robert is still in need of being placed in an institution that has definite limitations and restrictions." The last statement is vague about "institution," but the P.O. told me personally the juvenile should be sent to the Youth Authority or at least to the boys' ranch. Two months later Robert was arrested for violation of probation (taking an auto without consent of owner). The psychiatrist came to his defense with the following statement:

> It is indeed unfortunate that he has broken his probation, for, at this time, I feel he had moved toward significant improvement and that his further progress would be assured in the home and school environment and the therapy regime which he now has. Disruption of these factors at this point, in my opinion, could preclude benefit from future attempts at therapy with the minor and precipitate a regression. Certainly his violation of probation cannot and should not be minimized, but in dealing with this issue, I recommend careful consideration of the improvement he has made and the effort that has been expanded by him and all concerned in achieving this.

Robert remained at home, but I was informed of further difficulties by Robert but did not follow the case after the spring of 1965.

The psychiatrist's remarks could be made about anyone in therapy if the juvenile were fortunate to receive this kind of defense rather than Youth Authority incarceration. The police and probation view subsequent offenses as documentary evidence of criminality, but the psychiatrist's report forces a clinical interpretation that cannot be objectified or verified. A judge faced with a lawyer arguing as persuasively as the one quoted above would find it difficult to deny efforts to place the entire family in a therapy program. Parents seeking to mobilize resources to help their children under the juvenile court law are encouraged to do so by law enforcement agencies. Such action saves the county and state considerable monies, avoids the assumed negative influence of incarceration in an environment likely to expose the juvenile to the "worse" elements, and minimizes the stigma presumed to be forthcoming from the "community."

The presence of a lawyer who makes it his business to challenge all or parts of a case makes it difficult for the police, probation officials, and the court to invoke their conventional practical reasoning in handling cases, but does not resolve the question of who are the "delinquents" and how do they "get that way." The case in this chapter reveals how the entire process is managed and negotiated by socially organized activities amenable to direct study and observation. It should be clear how the object (the delinquent) or delinquent act can be transformed by invoking an ideology to reread the "facts," character structure, family structure, mental stability, and the like. The rereading highlights theoretical issues inherent in all decision-making and reveals the problematical structure of social control and judicial procedures.

Index

DATE DUE

DEC 4 '77			
APR 30 '78			
DEC 11 '79			
NOV 27 1980			
DEC 15 1980			
MAY 10 1982			
MAY 6 '83			
DEC 9 '83			
APR 17 '84			
NOV 9 '84			
MAY 10 '85			
MAR 7 '88			
NOV 6 '88			
DEC 09 '94			
MAY 01 1998			
GAYLORD			PRINTED IN U.S.A.